Between Two Worlds

Between Two Worlds

Politics, Anti-Politics, and the Unpolitical

Richard Hoggart

With an introduction to the American Edition

Transaction Publishers
New Brunswick (U.S.A.) and London (U.K.)

Library of Congress Catalog Number: 2001027975
ISBN: 0-7658-0097-7 (cloth); 0-7658-0946-X (paper)
Printed in the United States of America

Library of Congress Cataloging-in-Publication Data

Hoggart, Richard, 1918-
    Between two worlds : politics, anti-politics, and the unpolitical / Richard
Hoggart ; with an introduction to the American edition.
        p.   cm.
    Contains essays originally published between 1981 and
1998 and one essay not previously published.
        Includes index.
        ISBN 0-7658-0097-7 (cloth : alk. paper) — ISBN 0-7658-0946-X (pbk:
alk. paper)
        1. Great Britain—Civilization—20th century. 2. Lawrence, D.H.
(David Herbert), 1885-1930—Criticism and interpretation. I. Title.

DA566.4 .H537   2001
941.082—dc21   2001027975

CONTENTS

CONTENTS

For Mary; again

'In the destructive element immerse'
JOSEPH CONRAD

ACKNOWLEDGEMENTS

I AM GREATLY INDEBTED, in a variety of ways, to the following: Geoffrey Goodman, John Gordon, Alex Graham, Stephen Hearst, Paul Head, Muriel McNaughton, John Miller, Roy Shaw, Mike Shaw, Nicolas Tredell, Jonathan Pegg and all at Curtis Brown, Piers Burnett, Karen Ings and all at Aurum Press; our three offspring, Simon, Nicola and Paul; our son-in-law Richard Beck, and, of course, Mary, my wife.

SOURCES

THESE ESSAYS WERE first published as shown below. I am grateful to all the journals and publishers named for those first appearances. Almost all have been revised, some substantially. As a result, two or three have been made into one. A few elements have also appeared, since their first publication, in subsequent books of mine. I have sought to avoid word-by-word repetition and only retained these elements where they seem essential to the final essay as printed here.

Are Museums Political? The British Museum's Second Annual Franks Lecture, London, May, 1998. Parts have been incorporated from a paper given to a Woodrow Wilson seminar at the Smithsonian Institute, Washington D.C., 1996.

Noble Aspirations: UNESCO and Civil Society, A Memoir in *The Conscience of the World: The Influence of the NGOs on the UN System*, ed. P. Willetts, Hurst, London, 1995.

Broadcasting, Democracy and the Enabling Principle. From *Ariel at Bay, Reflections on Broadcasting and the Arts*, essays in honour of Philip French, ed. R. Carver, Carcanet, Manchester, 1990. Contains elements from pieces in the *Political Quarterley* and the *Daily Express*.

D. H. Lawrence's Country, in *Writers and their Houses*, ed. K. Marsh, Hamish Hamilton, London, 1993.

The Rainbow, Introduction to the Folio Society edition, London, 1981.

Women in Love, Introduction to the Folio Society edition, London, 1982.

Lady Chatterley and the Censors, in *Figures Mythiques*, ed. P. Vitoux, Editions Autremont, Paris, 1998. Elements also appeared in *An Imagined Life*, Chatto and Windus, London, 1992.

The Road to Wigan Pier, Introduction to the Penguin edition, London, 1989.

The State versus Literature, conference of the Working Party on Libraries and the Book Trade, London, January 1986. Reprinted in *Universities Quarterly*, 40/4, 1986.

Freedom to Publish: Even Hateful Stuff, 32nd Triennial Conference of the International Publishers' Association, London, 1998. Reprinted in the Proceedings of the Congress, *Books in the 1990s*, London, 1998.

Reviewers and Reviewing, in *Society*, 34/3, 1997, Rutgers University, New Jersey, USA.

Politics, Anti-Politics and the Unpolitical, conference on *The University into the Twentieth Century*, University of Victoria, British Columbia, May 1984. Published in *Proceedings*, 1984.

Gamekeepers and Poachers, in *New Universities Quarterly*, 22/2, 1978.

Between Two Worlds: Public and Private Discourses, Lecture at the University of Massachusetts, 1985, published in *Universities Quarterly*, 40/2, 1986.

Literacy Is Not Enough, talk at a Book Trust seminar, the British Library, autumn 1998. Published in *Literacy Is Not Enough*, ed. B. Cox, Manchester University Press, Manchester, 1998.

Figures from a Distant Past, Farnham, autumn 1999–2000. Not previously published.

Looking Back, conversation with Nicolas Tredell, London, 1993. Published in *P. N. Review*, 20/1, 1993. With elements from a University of Cardiff interview, 1997, published in *The International Journal of Cultural Studies*, ed. J. Hartley, 1/1, 1998.

Introduction to the American Edition

DURING A YEAR at the University of Rochester, New York, more than forty years ago, I took part in a day of lectures given by the faculty, designed to exhibit their fine scholarship to local benefactors. Afterwards my closest friend there took me for a walk and patiently rebuked me. What I had said about modern English literature was interesting; the way I said it wasn't. I sounded too relaxed and chatty, my audience expected academics to be solemn, their manner marmoreal.

In the mid-sixties I gave a named annual lecture at Columbia University in New York City. It was subsequently published, so was presumably adequately weighty. Afterwards, I walked to supper with Lionel Trilling. He said he had enjoyed the lecture (incidentally, that 'enjoyed' is a favoured word in Cambridge, England. You 'enjoy' but do not at such a time offer a judgment, even one which would be contained in, say, 'admired'). Trilling went on, roughly to this effect: 'I couldn't give a lecture in that manner. In the States we can't assume that sort of unbuttoned relationship with our academic audiences. We have to keep a kind of distance'.

Back home some years later a very distinguished academic at Cambridge remarked on my habitual use of 'we,' which suggests that I am talking to a known and identified audience; the descendants, perhaps, of Dr. Johnson's 'common reader', with whom he 'rejoiced to concur'. But, the distinguished academic went on, it is very unlikely that there is such an audience today. Readers of best-sellers, yes; and readers of technical works; and of course academics. But no substantial lay audience who find pleasure in reading for intellectual stimulation, to increase self-knowledge and widen their sense of the way their world is going. I think that critic would have agreed that many highly skilled professionals do read outside their professionalism; he doubted whether there was any sizeable body of, again, lay readers, amateurs in both the French and the English senses, some of whom may not be professionals at all. He presumably would not accept that, taken together, all those make up today's 'common readers'.

I believe there is still such a body in Britain. They are what Arthur Koestler described, after meeting them during the last war, as 'the anxious corporals'; they could be identified by the Penguin paperbacks sticking out of the back trouser-pockets of their battledress. Matthew Arnold glorified them as 'the saving remnant'. Others call them 'the intelligent laymen/women'. I spent the first dozen years of my professional life taking university evening classes in which such people predominated. In England today several hundred thousand go to evening classes. A good many of them write to me. I suspect that my Cambridge doubter was a little too much encased in those lovely walls. I mention all this because, if my American advisers above were right, much in the tone of this book may seem odd to American readers. But to whom do the authors of those very many intelligent and demotic books which appear in the States, and which uncompromisingly criticise all aspects of their society, assume they are speaking? It seems to me that they do expect an audience of intelligent lay readers.

Other English oddities within these pages include our continuing obsession with social class. Most American readers must be thoroughly used to that, and with today's fashionable assertion that class feeling has by now entirely disappeared here. A very upper-middle-class lady once said she quite liked a book of mine but 'You do go on a lot about class even though it's virtually gone. My cleaning lady is a friend." That she said 'cleaning lady' and not 'char-woman' no doubt validated her claim. To her. I wonder whether she invited the cleaning lady to her Christmas drinks party; or how she would have reacted if her daughter had walked in on the arm of the cleaning lady's son and announced that they were bent on marrying.

Then there is our tortured set of attitudes towards censorship in defence of public morals. It seems inconceivable that the (now defunct) Lord Chamberlain, the Royal Guardian of such things, required the sound of a lavatory chain being pulled, off stage of course, to be silenced before he would release one of Graham Greene's plays for public showing. The *Lady Chatterley's Lover* trial hilariously exposed the complex mix of the urge to censor with the maintenance of class feeling. Joyce's *Ulysses* was still being smuggled in here years after a Manhattan court released it on the grounds of its literary merit—grounds for the first time accepted in our new Act on obscenity, under which *Lady Chatterley* was prosecuted; and which the prosecution and the judge brushed aside throughout the whole week of the trial; preferring to rely on the fancied response of that stock figure, the Man on the Clapham Omnibus.

The debates about the public good and the State's wider duties towards its various forms thread through several of these essays. As to the arts, we have nothing comparable in size to the private philanthropy of the United States. In the last few decades we have released more public money than ever before for the arts. We still have endless arguments on whether the State should intervene at all; and on that band-wagon the would-be censors, the self-styled 'Moral Majority', ride high.

We can occasionally do better in these matters, especially in our commitment to the Public Service idea in broadcasting. That was conceived so as to ensure the political, financial, and structural freedom of this immensely powerful public instrument from possible damaging pressures by government or the advertisers. Like public libraries, public parks, the Open University and some other liberal inventions, they illustrate Britain's capacity suddenly to become socially imaginative, before curling up to doze again; our classic see-saw pattern. Nowadays we are seeing the Public Service idea in broadcasting put under pressures which may well destroy it.

Our universities, too, have traditionally enjoyed a remarkable degree of freedom from outside influences. As do the BBC, the British Council, and the Arts Council, they enjoy the protection of that curious instrument, the Royal Charter (granted, of course, by the Queen, not by Parliament). It provides a buffer between some great public institutions of a democratic and civil society—especially those which are bound to be involved with judgments of intellectual and artistic value—and, above all, the politicians; that is popularly called 'the arms-length principle'. Today, the universities, too, are being squeezed on two sides: from governments which are increasingly ignoring the safeguards of the Royal Charter and interfering as a matter of course, and from industry which offers money-with-strings. Oxford and Cambridge can attract donors without strings, and sometimes give the impression that they will accept money-with-strings without enquiring closely enough into possible academic implications. Other universities have to bite every proffered coin twice; not all of them recognise that necessity.

So one could go on. How should we describe this place where we live? I am English, certainly. In what sense am I British? That's really a political device as a title, though it has its uses. What is Great Britain? A political title again, meant three centuries ago to indicate the new political unity of these islands (now less of a unity than it used to be). Arriving in the United States it is better to announce your native country as 'the United Kingdom' since some immigration officers think 'Great Britain' is a boast; and can become churlish.

How does one describe oneself? I write in English and so am doubly an English writer. We do not speak of 'British' writers. Shaw, Yeats, Caribbean, Indian writers, and many another can be called English writers because they write in English, but they are not English. Worse: if you try to describe national characteristics you are walking through a minefield. The Scots and the Welsh will attack you if you describe as 'British' characteristics which they know to be uniquely weaknesses of the English; or, worse again, if you describe as British admirable attitudes which they know to be unique to them. Recently there have been half-a-dozen books teasing, often nervously, at these complexities.

A final word about the title, just in case it puzzles any reader. I have inhabited twice two different worlds. The first pair is: the world of my rooted, working-class, Northern, English, provincial childhood, and the world of the untethered intellectual. The second pair contains the world of the university academic, within the walls; and the world of national committees on matters of public moment, of Whitehall; and of huge international institutions.

I suppose it is possible to say, without being fanciful, that behind all the above may be a third, entirely internal pair of worlds. For much of the outlook bred by my peculiar childhood is still there, watching my every move; so is the outlook formed by today's world, that of a husband, father and grandfather, and of an endemic, hanging-from-the-chandelier, social observer—watching, above all, the way that childhood watches and influences me. Backwards and forwards. Englishmen, too, no less than Americans, can have 'complex fates'.

Richard Hoggart

INTRODUCTION

THIS CAN BE short since there are brief introductions before the separate pieces. Collected essays are not popular, often suspected of being rehashes of impermanent and transient writings, their reissue a form of self-indulgence.

These essays make up less than a quarter of those I have published over the last two decades. All except one appeared in books or journals with small circulations or were given at closed conferences. The exception is the Introduction to *The Road to Wigan Pier* and that is enlarged and greatly amended here. My justification for reissuing these few is that they contain the main lines of the interests to which I have turned again and again; and which are, to judge by the way they recur in public debate, still alive: the debates on culture and society, for example, on literature and censorship and on higher education.

I found myself, in the course of getting these essays together, writing some new pieces on the past and people I knew long ago, people whose stories seem historically and humanly worth recalling. So these are included towards the end.

As a finale, Nicolas Tredell's well-informed, patient and probing interview makes a better summing-up than I could produce.

Richard Hoggart
Farnham, 2000

PART ONE

SOCIETY AND CULTURE:
HOME AND AWAY

ARE MUSEUMS POLITICAL?

*T*his collection does not run chronologically, or 'Are Museums Political?' would appear near the end.

It is placed at the front because it tries to gather together some of the themes which have occupied me for many years and run through almost all that follows: about society and culture (in more than one sense), class, education (especially adult education), populism and relativism.

It differs from most other essays collected here in its ambience and audience. Most of those others were written to be read, in already sympathetic journals or books; my hoped-for audience was often among lay readers. This one was prepared as an annual lecture before an audience of specialists in the museum field, or of very well-informed lay enthusiasts in that and related subjects.

I am not a specialist nor very well informed in those areas, but I did spend fifteen years as chairman of the Judging Committee of the European Museum of the Year Award and so picked up a fair amount on the way. But my central interests are cultural change, in the senses listed above, English literature, and the interrelations between them.

So this was a slightly unusual experience before an unknown kind of audience; though a very polite and friendly one. How much they made of the argument I do not know. No 'Letters to the Editor' follow these occasions. Perhaps influence, if there is any, works in a different way then.

IF WE ASK: 'Are museums political?' it soon becomes necessary to look more widely than at museums alone. One might better ask: 'Is culture political?' For the interest in culture in virtually all countries, developed, developing and still underdeveloped, and with all sorts of mixed meanings, is one of the main sociolinguistic interests of the world today. So much so that the word itself has become a handy synonym for almost any aspect of society which intrigues us, and has come to have a coherent life of its own. We speak of 'the culture of literacy', 'the culture of television', 'the culture of enterprise' and so on. Soon, we may begin to talk about 'the culture of culture' – or perhaps 'the culture syndrome' – to indicate all the different ways in which we use that battered word.

My early days at UNESCO headquarters in Paris gave a deep immersion in that debate. UNESCO, like many UN agencies, is desperately nervous of division, of alienating any one of its scores of member states. Just before I arrived, the heavily pressed Department of Culture had produced a banner-heading motto of which they were quite proud and protective: 'All cultures are equal'. That escapist idea flew cheerfully round the Department like Dickens' hiccupping drunken fairy in *Martin Chuzzlewitt*. It also pleased some external advisers, many of whom had a high-minded vision of the imaginative unity of all cultures. Perhaps it seemed to them a step on the way to the realisation of that impossible and undesirable ideal. But what could it mean? For the more politically minded in some states it came to mean: 'Keep off any criticism of any practices of ours' – of enforced female circumcision, say – 'since we are now all officially equal. UNESCO says so.' A few of us went around adding our own Orwellian coda: 'But perhaps some are more equal than others'.

UNESCO is committed to freedom of expression even though that is not permitted in a number of its member nations. At an international conference of ministers of culture, the then Soviet Union put down a resolution which ran something like this: 'Member States will ensure that artists and writers produce nothing which insults their own culture or that of any other Member State.' No good would come of taking that head-on; it could have wasted a day. With help from a number of sympathetic delegates the Secretariat suggested a prefix to the resolution: 'Whilst respecting the freedom of the artist, Member States will ensure ...'. The Soviet delegation was happy that its form of words remained; presumably they guessed that the apparatchiks in the

Kremlin would not be likely to note the absurd contradiction. The resolution was passed.

Even what has been said so far is enough to show that culture can be poltiical; but not always, nor in all its aspects. As to museums, the suggestion would, to many, still appear irrelevant. Historically, and virtually up to the present, they have often seemed in the main social and cultural backwaters. Daniel Boorstin, until fairly recently Librarian of Congress, remarked that when you enter a museum you feel that 'something has died when the object was placed inside'. Earlier, John Burroughs complained that to enter one was to feel 'as though I were attending a funeral'. Chesterton claimed that museums invite us to cram ourselves 'with every sort of incongruous food in one indigestible mess'. Such attitudes survive today, but not in informed places.

There are at least three senses in which museums and sites may be called political. They are: the plainly corrupt and manipulative; the ideologically imposed; and the would-be-fair-minded but difficult.

Only a few weeks after I joined UNESCO there came a telegram from the Archimandrite of Alexandria. He invoked the Hague Convention on the protection of cultural objects and sites in times of conflict. He alleged that part of the monastery of Santa Caterina on Mount Sinai had been burned down by the Israeli soldiery and some of its priceless mosaics destroyed. I sent a splendid elderly Dutch admiral [to investigate] who returned to report, rather gleefully, that the destruction was to only one wing, a dormitory and without mosaics; it had been caused by Father Ignatius falling asleep with a cigarette in his mouth, after drinking deeply of the monastery's home-made cactus spirit.

Matters at UNESCO became more melodramatic. So much so that I am probably one of the few cultural workers who have been threatened with assassination five times, three times on the same day. Two of the later, post-UNESCO, death threats were not concerned with ancient monuments but with modern cultural affairs.

Four years after the Santa Caterina episode the Arab states put down a resolution accusing Israel of doing considerable damage to Arab monuments and sites in the occupied territories. I sent a pasteurised group of experts (no Americans or British, for example) to examine the allegations. They came back after several weeks to report that, far from damaging Arab cultural property, the Israelis were on the whole looking after it better than their owners had done. This unpleasant news had to be announced to the plenary session of the General Conference. Whether the Director-General's indisposition on that day was real or political was unclear, but I was deputed to present the report.

The result was a textbook example of the maxim: 'If it's bad news, kill the messenger.' That afternoon my secretary announced that an Arab terrorist group had telephoned to say I would be assassinated. There followed a similar message from another Arab group. In the early evening of that day I looked from my window over the Place de Fontenoy. A detachment of anti-riot troops – the C.R.S. – was heading in our direction. A young Israeli terrorist group had picked up the wrong message and was coming to kill me. Every morning in those last few months before we returned to England I had to feel under the car in case there was a *plastique* – a bomb – there.

So we came back to quiet old England, and I became chairman of the European Museum of the Year Award Judging Committee. A pleasant, quiet chore until the year in which we proposed to give not the main but a subsidiary award to the Israel Museum of the Holocaust. The ceremony was to be in Brussels Town Hall and the guest of honour was the Queen of the Belgians.

To my office at Goldsmiths' College there came that morning, an hour or so before I was due to leave, a message from our people in Brussels saying that an Arab group had phoned with the promise that if we went ahead with that particular award neither the Queen nor I would leave the platform alive. I was not by then impervious, but knew that at such moments one simply has to freeze emotionally, make what dispositions one can, and carry on. I asked that the Queen's office be told and added that I proposed to go ahead. Did the Queen wish to do that? The answer was, of course, yes.

The main prize is a bronze piece by Henry Moore; very heavy. Handing it to the Queen, I forgot the threat of imminent death, being intent on warning her, a slight lady, about the weight. Nothing happened. A few minutes later I presented the subsidiary awards. As he took his scroll, the Israeli curator whispered, 'We know everything, my friend Thank you.'

These quite dramatic incidents might be thought to prove that, in some situations at least, some museums have become political. That would be a mistake. They show that today's museums can be used – misused – politically; used as direct and distorted instruments. They tell little about the importance of museums in and as themselves, to particular societies. They tell no more about museums than a suicide attack on a fairground would tell about fairgrounds – except that both are places at which people gather and can be attacked.

We have to probe further, to where the word 'political' may indicate an assumed organic relationship between museums-and-sites and the perceptions of different national cultures. This is the second area of 'political' uses; in it there are, or were until 1989, two separate but related sub-types.

The range of new nations, especially numerous in Africa, and most of which came into being in the sixties, all wanted as quickly as possible to 'throw off the imperialist yoke' and create a sense of nationhood. How best to do that? Their boundaries, usually set by the retiring imperialists for political and economic reasons, might well include several tribes, several differing cultures and several languages. Ironically, the only more or less common languages might be those of the former occupiers. The new rulers quickly established an army, an airforce and perhaps a national commercial airline. They also commissioned a flag and a national anthem.

All that was not enough. They had to have a common culture. Whose culture, given the mosaic of tribes? And was there a body of written records? Before I joined UNESCO, an elder from Mali said at one of its conferences: 'When an old man dies in one of our villages, it is as though several volumes of our history have been lost.' That, incidentally, helped me a few years later to decide to work at UNESCO. In the new nations, not surprisingly, the culture which was chosen as national, publicised, taught in schools, invoked by broadcasters and the newspapers, was almost always that of the dominant tribal group.

I walked around the bazaars of Dakar with President Senghor, after an hour working with him on his draft translation into French of *Four Quartets*. Sengor, who promoted 'negritude' – Africanness – was also recognised as a French, not simply a Francophone, poet. On that Dakar walk he said how distressed he was that only a handful of truly indigenous woodcarvers remained; the rest were produced tat for tourists.

An African Minister of Culture said, movingly, in UNESCO's halls: 'Our culture is our identity card in the community of nations.' That, too, one did not forget. He was intent on discovering, consolidating and making that culture known. He disappeared in one of the military purges which racked his country. In such places culture is directly political, bound up with the painful, indeed often frightful, efforts at national cohesion. The price paid by individuals can be high, if not fatal.

A related form of this belief in the importance of culture was most strikingly seen in the Soviet Union. The bosses performed a double act. They insisted that the cultural integrity of the many nations which made up the Union was being maintained within Russia itself and throughout all its parts, down to the smallest ethnically distinct Asian component. They protested their virtue too much. It was a claim without much body or muscle, concerned more with nodding encouragingly at ethnic dance traditions than with political freedom for the different cultures to express themselves in their own ways. On those, Moscow superimposed 'Soviet Culture', an inorganic invention expressed in compliant novels, Stalinesque architecture and statuary, and manipulated, doctrinaire museums. Its prose about art was similarly untethered to reality: 'The art of Socialist Realism truthfully reflects ... the exploits of the people in building the new society.'

Early in my time in Paris we published a book on Byelo-Russian (now Belarus) poetry, edited by an Oxford don. It had an introduction which not surprisingly showed a greater interest in Byelo-Russian poetics than in that country's contribution to the total Soviet culture. Worse, the poet most praised had, we soon learned, been totally erased from the historic record since he had 'been a traitor during the Great Patriotic War'. My interview with the Soviet ambassador was torrid, and incomprehensible to both sides. He could not see why this particular apparatchik, for that was what he saw me as, could refuse simply to withdraw the book, since an involved member state had made an objection. He threatened to report me to the Director-General for insubordination.

Still full of the rich intellectual corn of Birmingham University, I told him – he was by now trying to lean on me noisily and heavily – that he could report me to the Queen, the Archbishop of Canterbury and the Prime Minister if he wished. He was plainly astounded. For a *fonctionnaire*, even a high-ranking international civil servant, to speak like that to a senior national diplomat was incomprehensible. He baulked momentarily – and then broke into a large smile: 'Ah, it is the famous English sense of 'umour.'

We were friendly after that. Meeting in a corridor a few weeks later, he introduced me to a deputy foreign minister who also smiled broadly and said he was glad to meet an exponent of the English sense of humour. Meeting him nowadays, one would be tempted, looking at Belarus, the Ukraine, Georgia and the rest, to ask how deeply the Soviet superimposition had penetrated and changed all those original cultures.

The Chinese, who joined UNESCO later, had a similar thrust to the Soviets but were much more assertive and brusquely bad-tempered. The embassy members set their wives to searching for anti-Chinese and pro-Taiwan references in all our many publications. They came upon a 12-inch recording of Tibetan temple music, one in a wonderful world-wide series which collected obscure and remote musical expressions. On the sleeve our Berlin contractors referred to Tibet as 'a mountainous country with a remarkable musical tradition'.

The Chinese ambassador appeared and upbraided me for 'this deliberate and plainly political insult to China'. There was no preliminary or gradual ascent; he started in a tone of such very high dudgeon that one felt he had spent a few minutes outside winding himself up before propelling himself at my office door. China had annexed Tibet not long before. It was useless to try to explain that one could say: 'Wales is a mountainous country with a fine musical tradition', or mention Scotland and bagpipes, without implying that either was an independent nation state.

The high-pitched tirade, so noisy that my secretary wondered whether to rescue me, ended with his going at once to my 'superior'. Being new, he confused ranks and reported me to our diplomatic affairs officer, who ranked lower than I did in UNESCO's immutable pecking order. That cheerful Brazilian soon telephoned to say all was well. He had told the ambassador that I was a temporarily detached English provincial university professor and perhaps not yet fully acquainted with all relevant nuances. But I was not a bad chap and would no doubt correct the fault in the second edition of the record. I reminded him that we had never had a second edition of any of the records. 'Yes,' said the ever-cheerful Brazilian, 'but he doesn't know that. So now you see, my dear Richard, why I am a diplomatic expert and you are a university professor.'

Are such instances evidence that in some countries 'culture' is now deeply political? Yes. They do not necessarily misuse cultural objects or events for their own direct terrorist ends, as did those in the first group. They are rightly convinced that 'culture' matters in itself, is at the heart of any nation's sense of itself; and that if you aim to create a new nation or to bind together a group of annexed or near-annexed territories, you would do well to pay great attention to cultural elements. For them, 'culture' is directly and deeply political, its definition and purity to be maintained by almost whatever force is necessary.

Now to the third and trickiest area. In the developed, sophisticated democracies of the West, can 'culture' be in any sense called 'political'? They do not in general have the political thugs of the first group, or the ideological bruisers of the second. The case looks easier than that of those others, but at bottom is not; it is more complex. This is a less dramatic area than the two so far described; but that is in the nature of democracy and does not make less important the effort to recognise and value 'culture' properly. The recognition and valuing is, though, more inward here than elsewhere.

Behind all this argument is the conviction that countries, societies, even 'communities' (to introduce a currently overused word), may not be 'civilisations'. This brings to the front the second large-scale definition of the word 'culture' itself. The first is the anthropologists': of culture regarded as 'a whole way of life'. Eliot and Orwell enjoyed playing tunes on this. The second is the Matthew Arnoldian definition: the best that has been thought, said, written, created through any of the arts. All these make up a society's historic claim to be something more – a civilisation.

These connections are, in Britain as compared with France, approached rather nervously; as though much in them is no better than it should be, morally, or at least is a little effete but still, and especially, morally suspect. This is odd when one recalls that in one art, literature, the British are recognised by many other nations as virtually supreme hardly surpassed by any of them; as even some French will admit.

As to the arts generally, British governments have in the last few decades given more attention to this. They still suspect titles such as: 'Minister of [or] for Culture'. Those sound too directional, intervention- ist. Eventually, they settled for 'Secretary of State for National Heritage' which comfortably suggested a preoccupation with old bricks and mortar. At present we are back with the face-saving forced marriage of 'Culture, Media and Sport'. That reduces the fanciness, comes down to earth with the mass television audiences and the crowds on the football terraces.

We have had recently some cultivated people looking after these things: book lovers, opera, music and visual-arts enthusiasts. But no Jack Lang, no one who has thought much in general terms about the roles of public bodies towards 'culture', the arts and the people. That sort of thinking is, we like to assume, 'very French', not really English; mercifully.

In many other areas where we try to order and assess our human inheritance, we have internationally respected extenders of many boundaries. If this is so, since this is so, where do we fall down, or at least perform less well than we should, in the cultural debate? In looking at this question we may arrive at a more convincing, as well as more complex, definition of the political nature of culture than we have reached so far in this paper.

I suggest three (it is strange how often some of us slip into making tripartite divisions on many issues. Is this due to nature or nurture? Is it bedded in the concept of the Trinity?) foundation ideas, assumptions, provisional assurances on matters cultural in societies such as ours today (again in the Arnoldian sense); and especially as concerns institutions such as museums. The first, which I mentioned at the beginning of this essay, is obvious and on the whole well honoured here. But it must be reiterated, again and again. The second is not so obvious and often approached in a surprisingly ill-thought-through way. The third is the most difficult, and important.

The first begins by insisting that integrity of scholarship is fundamental. A museum is a space within which we try with all the disinterestedness we can muster to define and assess our own past and that of others; and then make our findings available to scholars and others in the world outside. Museums are an important component of our collective memory, not simply of our sense of national identity and unity, if we have those, and also of our diversity – of our creative diversity, we may hope.

There is, one may gather from the profession's journals, still a tendency to gnaw at old but worrying oppositions, especially that of the claims of scholarship as set against those of wider communicating. That is an opposition which hides what might be a true compatibility; an opposition fed by the fact that we feel fairly confident in defining good scholarship, but as to effective, good, wider communicating – speaking straight to one another – we are in a mess, which does not lessen.

Scholarship, even of the very finest kind, is rarely, in the jargon, entirely value-free. What we decide to include and what to omit, what we decide to say by way of interpreting any objects – these are determined by our ways of looking, and we do not often enough look-at-our-own-ways-of-looking, our own hidden agendas. Our criteria for selecting objects and ideas reach down, often not altogether consciously, to our deepest sense of identity, personal and national, well beyond our conscious sense of the political. Richard Rorty was right to say that nations define themselves by what they choose to remember and by what they choose to forget; so do all of us.

What could be more challenging in this way than John Letts's efforts at founding a museum of Empire and Commonwealth? There, the sea of interpretation is massively rock-strewn and it would be a brave curator who argued that navigation is easy. We may not be able altogether to pull ourselves up by our own cultural bootstraps, but we can try. Otherwise we will be more than ever immersed in our own cultural climates, our national, class- and sex-determined climate. Our record shows how little we have exercised that boostrap-pulling. Many of those Jews who in this century were forced to uproot themselves and came here have done much to readjust our vision. Perhaps the other ethnic groups who have arrived in the last thirty years will similarly adjust our eyesight.

Area number two: audiences. To whom, in addition to fellow scholars, do we wish to speak? A recent paper has rightly asserted that one of the four main roles of museums is 'to inspire those who are receptive to inspiration'. True, but not sufficient. At this point I always quote Bishop Wilson in the early nineteenth century: 'The number of those who need to be awakened is far greater than that of those who need comfort.' With him, Gotthold Lessing a century earlier: 'We must not accept the wantlessness of the poor.' He was not or not only referring to the lack of material benefits. Two mottoes there for democratic education at all levels and of all kinds, including what should be practised in museums.

Those who have worked in adult education know that the 'receptivity to inspiration' is not only a matter of nature or even of nurture, not predetermined by social class or previous education. Properly approached, by someone trying to 'get across without selling out', a garage mechanic who left school at fourteen may reveal a more sensitive response to William Blake than the MA in Literature sitting next to him. A true example.

We are an undereducated society, so undereducated that most of us fall into the elephant traps of an aggressive, open, commercial, partial-democracy. A full democracy must be fully educated; in that, democracy is indivisible.

We are also a divided society and in some ways becoming more divided. A divided society is not a diverse society, but something less. The sense of class division is still strong, though it more and more shows itself as responsive to different forms of status, and as such has its own new forms of snobberies.

So the import of this second area is: do not assume you know all about your possible audiences; do not take present audiences as a sufficient guide to potential others; do not half-consciously assign some people to previously class-and-education bound slots; do not underestimate the capacities of many thousands outside. Only the best is good for anyone else, as we assume it is for us and our kind.

In prosperous societies the present divisions are unhappily revealed in any conversation about 'culture vultures'. Some culture vultures themselves may find no problem in the fact that the Royal Opera House has historically been accessible almost entirely to their own kind only. The provision of some cheaper seats way up in the gods has satisfied their social consciences. All this is assumed to be almost a fact of nature. Their critics then seize on this attitude as proof that 'high culture' is, as they have been repeatedly told and long suspected, merely a product of bourgeois elitism, separatism, consumerism; altogether class-defined and class-bound. There is then, it is believed, no point in helping young people to respond to Shakespeare or Mozart or Rembrandt; all that sort of thing is a class confidence trick.

This leads to the third and most difficult area: the condition of society as a whole today and some main secular tendencies within it, all of them bearing heavily on our attitudes towards cultural matters. Three common characteristics are prominent and interconnected: relativism and its siblings, populism and triviality.

The fear of making value judgements, the use of 'judgemental' simply as a dirty word, the predictable insistence that we are all and in all things as good as one another – all these are endemic. Of course we are each as good as anyone else before God if we believe in one, our consciences and the law; we are not equal in our gifts. They fall or do not fall on us without prior or relevant tests of worth in other areas. Yet the inevitable cry after you have dared to call a book 'good' and 'better than' some other is: 'Who do you think you are, to say that any one book is worth more than any other?' A senior official at the Arts Council found a discussion of this kind embarrassing. 'Look,' he said, 'I happen to like Mahler. This other chap likes riding fast motorbikes. That's all there is to it.' Private affluence and shared, public, imaginative squalor.

It is time to recover words such as: 'Good ... better ... lasting ... high quality'. We cannot absolutely prove the rightness of such judgements, nor ever will we; they do not belong to that kind of discourse. We can, with Dr Leavis, patiently lay out our understanding to the point at which we ask: 'This is so, is it not?' To which anyone is free to reply: 'No'. That sentence is usually only quoted so as to be dismissed today. But some may be persuaded to see its good sense; eventually.

This kind of society has little sense of its own history, of an intellectually and imaginatively three-dimensional past. 'Books are what is left of us,' the American critic Harold Bloom memorably said; and with more assurance than many of us can muster today. But it is a heroic thought.

Our sense of history and our forms of guidance to the present are selected and mediated by two main public voices: those of the advertisers and of the PR people. They echo back to us and constantly reinforce what they have helped to insert: judgement by numbers. These attitudes spread like dry rot through society. In a nearby town there is a new public librarian; I assume she is, as are most librarians, devoted, hard-working and well-intentioned. One of her first acts was to place near the entrance a free-standing display of the latest bestsellers. Why does she feel the need to imitate what WH Smith's can do more effectively? Perhaps to save money for her users, so long as they are prepared to wait until a particular bestseller reaches their names in the library's queue? That is not likely to be her main intention. She has set up her display because a bestseller has become a synonym for 'quality', simply because 'everyone' is reading it. But this is ridiculous. It is as if to assume that McDonald's hamburgers are the pinnacle of culinary taste simply because more of them are eaten than is food offered in three-star restaurants. The librarian would have done better to put on display: 'This month's great but neglected novel'. Her action unwittingly helps to subvert the exercise of free democratic choice and thoughtful exploration; it narrows and closes.

Not long after the present government came to power there was a party at Number 10 Downing Street for those thought to best represent

'Cool Britannia'. Two writers, man and wife, were there and looked around for others of their kind. They could see none. They may have been myopic or casual, but I doubt that. They did see the members of the latest, gruesomely uncivil pop group. What kind of prime ministerial adviser recommends such choices?

What, in all this, may be the role of the State? Not, itself, to accept uncritically, and so implicitly to reinforce, all that the engines of mass communication help make most popular, but to point to the better, to stand for more. The fact that this country publishes more than 100,000 books a year is no more than a triumph of technology and marketing, not a triumph of the mind. So it is with the whole of the Information Revolution. Information is not knowledge; knowledge is not wisdom. They have to be climbed towards, individually, in the end.

To return to the beginning, the three categories of culture and the sense in which they may all be called 'political'. A would-be civilised democracy will not abuse culture for immediate political ends, nor impose its own predetermined definition of culture on its people. It will be open, demotic, not bullying nor endlessly all-things-to-all-men-or-women. It will offer perspectives on the better and the best; its citizens will be free to be both inside and outside their own cultural overcoats.

The British Museum, London, 1998

Noble Aspirations: UNESCO and Civil Society, a Memoir

In a collection almost entirely about English matters, it seemed at first that this essay on UNESCO might not have a place. But it is partly about the United Kingdom's relationships with an international agency, and, more important, the underlying issues in those relationships – such as the rights of civil society, of freedom of thought and speech – frequently occur in later pieces here; and the consideration of them owes a great deal to English history and traditions.

UNESCO – THE UNITED NATIONS Educational Scientific and Cultural Organisation – is regarded by many as a sort of international joke; woolly, wordy, head-in-the-clouds. In some respects all that is true. It is rather like an unworldly professor who can be ignored most of the time by those who live in 'the real world' but who sometimes surprises outsiders by his tenacious, hard-headed grip on deep-seated discontents (here, a stronger word than 'problems') within that real world.

I begin in this way so as to indicate why, several decades ago, I decided to give five years to UNESCO's service. I do not regret that. In a book written two decades ago – *An Idea and its Servants* – I tried to describe the whole organisation, its weaknesses and strengths, from within. Looking back now, I think I undervalued a vital element in UNESCO's almost organic nature.

UNESCO is officially an intergovernmental body, and that brings both gains and losses. It is also more. To a degree and of a kind not common among other UN agencies it has another role and other constituencies: those with civil societies outside, with independent, free, voluntary associations, known as NGOs, non-governmental organisations. The constitution of its executive board, originally, also reflected this connection in its composition. The UNESCO National Commissions were meant to feed the connections with each of their societies at large and the organisation. All those have done good work, have been fine examples of civil society in action, finding a voice. But their freedoms have been progressively reduced under pressure from governments individually and collectively.

The central UN bodies provide arenas where matters of high governmental policy can be addressed, matters of war and peace, of security, of economic survival, those issues which need the full diplomatic attention of each government. Other affiliated agenices – labour, health, and the rest – clearly have narrower briefs, are officially more specialist. UNESCO is the odd man out. It is concerned with a very wide range of issues, some overlapping with the work of the UN Headquarters itself, some with the more specialised agencies. It has interests in peace, human rights, the environment; there and elsewhere it may overlap with one or more of the others. The difference, and it is fundamental, is that UNESCO is concerned above all with the intellectual discussion of anything to which it turns; it seeks to increase knowledge from the most basic level upwards. It is, or was meant to be, at its core the home of the specialist, the academic, the distinterested thinker, rather than of the tactician, the diplomat, the civil servant or politician. It has programmes on peace and peace-making, while the UN is urgently discussing how to stop war in some part of the world. The UN centrally is in that sense tactical where UNESCO is ultra-strategic, looking at the underlying and continuing causes of conflict and how to reduce them before they start; put simply, it concentrates on how such issues may be better understood. It is a research institution and, in a good sense, a deliberate 'talk-shop'.

That is only part of the story. In a more important aspect of its activities it seeks to be free from direct governmental intervention; in principle, at least. In practice, it has continually to deter some governments from interfering; for instance, from briefing its representatives at a conference not to look at the basic issues dispassionately but to impose their own government's prior conclusions on whatever the theme of the conference may be. The Soviet Union used to bring its firmly preconceived views on the causes of war to any UNESCO conference concerned with any aspect of peace, which left little room for freely ranging discussion.

UNESCO's real difference from the rest of the UN's agencies lies here. Its central preoccupations are some matters with which, in free societies, individual citizens are or should be directly concerned and governments less directly concerned, or concerned only under the ever-watchful eyes of their individual citizens: education (as compared with governmental indoctrination), individual human rights (which many governments still flout even though they may in international meetings profess to respect them), free communications of all kinds, and the disinterested pursuit of knowledge of all sorts, from the scientific to the philosophical.

In UNESCO's early decades, many societies were not in any way open democracies in which individuals were free in the above senses. Here one of UNESCO's glaring and continuing difficulties became plain: its constitution assumed virtues many governments did not and still do have, or seek. Of course, many governments are worse in this regard than others; and not only those among newer nations. UNESCO regularly stubs its toes on the unwillingness of some highly developed and sophisticated 'parliamentary democracies' to live up to the spirit of the constitution to which they have pledged adherence. All participants in UNESCO, NGOs no less than member states, feel this paradox; though for the congenitally aberrant member states the worry is slight.

From its inception UNESCO has had an executive board responsible, through the Secretariat, for the execution of its programmes. Initially, the constitution specified that the board's members should be 'persons competent in the arts, the humanities, the sciences, education and the diffusion of ideas, and qualified by their experience and capacity'; they should exercise their powers on behalf of UNESCO as a whole, 'not as representatives of their respective governments'. Excellent. The early boards had a good proportion of scholars, thinkers, admirable statesmen from much of the globe; they were the conscience of the organisation. Many other governments subsequently decided, if they had not done so from the start, that they could not leave UNESCO's main decision-making body in the hands of independent thinkers. Here, Japan has tended to take the lead. By 1954, the charter was amended, explicitly converting members of the board into government representatives. Even so, when I joined the Secretariat in 1970, something of the original spirit remained. The member from (not 'for', given the way she acted) Switzerland was an extremely impressive professor of philosophy. To hear her berate the board on questions of human rights was a joy to those secretariat members who daily tried to work so as to help fulfil UNESCO's purposes, and an embarrassment to those who did no more than follow instructions.

From eighteen, UNESCO's board membership grew to fifty-odd as more continents, regions and states were born and demanded places; its debates are therefore more drawn out and difficult. When the board members formally became nominees of their governments, a very important distinction was erased. Conscientious secretariat members regret this, but most have accepted it and make more and more tactical adjustments rather than following the institution's strategic lights. In November 1993 the General Conference finally eliminated the last vestiges of the principle that the members of the executive board serve as independent individuals working only for the great good of the organisation. The charter was amended again, to specify that substantive contributions to the board's work are not a prerogative of the people who sit on it but of the states who appoint them. All that remains of the homage due to UNESCO's powers in this respect is an obligation upon the states to submit to Headquarters the name and curriculum vitae of any person they intend to put forward as their representative. These progressive changes in the nature of the executive board were prompted by the unwillingness of governments to allow non-controlled representatives to decide the size and shape of budgets, which they would then have to fund and if necessary defend at home. That is understandable; but there could have been a middle way which allowed for both governmental responsibilities and free intellectual representation.

Something similar has happened to another of UNESCO's special inventions: the National Commissions. They were intended to be the living expression in each country of UNESCO's commitment to free intellectual life. They were to be composed of highly qualified and independent individuals, who between them would cover the whole spread of its interests. They would be able to advise their own governments and UNESCO itself. It was obvious from the start that in some states, such independence would be a myth. In some other states, they were genuinely free and their contributions most valuable. They spoke their minds when advising governments and expected the civil servants who administered their work to know the extent and limits of their own role.

That too has changed over the years and in much the same way as the executive board. A minister of government would replce a commission chairman from outside government – a university vice-chancellor, perhaps. The argument for this, and for a selection of commission members less representative of the intellectual community, was always predictable: if you wish to have any clout, you must be run by someone who can speak to and for the government of the day. Who then speaks freely for the charter? The NGOs, which had been used to looking for help from intellectually well-informed members of National Commissions, found that advice and support less forthcoming.

All such changes bore especially heavily on responsible members of the Secretariat. Except for time-servers and those from states which simply do not recognise the independence of the Secretariat, life became harder. The independence of staff can at least in principle be defended from one paragraph of the constitution. Article VI states:

> The responsibilities of the Director-General and of the staff shall be exclusively international in character. In the discharge of their duties they shall not seek or receive instructions from any government ...

(This injunction applies to all UN Secretariats.)

Each member state also undertakes not to seek to influence the staff. On joining the organisation all officials swear to uphold its basic principles, to become international civil servants rather than agents of their home governments. This allows the brave to point out to an erring committee that they are acting against the constitution, or to refuse an irregular request from the ambassador of a member state, or to remind colleagues that special favours for their own countries are against the rules, or to support an NGO by invoking the rules on its behalf against undue pressure from a particular member state. *Some* do that.

This long preamble has been introduced to highlight the unusual nature of UNESCO. In the following pages the NGOs are at the centre. They were born in the early days, when Julian Huxley's liberal intellectual spirit reigned, and on the whole have proved fruitful, right at the heart of UNESCO's purposes as envisaged by its founders. With the National Commissions as originally conceived, the NGOs may form two outside pillars of strength towards the fulfilment of UNESCO's purposes; in principle; if they are allowed to stand straight.

In the beginning UNESCO's relations with the NGOs were close. Metaphors can be tricky, but to compare this one with the relationship of the mistletoe to the host tree seems reasonable – to the mistletoe at any rate; and the tree in this instance does gain. The initial constitution, Article XI, section 4, runs:

> [UNESCO] may make suitable arrangements for consultation and cooperation with non-governmental international organisations concerned with matters within its competence, and may invite them to undertake specific tasks.

In the early years very close official and ad hoc relationships developed with a small number of international NGOs. By the late 1950s, their number had so much increased that it became necessary to specify in just which way each NGO might work with UNESCO.

In 1960 the General Conference formalised the whole system in a lengthy set of directives. They are detailed, helpful and precise as to rights and duties; they are also wide, liberal and enabling. An NGO must not have been established by intergovernmental agreement; its purposes and functions must be non-governmenal; there must be a wide geographic spread in membership; and good communications with members. 'Consultation' and 'Cooperation' are key words. Duties include: providing advice and offering technical cooperation; expressing the views of important sections of public opinion; and helping to prepare and execute the organisation's programme. The years since they were set down have seen successive attempts to alter them, usually under more illiberal impulses. Yet by and large they have worked well, in spite of the continuing increase in numbers – NGOs having one form or another of official relations with UNESCO increased from 187 in 1961 to 585 in 1991.

There are three categories of NGOs; all impost significant obligations with regard to liaison and the exchange of information. Category A NGOs have surprisingly high obligations and reciprocal benefits. They must make 'regular major contributions to UNESCO's work'. They are expected to expand those of their activities which are of special interest to the partner body and to promote cooperation between NGOs in their field. All NGOs may receive documents, attend meetings and make statements in all subsidiary bodies of the General Conference.

Good. Yet gradually the distinction between basic subvention and contract became blurred and some NGOs failed to account precisely and on time for the money they had received. Understandably, UNESCO took action. In 1991 the terms of reference of its Committee on International NGOs were changed to include examination of the Director-General's proposals to grant subventions. Individual amounts ceased to be determined by the Secretariat's judgement on the usefulness of each NGOs activities. Political decisions were now involved, and often ran in one expected direction.

From January 1996, subventions were to be granted solely to new NGOs or to NGOs from developing countries who were beginning to cooperate with UNESCO. New subventions are to be granted for a maximum of four years. Well-established NGOs will continue to receive contracts for work under UNESCO's own programmes. The possibility of more secure financial support, a limited version of the old subventions, remains open with a new provision for medium-term 'framework agreements' for NGOs to work with UNESCO. In principle it will still be possible for NGOs to maintain their independence, but they will be under direct scrutiny by governments and will be aware that from now onwards the price of taking a decision that is unwelcome to key governments could be the loss of financial support. Further: the concentration on NGOs from developing countries at the expense of others, though it may look well judged, is questionable. Developing countries need, let us say, substantial physical infrastructures and should have preference in money made available to their NGOs for that. NGOs also have other substantial if not physical needs. Intellectual, artistic, philosophical life and much else of those kinds are indivisible; you do not help developing countries to grow in those respects by neglecting some of the claims of NGOs in developed areas; they must feed and grow from each other; you do not encourage that by forms of selective starvation.

Nor do you improve cultural life in the widest sense by tying established NGOs to UNESCO's existing purposes. One impulse behind their foundation was that they would be free to think afresh, for themselves, and so to feed their new thoughts into UNESCO and to civil societies at large. Increasingly, direct governmental intervention may narrow the organisation's foundation purposes, be another movement away from the principles of 1946.

The third exceptional feature of UNESCO–NGO relations is still the degree to which it is formally specified that NGOs may be involved in policy-making. Category A members can expect in principle 'to be as associated as closely and as regularly as possible with the various stages of planning and execution of UNESCO's activities coming within their particular field'.

A generous set of guidelines have been weakened gradually over the years. What did the reality seem like, from the perspective of an Assistant Director-General in the first half of the seventies? I had an unusually wide and varied clutch of NGOs. One evening the ADG for Science was in my office waiting for a lift to a reception. He waited longer than expected because during a single half-hour calls came in about: an earthquake in Latin America with damage to important religious monuments; problems at a tricky social-science conference within the Soviet bloc; the latest eruption in the Arab–Israeli dispute to do with the alleged neglect of each other's holy places; whether a certain NGO was to be asked to give consultancy services somewhere in Asia; and a routine call from the Director-General's office checking that a paper we were preparing for him to deliver at a meeting on environmental problems somewhere in the world would be ready on time. The ADG for Science said he would not receive five such different calls in a couple of days, let alone in one half-hour and that after the end of the official working day.

NGOs can be polemical, addicted to lobbying and engrossed in their own virtually closed worlds. If there were an overall professional motto for the officers of NGOs, it would be: 'There's nothing like leather.' The style, the manner, the thrust will differ from type to type; so will the suggestion of rectitude and urgency, and the ease or difficulty of their intimacies with governments. Some will march into your office and harangue; others will try to persuade you to talk over lunch at an extremely expensive restaurant; some cluster in groups which change according to need; some think groups add strength, others are believers in the solitary word in the ear. They are all devoted and believe in the merit and priority of their cause. Given the range of interests represented by the NGOs, their officers are bound to be like a rainbow arc, from formalistic social scientists to the airily artistic, from disinterested scholars to forceful professional chauvinists; chauvinists for their professions, that is.

For UNESCO's relationships with the NGOs the towering key figure was the first Director-General, Julian Huxley. Huxley was a splendid example of a very special English type, a product of the intellectual and

scientific upper middle class; a free spirit, eccentric, entirely unbureau-
cratic. He was reputed to disappear between meetings to sketch the flora
and fauna of the Bois de Boulogne and to pass duller parts of official
meetings drawing in the margins of his official papers the birds and
plants he had seen. He was exceptionally inventive and delighted in
bodies where independent thinkers of all kinds were mixed with straight
governmental representatives. He was also inspired by that post-war
sense of hope for a more intelligently managed future which lasted less
than a decade, until the hard-headed pragmatists and the Cold War
warriors began to impose their dire spirit on UNESCO. Huxley loved to
tweak the noses of apparatchiks from East or West; most governmental
spokesmen bored him, but he loved talking to individuals and to groups
with intellectual or artistic passions. I cherish the memory of driving him
round Paris during UNESCO's celebrations for its twenty-fifth anniversary, in 1971. The old quirky spirit was in full form. He died in 1975.

So Huxley loved NGOs, but was rather cavalier towards the protocol
demanded by many member states. His own account gives the flavour of
his approach:

> In the hot summer of 1947, we also set up an International Theatre Institute
> (for drama, opera, films and ballet) ... The committee responsible for this
> comprised many well-known names in dramatic circles, such as ... Lillian
> Hellman from the USA. She was a strong liberal, but official US bodies chose
> to consider her a communist, and protested. However, we stood firm and
> succeeded in getting the Institute approved as another of UNESCO's inter-
> national non-governmental bodies. (*Memories II*, Penguin, 1978, p. 18)

In all this Huxley was ably supported by his Deputy Director-General,
Jean Thomas, a Frenchman. That pairing of nationalities was also apt,
since Thomas's personality well complemented Huxley's. Thomas was
typical of the best type of French intellectual *fonctionnaire*, precise, pene-
trating, and, like many from the Grande Ecoles, excellent at linking
management skills with the principles they are meant to serve. The
debates about the NGOs were, he said, some of the worst in UNESCO.

But Thomas, too, gave powerful initial pushes to some artistic
NGOs which were later to become major forces – such as the
International Council of Museums and the International Music Council;
as Huxley had done, particularly, to some of the scientific and environmental NGOs.

Huxley and Thomas were also responsible for establishing the principle of giving a basic, operating subvention to some NGOs. The debate over the proper balance between subventions and contracts continued over the decades. As we have seen, the noose has gradually tightened to the point at which permanent subventions even for long and well-established NGOs are now being phased out or threatened. Some governments do not at all like the idea of independent bodies which might say something critical about one or other of their practices; they certainly do not see why they should actually help those bodies to stay alive through free, without strings, subventions.

Huxley and Thomas would of course have vigorously opposed that. They believed that strong, professional, non-governmental international organisations were among the bastions of free thought and speech. They should not be led to conceive of themselves as lapdogs; they must be free to bite the hand that feeds them. Anyone in Britain who has had much to do with, for instance, the Arts Council or the BBC knows both that the clients of such bodies, being free-born Britons, do not hesitate to bite them; and that many people (especially some politicians and civil servants) find the principle hard to take. In authoritarian regimes the practice is, of course, incomprehensible.

It will be plain that I am very much a Huxley/Thomas man. Disinterestedness, like democracy itself, is very hard and perhaps impossible to attain; but it is the right ideal, the right condition to aim for, everywhere. Open capitalist democracies have their less evident, less unmistakeably punitive, ways of calling free speech and free enquiry into question. The arguments grind and drone on: 'The time is not ripe; it looks as though the losses will be greater than the gains; we will be misunderstood, thought to be unsure of our own purposes by other societies with which we are on ambiguous terms; surely there must be a limit, the point beyond which liberty becomes licence', and so, drearily, on.

Whatever the charter or the manual may say, the NGOs tend to feel like supplicants. So they woo the Secretariat, while often resenting their powers and higher salaries; or they woo delegates to conferences who come from important member states or regions or faiths or ethnic groups. Some members of the Secretariat begin to feel like powerful and generous patrons and may make vague – or strong – promises which have to be refused higher up the system. Some of the Secretariat are not necessarily susceptible to flattery but are politically vulnerable to pressures from their own countries.

All this should have been and on the whole was less likely to happen at the level of Director-General and ADG. They had to watch all the time as closely as the dense spider's web of communications allowed; they soon understood that an unwise promise lower down which was refused higher up could set off a fog of false justifications, exculpations and counter-accusations. It was of course easier for those who came from a reasonably open democracy such as the United Kingdom. Not once in five and a half years did the British Permanent Delegation try to put pressure on me or to woo me with compliments. I did not expect it. Moral courage is buttressed by such heartening considerations. One middle-ranking secretariat member, at home a civil servant, was forcibly recalled and posted to a tiny town in his native continental wilderness. 'Only one traffic light in the whole place,' he said sadly, 'and no Scotch.'

This was, had to be, a world of continuous lobbying by the NGOs for higher basic subventions and more contracts. There was political mingling with national delegations, conference representatives, secretariat members; in the halls, the corridors, the bars, the library, the rest areas and the restaurants; more shadowy encounters could take place in the tunnels connecting parts of the main buildings.

So strong was the public image of the larger NGOs that many visitors assumed they were a fully integrated part of UNESCO, members of the Secretariat. This was not what their best supporter Huxley had intended; but most of the relevant secretaries-general of the NGOs were not disposed to dispel the confusion. Some did not realise that in the long term and on a wider perspective it would be against their own best interests to be organically part of the funding body. The 'arm's-length principle' – keeping due distance from your sponsor – was valuable. One result of this narrowing of their vision was a tendency to look too much towards the needs of the developed world. Earlier we saw how important it was, for reasons of intellectual universality, not to yield to a General Conference disposition to focus the organisation's work too much on the developing world. Here, the reverse was true; some NGOs had to be reminded that their brief was worldwide and they should not neglect the developing part.

So the dance between the member states and the NGOs went on and goes on. Usually it was the non-democratic states which led the criticism, but not always. The democracies put their argument in more empirical, non-ideological terms, as a position which any sound person or government would instantly recognise. Lord (Arthur) Salter made a classic statement stressing 'the necessity of responsible *governmental* [my italics] participation in order to achieve effective organised international action'. In other words, he was putting the NGOs to one side.

Attitudes towards the National Commissions were in some respects similar to those towards the NGOs. In some countries the Commissions became progressively less free than at the start; in other countries they were born unfree. Much the same, as has already been seen, happened to the executive board itself. This progress was evident as early as the mid-fifties; members, it was noted, were by now not serving the Conference as a whole – 'they were speaking precisely for their governments'. The irony is that such speakers were given a more attentive hearing than those who spoke freely. The board enjoyed hearing the Swiss professor of philosophy but did not take many notes of what she said; it was not an expression of other government's policies which they needed to report back.

In all these movements the UK did not, after a few years, behave very imaginatively; it was not noticeably Huxleyan. Gradually, it began to convey an impression of only modest interest (I am not yet suffciently aware of how it has performed since Britain rejoined three years ago). Two earlier instances stick in the memory. In my early days a convention was drafted, with of course much professional help from NGOs, to discourage the illicit purchase and transfer of cultural property. Many poor countries were having their national treasures secretly depleted because of the financial allures of the western world; corrupt officials and sophisticated robbers saw to that. Most European powers, in particular West Germany, sent to the working party well-briefed and cogent experts. The United Kingdom sent a lawyer who was neither expert nor well briefed and who, according to orders, opposed the convention – in a nit-picking, fluting, superior voice which made me blush.

Three years or so later came a related but significantly different convention, also prepared with good professional help from the NGOs, this time on the restitution of cultural property. For example, if country X, being wealthy, has in its museums three examples of country Y's historic war canoes, leaving Y itself with none and unable to pay for any which might come on the market, then an exchange could be agreed (one of the three canoes for something valuable of which Y still has more than one example). Again, the British representative had instructions to oppose (shades of the Elgin Marbles). Luckily, after a private secretariat intervention on the evening before the working party began its sittings, the British position was revised.

But that had involved an intervention of substance by the Secretariat, an action not to be practised often. What if other secretariat members practised it but not in the disinterested way in which those on this occasion justified themselves? Such interventions can be practised in principle as upholdings of the charter; but the balance is tricky.

The UK's only mild enthusiasm was less damaging than the active political interferences of some governments. There have been fairly frequent efforts to make NGOs realise that they might lose their subventions and contracts if they did not toe particular lines: about long-standing, pre-apartheid, links on artistic matters with South Africa, for instance, or with 'The Chiang Kai-shek clique' in Taiwan. Even an NGO formally sympathetic to the battle against apartheid has a right to object to not being allowed to make up its own mind in its own time and, instead, being threatened through the power to withhold funds. Such a stand seems entirely beside the point to some member states.

During my time at UNESCO, PEN, a valuale air hole to writers suffering censorship in many countries, was violently attacked by Czechoslovakia because it had run an outspoken conference on current limitations on artistic freedom. That was another case in which the Secretariat, on behalf of the constitution, rallied support from other member states. The Czechoslovaks unwisely insisted on a vote, and lost it. An even more striking instance of direct intervention came in 1973 when Amnesty International, an NGO in Category B and admirably effective, arranged a conference at UNESCO Headquarters on the practice of torture throughout the world. Almost immediately before the meeting was to begin, objections were made, by those who knew the finger would be pointed at them, against the use of UNESCO's premises and facilities. They were supported by a prosperous western 'democracy' – France, I was told, but could not confirm this – which had economic interests to protect. Against my will and that of some others, UNESCO gave way and Amnesty moved to another venue in Paris. Chesterfield's well-merited cynicism about ambassadors always comes to mind on such occasions; but the subdued manner of some when they arrived to pass on their orders suggested that they knew there was another world out there.

NGOs can be involved with more helpful relationships. The Participation Programme uses money – not much – set aside from the core programme by the General Conference. Another good, free or nearly free, idea. The PP office can be approached by a National Commission with what it thinks a good initiative, germane to UNESCO's purposes and generally a model. It might be a conference or publication or modest research project carried out in the applicant member state but also involving nationals of other states. Almost inevitably, such proposals also involved NGOs. Once they were approved, UNESCO would match dollar for dollar towards the cost.

Participation Programme funds-and-NGOs could together provide an occasional escape hole for the more adventurous secretaries-general of National Commissions in, for example, Eastern Europe, if they wished to launch an initiative of a sort they believed valuable but suspected would be chewed over by their *politburo* and nervously rejected halfway up the usual channels. My own favourite among such secretaries-general would, having enlisted the right NGO, earnestly apply for PP funds and tell his bosses that there might be new money from UNESCO. I imagine he provided the rest from savings in his own allotted budget. By this means he carried out several projects of high intellectual calibre with the minimum of state interference.

So, at best, a good NGO might have a balancing role between the Secretariat, often under pressure to give way to expediency, and governments who were putting on that pressure. Those NGOs, if properly involved by the Secretariat, could help define and refine aspects of policy rather more effectively than the organisation itself could. Secretariat members may have been at the frontiers of their disciplines when they began to work for UNESCO; inevitably, the frontiers moved ahead of them as the years passed. So NGOs are essential to UNESCO if it is to keep intellectually up to date and retain the respect of the scholarly, scientific and intellectual communities. The Secretariat must know who are the best of old and new names to invite to conferences, conventions and the like, and must be careful of the temptation to invite again and again the members of their own, increasingly out-of-date, old-boy or old-girl network.

Looking over old notes, I rediscovered my early interest in NGOs. A month or so after arriving at UNESCO I drafted three criteria for our obligatory regular examination of NGOs, which was then due. Is it in the forefront of its discipline? Is it making reasonable efforts to widen its work and membership, especially in developing countries? Is its proposed programme complementary to UNESCO's? The order and the phrasing were deliberate, an attempt to recognise all at once the authority of intellectual life, the autonomy of the NGOs and the constitutional duties of UNESCO. Above all, the word 'complementary' recognised that the NGOs have a role beyond that of helping to fulfil UNESCO's official programme, that the last word does not emerge from an intergovernmental agency. A few members of staff were not enthusiastic. To codify the approach to NGOs might restrict some of their pleasant powers of patronage. But the criteria were adopted and went on the books. I think I would not alter them if I returned to the Secretariat now.

The founding idea for NGOs was, and still is, a fine one; a product of the democratic belief in freedom of enquiry and free circulation of the findings of such enquiries. The best officers of the NGOs are blood brothers of the most devoted among the international Secreatariat. In saying this one remembers yet again the high optimistic spirit of the immediate post-war years which gave birth to the United Nations itself and its independent agencies. The progressively more-governmentally-controlled view of UNESCO and, by extension, the risk of narrowing the definition of its relationships with NGOs, had best be regarded as an error; an error to which virtually all governments are prone but which should, progressively, be put right. A huge hope but perhaps not altogether forlorn; any gain would be worthwhile. All is not lost. There is some disparity between the attitudes of a few member states as they are revealed in restricted acts such as those described above and in the more supportive resolutions about NGOs passed by the General Conference in the last few years. To an eye used to UNESCO's codes, a late resolution against links with South Africa shows the modifying effect of more reasonable member states, helped by the drafting of staff members (this is not true of the anti-Taiwan resolutions). Earlier anti-apartheid resolutions addressed to NGOs were more restrictive and arm-twisting. The latest six-yearly report on NGOs in Categories A and B rightly urged more widening into the developing world and more cooperation with National Commissions; and this was within a general context of encouragement. The granting of subventions has not been stopped but is to some extent redirected unhappily. Still, the practice of awarding contracts to NGOs has largely survived a period of great financial stringency, particularly after the USA and the UK left, when the Secretariat might have kept more money to themselves.

All this is indicative of the tensions between member states and the executive board, the National Commissions and the NGOs, tensions which criss-cross in several directions, and tensions between the liberal intellectual spirit and the formalistic routines which dominate some other states. All these will continue to exist within each of those elements; and sometimes perhaps the good will win.

Farnham, 1995/2000

BROADCASTING, DEMOCRACY AND THE ENABLING PRINCIPLE

*T*his sad piece was written as a contribution to a Festschrift *for Philip French on his retirement. He had been for many years one of the staunch upholders and exponents of the public service idea in broadcasting.*

I have to some degree brought it up to date. That was not a large task; one did not need to be prescient even ten years or so ago to see which way broadcasting was inexorably going.

It is an insistent piece, more insistent in tone than I intended originally. But I think the hammering is justified. Consider only the lessons to be drawn from BBC staff today. Some have bent to the yoke and made the best of things – they have commitments, family, mortgages – and some of those go on fighting hard for good broadcasting. Others illustrate the rule that institutions as they change get the changing staff they need and deserve. Those will not regret the dying of the public service idea because they neither know nor care much about it; they have enlisted under another drum. Some have just given up and gone. And some, who might once have thought a career in broadcasting one of the best and most rewarding of professions, will by now be dissuaded from applying.

I write as the next main phase of dismantling gets under way: generic channelling; channelling by status and existing tastes; the end of the public service idea, of aspiration; but a safer aim: to be an audience masser, a coagulator. Already they are honing the language for the crime.

Of course, it's all to do with competition – and with a succession of governments which do not wish or cannot understand the need for civilised resistance.

N OW THAT BROADCASTING as we have known it has, within the last few years, begin to change almost out of recognition, and mainly, as now seems certain, for the worse, we ought to take stock and celebrate what we have had – which ought to be recognised, much as we dislike praising anything in the public service, as an exceptional achievement.

In the pre-radio-and-television era, what did most people do at home in the evenings? As to the people I knew, it would be pleasant to think that as a family we read, talked around the fire, pursued hobbies, made clip-rugs, very occasionally had a few neighbours in. Some did some of those things, especially where the husband was a handyman and a 'home bird', or the wife gregarious. For the majority, those would be myths. Many men went down to the pub or sat in front of the fire sort-of-reading their favourite popular paper, while the wives darned socks or tried to catch their husbands' attention with a titbit of local gossip, or turned over the pages of a women's magazine. None of it was horizon-broadening (a phrase which would automatically raise a laugh among many media operators today). Most homes were literally bookless; as they remain.

For most homes radio was, from the early thirties, the first ice-breaker: from the rather forced bonhomie of *In Town Tonight*, which nevertheless seemed to us up in Yorkshire remarkably metropolitan, to what also seemed the surprisingly varied programmes of the North Region, the memory of which by contrast shows up the programming of today's local commercial stations for what it is – poverty-stricken low-level audience-grabbing. BBC local radio stations usually range somewhat more widely, while taking intermittent nervous refuge in pop music.

And so on to early radio's most dramatic hour: the collective national shock – a greater shock even than the announcement of the abdication – of Chamberlain's announcement that we were at war. Even in that short span before 1939, radio offered two important changes in attitudes: the realisation, if we were willing to respond to it, that the world was wider and deeper than we had ever imagined in our enclosed backstreets; and the sense, beyond the late-imperialist blather of school, that we could, after all, and sometimes did, feel like one nation.

All that was only a small prelude to the post-war impct of television. It was a few years before it took off, but it then quickly established itself as the major cultural innovation of the century. It had both sound and vision; it came straight into our homes; it made immense panoramic offerings. But before we look at what changes it may have brought about, it will be as well to look at what it did not alter.

Most people, before they make changes in their ways of life, have a powerful capacity for not changing their habits but rather for converting new offerings to fit their traditional ways. *The Royle Family* captures this well among working-class people. They have absorbed television by making it part of the circle around the hearth, but, since they have no hearth now that central heating is almost universal, television has become the equivalent of the hearth. If these see, collectively of course, something surprisingly new and different they may still, led by the mother, say: 'Fancy that!' and immediately absorb it, or make it into a small oddity peered at from within their habitual life. *Coronation Street* has become so much a part of the leisure fabric of their lives that they call it simply 'Corrie'. Two or three years ago I saw a long queue outside a new chocolate shop in Farnham and asked what they were all waiting for. 'Oh, Vanessa's doing the opening.' At the time I did not know who Vanessa was; my informer simply assumed I did. The traditional love of a flutter continues and finds new forms, not only that provided by the National Lottery. Once again, *The Royle Family* hits the button. They watched *The Antiques Roadshow*. Widening their horizons? No. They place on the coffee table advance bets of twenty pence on who comes nearest to the likely value of each object as announced by the expert. Well-observed absorption.

But, and it is a very big but, British broadcasting has persisted in offering far more varied programmes than most people knew they wanted, and in some ways has had its effects over the years much more than we always recognise: in awakening pity for people in great distress across the poorer parts of the world (as shown in, for example, the response to programmes about the famine in Ethiopia); in lessening the class-related nature of some sports and in introducing new participants to other recreations (as in rock-climbing, which, though, has long had a small proportion of other than middle and upper-class participants; and snooker, which has been invited to lessen its raffish image); in widening the appreciation of music, of archaeology, of bird-watching, of home care and of a dozen or more other such pursuits and interests. The influence of all those is not evenly spread by social class, age or sex; but a wider spread there is.

As was hinted earlier, and though it is difficult to avoid seeming Little Englandish in saying this, television even more powerfully than radio can at times evoke a sense of our common nationhood, especially through capturing great public events. An aspect of it naturally shows itself in international football matches, but the Britishness there is inherently shallow and transient. The funeral of Winston Churchill was on a different level, speaking to something even in those of us who had many reservations about the Great Man and his post-war record, but who shared the experience of the last war. There is something of showbusiness in all such events, but they do appear to draw on certain shared patriotic, not necessarily chauvinistic, feelings.

There is a less obvious and more important way in which television can tap into a common national consciousness: in comedy. It is in itself a tribute to the broad definition of public service broadcasting which was pioneered by the BBC; from *That Was the Week That Was* through *Morecambe and Wise* and *Monty Python* to *The Fast Show* and many another. Their importance is that they reveal a funny bone of a type that seems to be common to all classes and ages – dukes to dustmen. It expresses itself in zany, irreverent and often subversive situations and language to match. Foreigners either love it or simply cannot respond to it and decide it is 'very English'. It does seem to be a collective capacity even more than the response to a great statesman's funeral; a demonstration of a shared sense of humour.

At the other extreme today we have the efflorescence of audience-participation shows, of which a prime example is the BBC's Saturday-night presentation of the National Lottery results. It is a frenetic, mindless, whipping-up of near-hysteria of which the Corporation should be ashamed; and which Reith would have rightly scorned.

It is a truism that different national governments established broadcasting, its control, structures and financing, in one or a mixture of three main ways: state control, by which citizens heard and saw what the authorities thought was good for them; commercial control, by which the spread and types of programmes were decided by what best suited the pursuit of advertising revenue; and the not-state-controlled, not-advertisement-led, more-or-less-democratic systems. Britain, in one of her moments of social imaginativeness, opted for the third kind, which she called the idea of 'public service broadcasting'. This meant broadcasting in the interests of the public as widely conceived. Not for the government, not for the advertisers, nor, most of all, for only a few successive chosen segments of the audience, no matter how they might be defined (by cash or power or political considerations).

Few have realised how striking a concept that was or for how long it survived in more or less good shape, though under increasing battering. The prescription looked and looks simple: 'inform, educate and entertain'. The order is deliberate, the simplicity only on the surface; underneath, the demands are formidable. It is above all a trio of positive injunctions. That is the strength, sometimes more potential than actual, of British broadcasting legislation on the whole. It says 'thou shalt' before and more strongly than it says 'thou shalt not'. The BBC has the Royal Charter; commercial television has an Act of Parliament, which is explicity both more restrictive and looser. Obviously, a board of governors committed to the pursuit of the public service idea and working within the terms of the Royal Charter can be freer (not 'looser') than a board even composed of the great and good which has no such charter, and is aware of a set of profit-seeking bodies seeking to breathe on their individual necks. This in a country where, in spite of its invention of the public service principle, the excellent implications of that principle, properly understood, are in fact very little understood even at high levels. The most recent version of the Television Act, under which the commercial television board works, is even slacker than its predecessors; some things are no longer required under the Act. Our local commercial company at once made redundant its educational and arts officer. 'Freedom', the Act calls that. Freedom to what end? To commercialise television. To exploit viewers by reducing their freedom of choice; to make a fast buck at the expense of others' access to a richer world than they, the exploiters, can even conceive. All in the name of democracy; by people who dismiss their critics as 'moralisers', as though for them that word has the weight of 'paedophile'.

The reference to the Royal Charter just above is too starry-eyed. Governments of left and right cannot resist intervening and so damaging the powers of the chartered body. MPs speak in the House in ways which indicate that they do not even know what the constitution of an institution with the Royal Charter means. As I write the final version of this paper, a Labour Secretary of State calls in the chairman of the BBC Board of Governors to criticise the Corporation's programming. Quite out of order. Do his civil servants not advise him on the limits of his role? Technically, he may have the right to join in the debate; if he does so in the above way, he risks damaging a very good democratic convention. The monarch is brought in, via the Charter, to protect that convention.

Broadcasting in the public service means aiming to cater geographically for everybody, not just for those massed in the conurbations; in that, it is like the Royal Mail. It means catering not only for known majorities but also for as many minorities as possible, some small, some almost majorities. An important point here is that these groups are not in watertight compartments separated from each other; they overlap and shift in and out. We are all at some time members of majorities and also of different minorities. Public service means catering for all ages and all levels and kinds of taste (short of those at present prohibited by law, such as hardcore pornography). It means offering audiences not only things they already like but also things they did not know they would like until they are offered them. It means not simply 'giving the people what they want', nor what some powers-that-be want to ram down their throats for their own purposes; it means offering very much more of interest. 'How can I know what I like until I see what it is possible to have?'

A splendid moment in the usually mere simulacrum of a debate on this subject came when T. S. Eliot appeared before the Pilkington Committee on the Future of Broadcasting (1960–2), and was asked to comment on this false antithesis. Mr Eliot was by then old and had been very ill, but looked magnificent. I was deputed to ask him on behalf of the Committee what he thought of the commercial broadcasters' favourite justification. He raised his head, paused, and then uttered in impeccably phrased and punctuated prose: 'Those who *claim* to give the public what the public *want* [pause] begin by *underestimating* public taste [longer pause]. They end by *debauching* it.' There is little one can add to that crystallisation of the reality, though whether the profit-makers will recognise its force and truth is unlikely.

The enabling principle expresses well the key thrust of the public service idea. So much is easily said. But the matter of minorities and their rights demands a very hard look. One of the trickiest minorities for which to justify 'adequate' provision – trickier even than the justification of programmes about homosexuality – is that which appreciates the arts.

So few are even aware of the issue. What is the justification for their having broadcasting time? It cannot be a matter of counting heads. The justification is founded in the belief, which goes beyond numbers, that the arts matter to our intellectual and imaginative health; that they represent the height of our understanding and interpretation of our world in all its dimensions. That they and such claims on their behalf mean little or nothing to very many people is a great shame and to some extent, but not altogether, a consequence of inadequate social and educational opportunities. That does not weaken the case for promoting the arts. It increases the case for better education and the reduction of other such barriers, especially those of routine social divisions. 'The arts must be kept up.' That only a minority turns to them nowadays is a sad fact but, to repeat, does not weaken the argument that broadcasting should pay attention to them way beyond the increasing addiction to numbers alone. Potentiality is all. When one thinks, by contrast, of the time blithely given to, say, football, one is depressed at the truncated definition of a mature democracy. These are crucial points of judgement, watermark tests of that maturity. In essence, the job of public service broadcasting is not only to reinforce existing taste but to seek to widen it. We must gamble on our own and our fellow citizens' possibilities.

The proper definition of broadcasting in the public service discourages formulaic programming, or programmes merely copying known successful patterns (but perhaps with knobs on, with slight new angles). It means, rather, pushing the boat out, having what seemed a good idea and being free to try it out. Without that non-stereotyped approach we would not have had so wide a range of those good comedy series, from *Dad's Army* through *Steptoe and Son* to *Till Death Us Do Part* to *One Foot In The Grave* and after; or news and current-affairs programmes with large and serious horizons, a feeling for issues of great moment; or inventive programmes on the arts; or, perhaps most surprisingly of all, earthy, unsentimental, documentary programmes about where we fall down as a society – on drugs, violence, home-grown poverty – programmes which would predictably be 'a turn-off' for mass audiences but which ought to be made, had to be made, for those who would look and listen. We know by now that that last group can be larger than market indicators might suggest.

That was the first implicit general rule: spread, experiment, respect not only what your audiences already like but what they would like if they had the chance. Even as I write this I can hear once again in the background the cynical laughs of the commercial broadcasting tycoons; but so be it. Cynicism's cousin is humbug and we have to learn to recognise and live with both. Broadcast news at its best – it falls down more often than one would wish nowadays – can be a good example of the honest and responsible operation of the public service idea.

It would have been easy to provide tabloid news for 'the masses' and 'heavy' news for the particularly literate; not that the 'heavy' newspapers are particularly heavy nowadays. What we have had instead, and in spite of the fact that many people are inadequately educated, is straightforward, not hyped, news, news which assumes if not wide reading then certainly shrewdness and the capacity to accept ideas presented clearly and straight. Current-affairs programmes extended that process. Who would have guessed before television appeared that the programmes on famine in Ethiopia mentioned earlier would attract not a mass audience but a very large one, a substantial minority, many of whom went on to pledge donations to charities. At best, domestic issues have been consistently treated in depth by such programmes as *Panorama* and the late *World in Action.* Some politicians did not like them because they often exposed 'the quarrels of this society with itself' (a fine phrase used by a BBC senior executive when harried by MPs) – but that is a fundamental democratic aim, and implicit in the very definition of the public service for broadcasters.

The praise for current-affairs and news programmes above is by now out of date. As I revise this essay, the death of Paula Yates, a television presenter, is announced and in suspicious circumstances. Clearly, most people in Britain know her name and unhappy history. In their main early evening news on that day both the BBC and ITN led, and at length, with that event. That is one of the worst, most cheaply populist acts, committed recently by both channels; the sense of the relative importance of different public events has completely collapsed. That collapse is partnered by increasing near-literacy among those who write the news and broadcasting journalists at large. One reporter in Northern Ireland recently described the terrible internecine murders on the Belfast's Shankhill Road. His next sentence began: 'This close-knit community ...'. This is reporting as by rote, cliché-rote, as a sort of tic.

After that, it is almost a relief to turn to soap operas. Most are formulaic and conventional and, as such, in a straight line of descent from the novelette serials in the popular women's magazines of half a century ago. They differ in two important respects: they seek a much wider audience, in class and education and age terms, than the earlier magazines; and they are on the whole written by cleverer people. They have to 'tell a good story' and keep the audience cliffhanging from one episode to the next. The best are, at their best, rather better than that. To some extent they tackle subjects the earlier stories dared not tackle. That timidity was partly an aspect of the conventional attitudes of their time and culture, partly due to their fear of what might put off their relatively narrow audience, and partly due to that greater cleverness of today's scriptwriters – who become bored and decide to push the boat out, probably egged on by an inventive director or producer. Of course they cannot stray too far or too often or they would lose audiences. Yet from time to time *EastEnders*, for example, might without much flannel or periphrasis, but sometimes over-theatrically, treat homosexuality, lesbianism, racism, violence in the home, drunkenness, one-parent families, prison.

Here we meet the question of quality and its definition. The first thing to say is that quality, much like the nature of 'a free society', is indivisible. Quality does not automatically inhere in 'highbrow' programmes and rubbish in the rest. A popular programme may be of high quality; a 'highbrow' programme may be conventional, snooty rubbish. That is a simple truth but one not always seen or followed; dead ends are followed instead, in almost all discussions. Or broadcasters themselves, in the BBC as elsewhere, consciously or unconsciously invoke the *boule de suif* principle: let the whore be used to buy time for the aristocrats. Translated, that becomes: 'Yes, we do some lousy programmes for the mob; but that keeps our competitive numbers up and so we can safely put on at least some "good" programmes also.' The odd flower floating on a sea of sludge.

Manifestly, commercial broadcasters are usually happy to equate quality with the numbers viewing. Occasionally, frankness intervenes and they change the title of an annual prize from that for 'The best such-and-such a programme' to that for 'The most popular such-and-such a programme'. An astonishingly unexpected flash of candour, of honesty.

Huw Wheldon, one-time head of BBC Television, liked to talk about quality in a deliberately down-to-earth way. Not definable in abstract terms and that wouldn't help anyway, he would say, and went on in this manner: 'My first test is whether I personally like a proposed programme and am supported by most of my colleagues; we respect it, find it interesting, and guess that many others would also respond in those ways. I heartily dislike programmes made for "the masses" which the makers themselves secretly despise. Respect the programme and those who might become its audiences. Nothing else is as important.' Very British, that; pragmatic, full of sound sense; not to be dismissed as 'Welsh waffle', but asking the right questions about programmes and people. A tighter expression of the same aim, attributed to Wheldon and sometimes to Bill Cotton, is: 'We should aim to make the good popular and the popular good.' It is almost impossible to imagine hearing that within Broadcasting House today.

By principles such as those the BBC became the benchmark for many other broadcasters, here and abroad. One commercial television top executive went so far as to say that 'the BBC keeps us all honest'. It was, for those who would see, the conscience of British broadcasters. Some could never see, could not or would not.

All this is maintained by the BBC's unique funding system, the licence fee. Again, here is something widely misunderstood. The overwhelming justification for this method is that it keeps the BBC independent of both governmental control (which a direct governmental subvention would risk inducing) and from the pressures of advertisers for bigger and bigger audiences all the time and to hell with 'quality'. That is overridingly the best justification. Second, and again a point which few recognise and the commercial people do not want us to recognise: the licence fee is far and away cheaper than any of the new commercial systems. For what the BBC gives, you will pay several times more to receive that range and variety by cable or satellite. The Murdoch press habitually tries to undermine the licence-fee system. The full subscription to BSkyB is about three times the licence fee. If you ask people simply whether they would like not to have to pay a licence fee, most will say yes. If you lay out comparative costs and ranges of programmes, the majority opt for keeping the licence-fee.

Many MPs simply do not wish to accept this fact; they think it more 'democratic' (for what multiple purposes, many of them cock-eyed, is that word wheeled out!) to oppose a public fee 'upfront'. I remember a wearying half-hour with a Labour MP who was rigidly impaled on a phrase he found attractive: 'I dislike the licence fee because it's a regressive poll tax.' Language such as that is an escape from thought. He was, I suspect, objecting to the fact that all pay the same fee; but this is nothing new – it exists in the postal service, in dog licensing and elsewhere.

Then there are all the other MPs who somehow think that to support commercial television and reject the 'state' system of the BBC is to strike a blow against elitism and for democracy. For them the fact that for its deliberately mass-focused programmes commercial television often gains larger audiences than does the BBC, is itself a pure example of 'democracy' at work and one they hesitate to do other than supinely acknowledge; fully to recognise the implications of their position would be to reveal wholly undemocratic horrors. At such moments one thinks we would do well to offer in the House, to MPs and peers, regular and continuing classes on the intricacies of democracy.

These are unpopular judgements. The late Hugh Gaitskell, when leader of the Labour Party, was infuriated when on television I accused his party of being stuck with these attitudes; he invited Richard Crossman (we were about to meet) to 'kick my arse' – very vulgar. Harold Macmillan, Tory Prime Minister, faced in 1962 with the Pilkington Report on Broadcasting which they found unpalatable, asked who had written it. He was told, wrongly, that it had 'been written by a *provincial university lecturer*'. Perhaps an Oxbridge graduate would have had better manners. Middle- and upper-class snobbery has many forms.

The 'new' Tories are natural proponents of the commercial idea in broadcasting. Awkward considerations on the admirable British record in this most pervasive form of mass communication interest them hardly at all. They reduce almost everything to simplistic assertions about 'the free market' and 'individual choice'. They set about creating a wasteland and call it freedom. Paragraph 1000 of the Pilkington Report is worth recalling: 'It was argued in favour of the introduction of a service of subscription television in this country that the equipment developed for it, and films made to supply it, would be saleable abroad. If it were desirable to introduce a service then the incidental advantage of selling equipment and films abroad would accrue. But obviously the first duty is to promote the service of broadcasting in this country; and this could not be disregarded so as to secure the incidental advantage.' We do not hear so thoughtful a note from politicians today.

Television has its limitations, of course; and its less-than-happy effects. At this moment we should celebrate and fight to sustain its achievements because, from the 1990 Broadcasting Act and onwards, all that has been at risk. That false assumption, that more channels, commercially run, will mean more choice, rules. As we have already seen, it means less choice, worse programmes. One begins almost to despair of the short-sightedness of recent governments. Their distorted view of British life and their resulting acts verge on the socially and personally indictable.

Technological advance becomes self-justifying and overrides thoughtful policy-making. Digitalisation, insufficiently understood and controlled, will accelerate the damage. Recently, two economists, Graham and Davies, firmly summed up their findings: the future will bring great concentration of ownership, huge fragmentation of audiences and less real choice for all (because they will all be chasing each other's tails). We will lose variety in the senses described above. Most channels will be dead-centred on mass audiences. For profit. There will be room for minority audiences so long as they too can be made profitable. There will be services addressed to small and specific and virtually enclosed tastes; and that is altogether a lesser and less interesting thing than we have so far had. Market-massing and status-differentiation; those will be, both under and above ground, the dominant thrusts. No more coming together as a whole communty, whether for fun or in shared respect; no more taking great risks to move into new territory; no more assuming that people are capable of responding to more and better than we might originally have thought. It may be almost time to say R.I.P. to television conceived in the public service and interest. We are lucky to have known it.

Farnham, 1990/2000

PART TWO

A VERY ENGLISH VOICE

D. H. LAWRENCE'S COUNTRY

THE TOWNSHIP OF Eastwood and its surroundings incorporate to a remarkable degree some important elements in English social and cultural life. They can still remind the visitor of the old rural England of farm and forest and river; they also recall a people and a landscape greatly damaged by a thoughtless and often grasping capitalism. From the mid-nineteenth century, coal mining on a large, industrialised scale was developed in those parts. The working people were meanly dragooned into uniform 'estates' (a strange adoption of a word with grander meanings). Such housing was built in many parts of the country, but especially in the Midlands and North, Scotland and Wales, as the Industrial Revolution reached its peak. The men were overworked and underpaid by the mining bosses. Ironically, the large houses on the 'estates' of the big landowners, who by law owned the mining rights under their land, often overlooked the miners' huddled dwellings, but were far enough away to have their own enclosed space.

Typically, Eastwood in D. H. Lawrence's day exhibited also the resilient culture of the working-class people themselves, a culture which could hold a complex balance between the men and the women. The men were of course physically strong, but psychologically the women were often the stronger; they had to be. The men could take refuge in the pub and its beer after the back-breaking work. It was often left to the women to 'make do' on what money was given to them: to make sure the rent was paid, to provide enough nourishing food, to keep the house clean and tidy, to look after the kids; all in all to make sure, if at all possible, that they didn't run into debt. Most embodied a determination to survive respectably, and in that effort the twin pillars were self-help and, almost but not actually paradoxically, neighbourliness. They held fast to church or, more likely, chapel. Most of them would not allow themselves or their families to be brutalised by living conditions hardly better and in some ways worse than those their forebears, pre-industrial workers, above ground, had known on that same land. Some men congenitally drank too much and, unless the wives could effectively discourage them, the household slid down the slope towards acute poverty.

In this place in 1885, into a miner's family, D. H. (David Herbert, but known to Eastwood as Bert) Lawrence was born. Frail and sickly but, with his mother unshakeably behind him, determined to make his own kind of life in his own way, he wrote ceaselessly. An old miner said to me in the nineties, as one offering remarkable and hardly conceivable information to a visitor for whom he expected the fact to be as strange as it was to himself: 'Lawrence lived by 'is pen, yer know. That teks some doing, for a miner's son.'

Eastwood sits on a hilly spine of land nine miles north-west of Nottingham. The main street runs roughly along the spine, and its north-west-facing slope looks over the last half-mile of the county of Nottinghamshire towards Derbyshire; the border is marked by a small and sluggish river, the Erewash. To a visitor it seems a small mongrel of a river, but, like most mongrels, it is loved by those who know it well, as Lawrence exceptionally did. It figures in his writing as powerfully and memorably as do the great rivers of mainland Europe in some Continental novels. Even today the view from the top of the town, over the fields, hills and woods of what Lawrence called 'the country of my heart' is little changed from his time. There is, of course, one most dramatic change: even where their buildings have not been knocked down, and many have, the mines are silent, worked-out, dead.

Eastwood's population has grown to 12,000 from the 3000 of Lawrence's day. Yet again, it is remarkable how little the general appearance of the town has changed. There are, of course, the new chain-store shops – outfitters for women and men, chemists, video and general electrical shops, fast-food outlets (but still the old-style fish-and-chip shops); and there are new housing areas on the fringes. But Lawrence would have recognised the town at once; its odd geographical position has kept much of the centre largely as it was a hundred years ago. True, there is a

White Peacock café, named after Lawrence's first novel, a small factory called the 'Lawrence something or other', and a few similar fribbles. But, even if one worked only from an old print, the main frame of the town is instantly recognisable and its Lawrence landmarks easily traceable. Most striking of all: the four houses in which the Lawrence family lived are all still there and can be seen in a circular walk of less than a mile. Two of them can be visited and luckily they are the two most interesting of the four.

Any visit to the town starts best at the new public library, set just back from the main street. It contains a special Lawrence Room, which, among much else, has the Hopkin collection. William Hopkin was a prominent local socialist and writer who befriended the adolescent Lawrence, remained a friend for life and was sent copies of most of the books as they appeared. Years ago I met his daughter in Santa Fe, another of Lawrence's adopted territories. She was then very old, had been born some years after Lawrence but remembered his visits vividly. She had the intelligent sparkle Lawrence admired in some of the Eastwood women.

From the library it is only two or three hundred yards up the same side of the street to Lawrence's birthplace, 8a Victoria Street. It is a typical terrace of miners' houses, each opening directly on to the pavement, looking across at the neighbours opposite. 8a is slightly different from most around since its front window is larger than usual, an oblong. A visitor from a similar background knows at once that 8a was used as a shop, of the sort that appeared at intervals in working-class terraces. Mrs Lawrence sold household linens and baby clothes from a display in that window.

The front door opens directly into the living room and that in turn to the kitchen. They and the bedrooms are furnished as nearly as possible in the style of the Lawrence's time there (they left in 1887, when Lawrence was two years old). There are two identified pieces of furniture from the Lawrences, a chiffonier and a single-legged but broad-based bedside table which can be adjusted up and down and across, so that the table's surface may be placed over the bed – to help feed an invalid, for instance. Both pieces, slightly genteel for a miner's home, poignantly remind us that Mrs Lawrence was from 'a better class' of family than her husband; she had been a schoolteacher. Presumably most of the Lawrence furniture passed, when the family home was broken up, to the children and other relatives, or was sold to a 'house clearance' entrepreneur for a few pounds.

8a Victoria Street is not the poorest kind of miner's dwelling; nor are the other three Lawrence houses. It is, compared with a typically basic miner's home, quite substantial, the living room a good size with a warm and solid feeling, the bedrooms not cramped, and a large attic running across the whole floor area. The 'main' or front bedroom, its big iron bedstead and simple bedspread, are deeply evocative. You may easily imagine the knocking on the party wall, indicating to the neighbour that labour has started and the local midwife had best make haste. David Herbert came into the world here as the fourth child and third son. Mrs Lawrence was to have her fifth and last child, a second daughter, in their next home. Through the main bedroom, in a room which did not then form part of the Lawrence's home, is a short presentation, mainly photographic and about the local area, of Lawrence-related material.

Just below the house, dropping down the hillside, were in Lawrence's day rectangles of mean miners' dwellings known as The Squares. Lawrence hated them, with good reason. They were what the colliery owners, secure in their handsome mansions, had thrown up to contain their workers. Compare the beauty of the hill towns of Italy, Lawrence cried, in a passage which is often regarded as excessively romantic. He had a point. Grouped housing, even for people who cannot pay much in rent, does not have to be as basic, as ugly, as uniform, as neglectfully blind to the surrounding natural features, as this. This was housing by people whose god was Mammon, who regarded their workers as little more than beasts of burden, and whose interest in grace and beauty started and stopped within their park gates. Areas such as The Squares, squalidly planned, squalidly thrown up, encouraged squalid living.

It is no wonder – but not a sufficient excuse, especially to women such as Mrs Lawrence – that many miners spent too much of their spare time and their wages, after a long hot day down the pit, in the male camaraderie of the public houses, such as the one to which Lawrence gave the name The Moon and Stars in his first major novel, *Sons and Lovers*. It still stands, in a backstreet only a couple of hundred yards from the public library; its real name is The Three Tuns. It too has a Lawrence room now, and a few other bits of self-conscious catchpenny nonsense. They might have done better to arrange it to the memory of Lawrence's father, with pub material of that time. But the atmosphere, at least from the outside, survives, and easily evokes the shade of the father, stumbling out and heading for home and a tongue-lashing.

Of The Squares, one row of houses has been retained, though now pedestrianised and artifically cobbled, so that it needs a feat of the imagination to recreate the noise and smell and the clinkered dirt of the streets as they were. You are a hundred and fifty yards from 8a and, as you turn right along the gentrified recreation, are heading for the second home of Lawrence's childhood, in a group of houses called The Breach. The family lived there from 1887 to 1892, from the second to the seventh year of his life. In *Sons and Lovers* The Breach is called The Bottoms and the Lawrence's time there memorably evoked – the house itself and the melodramatic life they lived within it – in the first half of that book. The Bottoms is a more accurate name than The Breach for the cluster, since the houses sit almost at the bottom of the ridge on which the town stands. A field away is the Erewash and Derbyshire.

These houses were, again, larger than the generality of miners' dwellings and a step up in size from 8a Victoria Street; 'substantial', Lawrence said. Much of the group still stands, though now surrounded by more modern houses. Lawrence could look from the back bedroom over the fields to Derbyshire, or from the front at the slope up to town, then parcelled into allotments which some miners tended. The allotments have given way to semi-detached houses and a school, and the road has become, entirely unsurprisingly and unimaginatively, Garden Road. At least it hasn't been called Lawrence Road; but the house has been renamed Sons and Lovers Cottage and its upper part is let to holiday-makers, most of whom want to explore the surrounding countryside and, I was told, have not heard of Lawrence.

Mrs Lawrence was pleased that hers was an end house and so only half attached to the rest of the terrace. It cost sixpence a week (two and a half new pence) more than its neighbours, but gave her slightly more privacy and a bit of side garden, and was not overlooked. She came to dislike the house intensely since it shared with the block opposite, at the back, a dirty and noisome alley (still traceable). Her gentility made her strive constantly to pull her family and especially her children out of the drab, often brutal and totally unperspectived life of the miners.

At the bottom of the narrow little garden is a small brick shed which recalls the harrowing scene in *Sons and Lovers* when Morel (based on Lawrence's father), drunk and violent, locks his wife out of the house, and she wraps round her an old rug from the 'coal-house' nearby until she can get into the house again.

Here too is a recreation of a miner's home of the 1880s and 1890s. The 'best front room' would only be open on special days – Christmas, weddings, funerals, some Sunday visitors. Most of the time it looked much as it does today, chill and formal, frowned over by an upright piano out of proportion with the size of the room itself. It recalls Lawrence's haunting poem, 'Piano':

> Softly, in the dusk, a woman is singing to me;
> Taking me back down the vista of years, till I see
> A child sitting under the piano, in the boom of the tingling strings
> And pressing the small, poised feet of a mother who smiles
> As she sings.

The back kitchen, where the family would live most of the time, has a black-leaded range, a centre table and a few simple chairs. It is best to enter by the back door as the family would, coming from the pit or school, through the tiny scullery with its simple utensils for cooking and the washing of clothes, to the heart of the house. The front door would have been opened only for those special occasions and for greatly respected visitors. A coffin would be taken in that way and placed on trestles in the front room until it left again by the front door for the cemetery; as it is in the most poignant of all scences in *Sons and Lovers*, after the death of Paul's older brother William.

These two, 8a Victoria Street and the house in The Breach, are much the most evocative. But two remaining Lawrence homes, both within a quarter of a mile, do add something to the atmosphere. You climb three hundred yards up the hill towards the town and find Walker Street. Here the Lawrences lived until 1902. Mrs Lawrence's slow but steady climb to near gentility is illustrated by the bay window, a very important signifier to those who know the social codes. Being high, these houses have a splendid view over the country of Lawrence's heart. This was not the claustrophobic setting for family fights like those at The Breach. As you look over the road at the sweep of countryside, you remember more the settings of Lawrence's first novel, *The White Peacock*, and other passages in novels, short stories and essays.

The Walker Street house has no plaque and visitors are not received. The fourth of the houses has at least a plaque. It is even further up the hill, just behind the town centre and has no view, being in a street where houses face each other at right angles to the panorama: 97 Lynn Croft Road. But it was, in the finely graded terms of such communities, yet another step up, and even Lawrence was proud of its style and standing. He was still young enough for such pride, being only sixteen when they moved in. It was here that the family lived until 1910, the year of Mrs Lawrence's death. This house, we may say, marked the end of Lawrence's early life; just as Paul after his mother's death moves out and away, and *Sons and Lovers* ends.

That, then, is the essential town walk. Apart from a few with literary tastes, inhabitants of the modern town are not greatly aware of Lawrence and his achievements. More have at the back of their minds the fact that he wrote 'a dirty book', called *Lady Chatterley's Lover*. The town goes about its perennial business as, in a phrase from Lawrence about the banal inevitability of most of our lives from day to day, 'it has to do'.

So we leave Eastwood. It would, though, be a pity to do so without seeing something of Lawrence's much-loved local countryside. North-west on the Mansfield Road you pass the home of the Walkers, who, with the Barbers, owned the local mines (later, the house became the offices of the National Coal Board), past the mine offices where young Paul Morel queued miserably for his father's wages. Then up the hill towards Underwood, down a lane off whch a private gate leads to the ruins of Haggs Farm – the Willey Farm of *Sons and Lovers*, where Lawrence formed his relationship with Jessie Chambers, on whom the character of Miriam is based. A quarter of a mile on, you can leave the car on the verge and walk in woods Lawrence knew well. Then to Moorgreen Reservoir, the setting for the water-party chapter in *Women in Love*. On a slope nearby is Lamb Close, still the home of the Barbers and decidedly not open to the public. But it can be glimpsed through the trees. It figures as 'Shortlands' in *Women in Love* and elsewhere. As a countryside 'lung', the area is now much used by walkers and their dogs.

A second, south-easterly trip goes above all to Cossall, still a virtually untouched village with good, solid houses grouped around an old church. Though nearer Nottingham than Eastwood, and now within sight of the motorway between London and the North, it sits quietly there as it has done for centuries. The cottage to the left of the church, double-fronted and well-proportioned, was the home of the Burrows family, to whose daughter, Louie, Lawrence was for a short time engaged. It was the model for the cottage of Will and Anna Brangwen in *The Rainbow*. One may then go a few miles further east, cross the motorway and come to the hamlet of Strelley, which also looks much as it must have looked when Lawrence knew it, and described the Brangwens seeing it from across the fields.

So what does all this wandering add up to in terms of our understanding of Lawrence's work? Can such a visit do anything to increase our appreciation? Or is it a harmless form of biographical gawping, intrinsically no different from shufflings through country houses, about whose history and the lives of their inhabitants we learn only a little and that on the surface?

There is no substitute for trying to read the works themselves in all their complexity, and there are no short cuts in that effort. The backgrounds of some authors may be virtually irrelevant to our understanding of their works. With Lawrence, such background, though it may do little if anything to help us appreciate the works, can help us to understand better the culture from which he came and the contributions it made to his work – in all that culture's crudenesses and complexities, its weaknesses and strengths, its brutalities and pieties. We realise then, very much as from outside, how much more penetratingly Lawrence saw into that culture than we could ever have done, even if we too had been born into it.

It follows, very importantly, that a visit may bring home to us with renewed force something of the ways in which a gifted writer can take material which looks to an external and unendowed eye simply poor and deprived, and can see in it and recreate the power and passion, the splendours and miseries, of those lives. And can do so in such a way that we cannot any longer, if we have been so tempted, dismiss such lives as of little interest or consequence. That can be one of the greatest gifts of the novel, as Lawrence knew.

Similarly, to see the landscape Lawrence loved so much and to recall his recreation of it is to realise how relatively blind most of us are, as compared with him. The eyes and ears and touch and smell which he learned to exercise on that pleasant but undramatic home landscape were later to blossom in Australia, Sicily, New Mexico, Sardinia, the South of France. More dramatic landscapes, all of those; but in the contrasting light of them, as we visit Eastwood, we are reminded that, to a creative eye, no landscape is in itself uninteresting, dull.

Lawrence was a great evoker of landscape, a fine essayist and critic, a considerable poet and short-story writer and a superb novelist. His great-est single achievement was in the exploration of often deeply hidden and complex human relationships. A reading of the novels might best begin with *Sons and Lovers* and then go on to *The Rainbow* and *Women in Love*; after that, the road is plain.

So: to stand in The Breach house does not in itself help us to see further into Lawrence's achievement. The process by which art comes about is too subtle for that. But a visit to Eastwood may help us to see how, from the most unpromising of circumstances, the individual creative imagination can transmute events and places and styles into a kind of universality; that is, may speak deeply and relevantly to readers of all times and places.

Eastwood, 1993/2000

THE RAINBOW

SINCE THEY FIRST appeared, the works of D. H. Lawrence have sharply divided scholarly and non-scholarly opinion, the critics and the 'intelligent lay readers'. They have also shocked less informed public opinion, egged on as always by the moral-gatekeepers, especially those in the popular press; and of course the censor at that time took action. *The Rainbow* had to be withdrawn when it first appeared. Although the general level for being shocked is less today, virtually the same range of reactions can be found (having been stirred up in mid-century by the trial over *Lady Chatterley's Lover*, whose effect remains to some extent alive after a couple of decades) still dividing critics, non-professional readers, public authorities and the rest.

The case against Lawrence brought by those who claimed to be the voices of 'the common man' rests almost entirely on his explicit attitude towards sexual matters. He was, for instance, quite open only eighty years ago about the fact that women feel sexual desire, that they can lust after different men – and sometimes women – at different times, that their sexual sense comes and goes, and is as integral a part of the rhythms of their life as eating or sleeping or menstruation. I know of no reference by Lawrence to that odious would-be joke about English women's recommended uninvolved attitude to the act of sex – 'Lie back and think of England' – but can easily imagine his contempt. So it was quite shocking in 1915, and in spite of the relaxing influence on sexual habits of the First World War, to describe one of his characters – Ursula in *The Rainbow* – in the way quoted below. So frank is it that we may fairly guess it would shock many women, and perhaps many men, even today. They might well be reinforced in the conviction, usually reached at second hand, that Lawrence was an obscene writes: 'And in this state, her sexual life flamed into a kind of disease within her. She was so over-wrought and sensitive, that the mere touch of coarse wool seemed to tear her nerves'. Lawrence acknowledged also that many men could have homosexual as well as heterosexual desires. In short, he insisted that the full extent and implications of our sexuality had to be faced, and especially the intricacy of our sexual relationships with those closest to us, just as much as our relations with them at the conscious and workaday levels.

The publication of *Lady Chatterley's Lover* not long before Lawrence's death confirmed these objections. It seemed more shocking even than his earlier books, not because it probed love-and-sex relationships more successfully than they did – it did not – but because it used explicitly and freely that magic-horror word, 'fuck'. That was enough to bring out the English legal and political establishments against it then and later, and to shock many non-literary people. But not all; among other things, the book's trial, thirty years after it was written, revealed that great changes had been taking place in British attitudes since Lawrence wrote the book. Rough labourers who use that shocking word frequently might have been shocked to see it in print; but that was unlikely to happen.

It will be as well to say early that Lawrence was something of a puritan, a believer in marriage and in tenderness above all else in sexual relations (*Lady Chatterley* was at one point called *Tenderness*) and very much against any prurience or sniggering in sexual matters. Aldous Huxley tells of being rebuked by Lawrence when, as they were working together, he made a smutty remark. Lawrence, very angry, told Huxley how wrong it was ever to make jokes of that kind; they 'did dirt', or something to that effect, on life. Lawrence was also in favour of frank-ness and directness, and when necessary of the 'burning out' of sexual shame by intense passionate activitiy; as in the passage in *The Rainbow* where Will and Anna cross just such a frontier and reach a new space where they can live together emotionally, less encumbered.

Informed critical opinion on Lawrence divides not so much on his attitudes towards sex as on his achievement as a novelist of individual and social perceptions, on his psychological and social analysis, and on his insights into intricate human relations above all. Nevertheless it is not easy to refute the accusation that he wrote some silly and some cruel things, that he sometimes uttered authoritarian, neo-fascist and anti-Semitic sentiments, that he could be shrill and hysterical, and that hence some passages in his writing, including the novels, are inflated and wrong-headed. By contrast, it is a huge relief to move from those to some of his books on travel or to essays on other writers or to the poems. But there is no point in denying the faults or trying to minimise them; it was very much the same driven, often sick, gifted man who wrote them all. It is fair, however, to add three qualifications: that those elements are small in relation to the great bulk of his work; that that work contains overwhelmingly what he might have called 'life-enhancing' attitudes; that he was, for virtually all his life and increasingly, in the grip of an advancing consumption with only intermittent relief; and that some of these attitudes − for example, the half-baked leader-cult arguments − were in the air just before and after the First World War (though that last is not in itself much of a justification, and his company in that area not attractive).

I agree with those who claim that his finest work places him with the best half-dozen writers in English of this century. In discussing *The Rainbow* − a text of great richness − I will try to isolate the core of that achievement in fiction; a core whose quality will, I hope, seem virtually indisputable even to those who have serious doubts about some other parts of Lawrence's voluminous and varied body of work.

It was an achievement, over a life of only forty-five years, for which almost nothing in his background might seem to have prepared him; nothing intellectual or imaginative or 'bookish', that is. For a mind of his kind as for some others, it was a most fruitful background − as a witness to the industrial horrors of late-Victorian England, to the changes it was then undergoing, to lives burdened by labour and poverty, but, above all those elements, to relationships in that environment no less complex than, say, those of people of the middle class. Lawrence's early novels, particularly *Sons and Lovers*, show this background best. Especially in the first part, he is the privileged observer, looking on from the kitchen table, privileged by his gift. In the second half he is more directly and personally involved, beginning to hone relationships, especially of love, up to the point at which he leaves home.

Lawrence's father was a superior sort of coal miner in Nottinghamshire (to be exact, a 'butty', a kind of charge-hand at the coalface); his mother had a more gentle background and certainly more social aspirations. Just how far his father was as solidly working class and his mother as grippingly would-be genteel as Lawrence portrays them in *Sons and Lovers* has long been a matter of dispute. Lawrence said later that he had been hard on his father in that book. It was a classic pattern; the ailing, bookish boy cleaving to his mother and finding his father and his father's ways dreadfully unattractive. For all his skills – even in that early period – in separating the artist from the tale, Lawrence did not adequately work out those tensions in fictional terms within that novel. It is, though, a book which has to be read, replete with memorable parts. One doesn't have to excuse it on the grounds that it was written by so young a man; the talent was already abundantly there.

Lawrence went, with a grant, to Nottingham High School, became a 'pupil teacher' and then on to Nottingham University College, and so became a qualified teacher. He taught for a while in Croydon (which we can see mirrored, as was his pupil-teacher period, in some of Ursula's experiences, and in his poetry). He was torn about teaching. His writing shows both the physical and the psychological demands it made on him and also, much less common, his marvellous sensitivity to the challenges and opportunities teaching can present, even in most difficult circumstances. As in 'The Best of School':

> This morning, sweet it is
> To feel the lad's looks light on me, Then back in a swift, bright flutter to
> work:
> Each one darting away with his
> Discovery, like birds that steal and flee

He meant to be a writer and all his spare time was consumed by that. Personally, then, it was bound to be a very hard time; but what periods in Lawrence's life were not? He lived life hard and to the hilt. His relationship with Jessie Chambers, the Miriam of *Sons and Lovers*, ended; but not before they had had unsatisfactory sexual relations. He also had some sexual experience with a 'liberated' married woman in Eastwood, his home town. He was not a hermit, but neither was he sexually promiscuous. The key thing to say about the women with whom he formed relationships early in his life (there were also 'Louie' – Louise – Burrows, especially, and Helen Corke) is how intelligent and articulate they were. Eastwood and its surrounding countryside were not in some deep semirural sleep; it had something of a continuing radical, political and intellectual tradition. Those early women in Lawrence's life were better educated, more solidly sensible than most of the women whom he allowed to dance attendance on him in his famous years. I noted in the preceding essay a meeting not long ago with one of the Eastwood acquaintances a dozen years younger than Lawrence – not one of his lovers, but a friend. At the time we met, she was in her eighties. The shrewd, well-informed, humane, lively intelligence was as active as ever.

In 1912 Lawrence met Frieda Weekley, the wife of the professor of French at Nottingham University. Frieda was a von Richthofen, already the mother of three children and a few years older than Lawrence. Her sense of unreckoning freedom would have put off if not frightened many men; but not Lawrence. Within a very short time indeed he had taken her away from her husband and children – they eventually married, in 1914 – and set off on a life of wandering around the world in search of a way of life more spiritually satisfying than that of the mechanised-industrial societies of what Lawrence now thought of as the deathly West. All the time he was writing furiously. The effort, especially for a man rarely in good health, was formidable. If a book, written at great cost and great length, did not at all satisfy him, he would prefer not to amend it but to write it afresh; 'overpainting', one critic called it; a total overpainting.

The search took them to Germany, Italy, Sicily, Sardinia and, by 1922, to New Mexico. During those years he produced almost a dozen novels, many short stories, several plays, and a number of fine travel books (*Kangaroo*, the novel set in Australia, is thought by many Australians to contain one of the very best evocations of the Australian landscape). He spent only a few weeks there in 1922, before New Mexico. His sense of the land and of nature and of their interactions with the human spirit was phenomenal.

He also produced a body of brilliant critical work on literature and on social matters. He had more than one effective style. Some of his social criticism is so direct and idiomatic that it opens new doors, especially to those who come from similar backgrounds. We need not necessarily try to imitate him; but we can learn much from his blazing of trails. In addition to all this, he wrote a body of verse which gives him a claim to be one of the best of twentieth-century English poets.

Gradually, Lawrence's consumption took a greater hold, until they had to move from the ranch in the hills about sixteen miles above Taos in New Mexico (itself about eighty miles from Santa Fe) to Europe again. This was in 1925. Later, Lawrence went into a sanatorium at Vence in southern France and that was where he died on 2 March 1930. Subsequently his ashes were brought back to the New Mexico ranch by Frieda and her new husband (formerly a joint friend) and interred in what was called 'the shrine', a couple of hundred yards above the ranch, among trees.

It was an astonishingly packed achievement, all produced in only thirty adult years, years regularly wracked by illness. It is hard to imagine the sheer physical labour of it, the driving of himself which must have been needed, the strain on even a fit man of writing and rewriting at such speed. Lawrence was in more than one sense a very driven man, driven by his genius, his daemon.

It seems likely that, if he had had to make a choice between his different kinds of writing, and that task would probably have been uncongenial, Lawrence would have chosen the novels. Within that body of work, by almost common consent, the peak comes with *The Rainbow* (1915) and *Women in Love* (1920). Those two, Lawrence said, 'are really an organic, artistic whole' and in some ways that is a simple truth. Published as one, they would have made a Victorian-sized volume, though lone even as that, running to about one thousand pages of average printing. Though they appeared as separate novels, they deal centrally with one family, the Brangwens, from the early nineteenth century until just after the First World War. If they are regarded as two distinct novels, then *Women in Love* is the more successful; but *The Rainbow* is the gateway to it, the necessary gateway, and very important in its own right. Taken together, these two constitute not only the peak of Lawrence's achievement as a novelist but one of the peaks of English fiction.

Inevitably, they have attracted an enormous amount of criticism, and the bulk increases yearly. Some of it is brilliant and illuminating; a larger amount is useful, in one way or another; some is tendentious or pretentious. This last group of authors have seen in Lawrence's work predominantly what they wanted to see, what they themselves wanted at a particular moment in their own lives, or what they thought might further their careers as a new and startling point of view – whether on his 'philosophy' or in finding new symbols or redefining his approach to sexual matters. They remake Lawrence in the images they pin on him. Before we decide what of all the criticism – if indeed any – can help us and which we can pass by, it is best to bed ourselves, to buttress ourselves with, a solid first-hand knowledge of the novels in themselves.

I mentioned Lawrence's use of symbolism a few lines back. Symbols of varying length and types and effectiveness weave through *The Rainbow*, as they do through almost all his novels. They were an integral part of the strategy of novel-writing for him. The key symbol here is, not surprisingly, the rainbow. It, together with the image of the protecting arch and that of a gateway, has several interlocking meanings. It recalls God's signal to Noah after the Flood, Lawrence said himself; so it suggests the possibility of putting things together again after dissolution and fragmentation; it suggests protection from above. This is clear at the end of chapter three, when the young Anna realises that her mother and her stepfather have now moved into a deeper and surer union as a couple:

> Anna's soul was at peace between them. She looked from one to the other, and she saw them established to her safety, and she was free. She played between the pillar of fire and the pillar of cloud in confidence, having the assurance on her right-hand and the assurance on her left. She was no longer called upon to uphold with her childish might the broken end of the arch. Her father and mother now met to the span of the heavens, and she, the child, was free to play in the space beneath, between.

The rainbow and the arch also symbolise a gateway through and under which one passes to a purer and fuller life. As in the rather inflated final paragraph of the book, as it leaves Ursula:

> And the rainbow stood on the earth. She knew that the sordid people who crept hard-scaled and separate on the face of the world's corruption were living still, that the rainbow was arched in their blood and would quiver to life in their spirit, that they would cast off their horny covering of disintegration, that new, clean, naked bodies would issue to a new germination, to a new growth, rising to the light and the wind and the clean rain of heaven. She saw in the rainbow the earth's new architecture, the old, brittle corruption of houses and factories swept away, the world built up in a living fabric of Truth, fitting to the overarching heaven.

The symbols apart, two main features of *The Rainbow* must be approached in any discussion of it. First, the degree to which Lawrence here developed a form of novel in which he had precursors. His nearest creditor in time and the one with the strongest influence on him in this respect was Thomas Hardy. We know that Lawrence reread Hardy's novels while writing *Sons and Lovers*. Quite soon after, he wrote a perceptive essay on

Hardy. From Hardy, above all, he learned a great deal about how to shape, shape up to one might also say, the psychological-and-social novel which extends over a good span of time, which moves through more than one generation and many changes in individual personalities, and which at the same time gives a sense of a society undergoing great cultural – in the widest sense – changes. Such a novel, if it is to succeed in the way the best of Hardy's works do, must not simply use the changes in society as a sort of theatrical background to characters who might have lived at any other time; it must interweave, inter-integrate personal and social change; it must indicate the ways social changes themselves get inside us, affect the very way we look out on the world, how social change inter-plays with psychic change.

Hardy's *Tess of the d'Urbervilles* is an important forerunner here. In it we can sense more fully than in virtually any earlier novelist (except perhaps George Eliot) the nature of a society which is changing from rural to urban, because we also feel it on the pulses of a young country girl who is ground by those pressures, caught and destroyed by them. That kind of exploration was carried through to *Jude the Obscure*. Jude feels directly and painfully the forces of modern life changing his actual and defining his potential relationships; his own consciousness is affected and altered by those pressures. Thus it is not at all difficult to see the similarities – the almost brother-and sister-similarities – between Jude and Ursula, Ursula who more than any other character carries the weight of change through from *The Rainbow* to *Women in Love*.

We see the rural encroached upon by the urban, with the coming of the canals, the railways, the coal mines, the mechanical threshing machines. We follow three generations of Brangwens, separate genera-tions but emotionally interlocked, a flux (the word is one of Lawrence's favourites) of mutual attractings and repulsings, forever swaying back-wards and forwards yet in the end always moving forward like an advancing tide. The first generation, of Tom and his Polish widow, Lydia and her little girl Anna, find themselves after many hard patches with a marriage that works well in most of the right ways. Still, Tom always regretted that he never quite had with young Anna the close relationship he had longed for. We need only read some of the scenes between these two to acquire a sharp sense of how well Lawrence could write about deep and largely inchoate connections. The second generation is that of Will and Anna, and that relationship works less well. It is stiflingly uxorious, with the fecund Anna dominant (Anna Victrix); so that even near the end Lawrence says:

> Brangwen had kept his carelessness about his circumstances. He knew his work in the lace designing meant little to him personally, he just earned his way by it. He did not know what meant much to him. Living close to Anna Brangwen, his mind was always suffused through with physical heat, he moved from instinct to instinct, groping, always groping on.

For the third generation, represented here by Ursula, there is in this book no marriage but instead a relationship with Anton Skrebensky which ends in humiliating failure for him, but for Ursula, as the book closes, in a confidence that she can make her own future, that she now knows better what it is she seeks.

It is Ursula who is, as it were, the dividing range between the last remnants of the old rural life, whose styles had been gradually weakening from old Tom through to Will and Anna, and the new self-conscious urban life. Ursula is one of the first group of emancipated, self-defining women who move through British fiction in the first two decades of the century (Well's Anna Veronica is another at about that time; one might, too, look further back to Jane Eyre). Ursula has been to university and so has broken from the hearth; she is sexually freed; she will decide things for herself. She reacts against the absorbed fecundity of her mother and from her father's baffled but equally absorbing uxoriousness. Home is suffused with the smell of mother's milk, the sight of one breast-feeding child after another – to the number of nine. It is always too warm and confined; she must break away. But they will not allow her to go south to teach; she must teach locally and live at home. Lawrence also indicates in all this that the provision of educational opportunities for 'ordinary' people, the nature of that provision, its direction and its limits, that these are themselves defined by and so become examples of the power and the needs of the new industrialism. People were now required to be to a certain level literate and numerate so as to man the new mechanised/technological society; not much more. So Ursula herself receives the training thought appropriate to those who will staff those schools; she becomes part of the new lower-professional caste of local-authority schoolteachers.

Ursula reacts also against the brittleness of personality which the new mechanical society could induce: against, for instance, the hard, mechanised soul of her Uncle Tom, the colliery manager. She has a short-lived lesbian affair with her own teacher, Winifred Inger, but is horrified when the older woman becomes the mistress – eventually the wife – of Uncle Tom. All the time, though at first without realising, she is looking for something new and different in her closest relationships, a relationship in which she neither submits to another nor dominates by her own power of will (of which she has plenty). She is a sort of early feminist but hardly at all politically interested and certainly not a suffragette. Indeed, like Lawrence, who also distrusted politics and sometimes yearned for a leader, she is a sort of aristocrat, or elitist in that she is distinctly anti-demagogic; and here, as in life, it is not always easy to distinguish well-founded anti-demagogic from anti-democratic attitudes. She is seeking freedom to find more purpose, meaning, significance in her own life; so for her, as for Lawrence, the attempt at honesty before the self is all-important. That drive is focused in her affair with Skrebensky, an affair which has some great and indeed brilliant moments, but which is yet never, and for very deep-seated reasons, quite right. She feels passion for him and, when he returns from the Boer War, they are fully lovers. She even has a hot-blooded quasi-honeymoon with him which reminds us of that of her mother. But she does not feel she has to marry him before that happens or afterwards. She allows herself to become engaged but underneath knows that cannot work. He is incapable of the necessary frankness before her and before himself. The engagement is ended, Skrebensky marries his colonel's daughter and goes to India.

Ursula subsequently falls ill, has a miscarriage and then slowly awakens to the possibility of a fuller and more meaningful life; and so the book ends. She has tried to be honest before herself and others with whom she has an intimate relationship. As a result, she is now alone, isolated from her family background and from close relations. But she is ready for new and more worthwhile relations. This ending markedly echoes that of *Sons and Lovers*, where Paul, his mother dead and his affair with Miriam over, sets off for the town and a wider future. Ursula is 'up against her own fate' and has chosen that it should be so; that stage is an essential one on the road to self-awareness, to the arrival at a firm hold on the search for integrity towards oneself and others with whom one chooses to share one's life. In that process, Ursula is carrying something of the consciousness of the emancipated women who came up through the nineteenth century (among her cousins are, as we saw, Tess, and Sue

Bridehead in *Jude the Obscure*). She is of the company of those who have to struggle to find a balance between their refusal to be the submissive subjects of the men in their lives and their wish to accept their femininity in its fullness.

All the above is only a sketch of the intricate manner in which *The Rainbow* traces the interweaving of social and psychological change through the larger part of a century. It is an important achievement in itself and a valuable extension of the work of those from whom Lawrence learned.

The second main feature of *The Rainbow* is even more important than the first, more a breaking of new ground; that is, Lawrence's handling of psychic relations in themselves and below the conscious level. This is what differentiates Lawrence's explorations here from those of others mentioned earlier; they are deeper even than their actors could know; Lawrence is working on virtually new ground. They exist especially but not exclusively between men and women; and importantly – but again, not only – between women and men who are not married but have at least what today would be called a 'partnership', but that word is inadequate, since it sounds like a civil contract; let us rather say: an understanding between people who have a serious sexual relationship outside marriage. Here lies the greatest of Lawrence's achievements; this is what he took further than any English novelist before him. This is what the early, semi-inchoate or articulate-mainly-in-the-head relationships between Paul and Miriam and Paul and Clara in *Sons and Lovers* were pointing towards and which Lawrence subsequently aimed to surpass; and did. Other English novelists had of course treated love relationships with great subtlety. But the combination of Lawrence's period – things could now be said explicitly which could not have been said earlier, though still not without stubborn attempts at censorship – and advances in psychological analysis, combined with the special trust of Lawrence's personality, all forced him towards the explicit in-depth analysis of individual feelings and relationships at subterranean levels. Above all, it rested on the sense that 'character' is not fixed, settled; rather, it is always fluid, and so are relationships. Yet underneath, one comes again on a fixedness, an unchanging solidity.

Lawrence knew he was moving into something new and intensely difficult. At one point he described the book to Edward Garnett, one of his early supporters, as 'a queer novel, which seems to have come by itself'. He also told Garnett, with the aggression he understandably showed when engaged on a hard pioneering task, and knew that what he had achieved or was seeking might well not be understood: 'It is the real thing, say what you like. And I shall get my reception if not now, then before long.' He knew too – who better? – just what he was trying to do. He wrote in June 1913: 'You mustn't look in my novel for the old stable *ego* of the character. There is another *ego*, according to whose action the individual is unrecognisable, and passes through, as it were, allotropic states which it needs a deeper sense than any we've been used to exercise, to discover are states of the same radically unchanged element.'

To appreciate what Lawrence was seeking, one need read only the first three pages of *The Rainbow*. They are not the peak of his success in this mode, but they give a good indication of what was to come. Rhythm is central to these pages, as it is to all Lawrence's writing at its most powerful. That is why he repeats certain words in an incantatory way. He was, he admitted, criticised for this recurrent rhythmic beat in his writings and answered, in his foreword to *Women in Love*, that it was 'natural to the author ... this pulsing, frictional to-and-fro'. One may see it on the second page of *The Rainbow*, where he talks of the earlier Brangwens' communion with the land and seasons:

> They knew the intercourse between heaven and earth, sunshine drawn into the breast and bowels, the rain sucked up in the daytime, nakedness that comes under the wind in autumn, showing the birds' nests no longer worth hiding. Their life and inter-relations were such; feeling the pulse and body of the soil, that opened to their furrow for the grain, and became smooth and supple after their ploughing, and clung to their feet with a weight that pulled like desire, lying hard and unresponsive when the crops were to be shorn away. The young corn waved and was silken, and the lustre slid along the limbs of the man who saw it. They took the udder of the cows, the cows yielded milk and pulse against the hands of the men, the pulse of the blood of the teats of the cows beat into the pulse of the hands of the men. They mounted their horses, and held life between the grip of their knees, they harnessed their horses at the wagon, and, with hand on the bridle-rings, drew the heaving of the horses after their will.

Few novelists have so well caught the psychic ebb and flow of relations below the conscious level. It makes the usual family-chronicle novel seem two-dimensional. It reaches into realms of meaning, intuition, consciousness, response which the novel – and most of us for that matter – rarely penetrates. The achievement was all the greater because there was not easily available a language in which to describe these things. There was a language for the normal, extensive and overt ranges of morality; there were abstractions in plenty to point towards remoter things; there was not a fit language for describing the 'thisness' of these other rhythms and movements, for indicating and describing how we are inhabited by rhythms more elemental than we recognise, lived in by forces more powerful than we can consciously command.

There are a host of examples: the women looking beyond the land all around and sensing another kind of life, a page or two after the description above of the men's deep attachment to the land; the ebb and flow of passion, the nearness and remoteness in the early married life of Tom and Lydia, especially the passage in chapter two beginning: 'She was sure to come at last and touch him. Then he burst into flame for her, and lost himself . . .'; Tom and Lydia settling later to a very stable relationship as each learns to recognise the other's 'otherness'; the intense movements in the relationship between Will and Anna, his first child; the horrifying sensuality of Will's encounter with the girl in Nottingham; Will and Anna among the sheaves in chapter four; Ursula with Skrebenksy in the stack-yard; and so on. The examples are many and all full of intensely, closely observed detail of the deepest movements of our deepest relationships.

These are examples of what one critic, Julian Moynihan, has called 'ritual scenes'. Perhaps the finest introduction to Lawrence's powers in this manner within *The Rainbow*, and one of the most powerful descriptions of passionate love-making in English fiction, appears when Will and Anna have their honeymoon in the cottage. It is in the very purest sense immensely erotic; it traces lyrically the total absorption of a young couple in each other's bodies. It is also and without discordance very funny, especially when she eventually turns him out because she wants for the first time to 'bottom' (thoroughly clean) the cottage and make it smart for visitors. He is like Adam cast from Eden, or a lost bull-calf wondering what has hit it.

Some critics think the final chapters overwritten, merely making statements about relationships which the earlier chapters have fully brought to life. There is something in this criticism. But consider the late pages where Ursula's relationship with Skrebensky fails. He is all will and rationality, separated from his own deeper self, ruled by mental consciousness and divorced from true spontaneity (I am using here phrases from Lawrence's own writings). She forces him to face this barrenness; the scene culminates in the terrible and terrifying sexual encounter on top of the dunes. She forces him also into elemental passionate experiences, and that destroys him in the sense that it breaks apart his carefully composed sense of what he himself is. It has to end.

The above is an attempt through generalisations and abstractions to describe a scene which, like so many in Lawrence at this period, reach into new recesses of our emotional life, and are not to be adequately paraphrased.

As the book draws to its close, Ursula is left looking towards the future, Gudrun has begun to move forward from the shadows, and we the readers are ready to move to *Women in Love* and a wholly new set of relationships. *The Rainbow* can be read as complete in itself. Yet without going on to read *Women in Love*, one misses not only another great novel but an enhanced understanding of *The Rainbow* itself.

Farnham, 1981/2000

*W*OMEN IN LOVE

D. H. LAWRENCE NEVER SPARED himself on a novel once he knew it was going to be important for him, for what he wanted to say and for his development as a novelist; it had to be seen through to the end. This was nowhere more true than when he was working on *Women in Love*, which is by fairly general consent his finest novel. Its companion and precursor, *The Rainbow*, had appeared in 1915 after the sorts of delays which became endemic with Lawrence's novels, such were the fears of publishers and the suspicions of the censoring authorities. By then, *Women in Love* had been two years in the making. Lawrence had begun it in March 1913, in the Tyrol. He worked on it for about four years but still wasn't satisfied. He then did something which he did more than once, such was his drive, something most of us would find impossibly daunting even if were were in the best of health, which Lawrence was not. In 1917, in Cornwall, he set to and rewrote the novel. That was his way of avoiding the flagging and disjointedness which can easily appear in spite of the most careful invisible-literary-mending. He wanted to keep the surge and thrust and flow – his kind of words – so he started at the beginning and wrote the whole thing again. It was published in 1920, in New York, and in Britain in 1921.

Yet this, the year of the rewriting, was a particularly bad time for Lawrence. He and Frieda were harassed, to some extent because she was German. Lawrence himself hated the war with an intensity fed by the conviction that European civilisation was on its last legs. He dreamed of a kind of commune or community of like souls. But his experiences in trying to promote that were anything but encouraging. It may well be that the unresolved strains that *Women in Love* shows, in spite of its tremendous strengths, reflect the terrible strains within Lawrence himself at the time of final writing.

I said a few lines above that *The Rainbow* is the companion to *Women in Love*; after all, they were originally thought of as one novel and the interconnectings are obvious. But from some angles *Women in Love* can be regarded as a different and quite new book. It goes much further than *The Rainbow*, tackles more difficult fictional problems, is more dense. Yet the links, the continuity, are there, so it will probably be useful to look back at the bare bones of *The Rainbow*. It follows the fortunes of three generations of the Brangwen family, of Tom and Lydia, Will and Anna and, last, Ursula and Skrebensky. The first two couples marry and have children; Ursula in the end rejects Skrebensky. *The Rainbow* ends with her assuming responsibility for her own destiny, a modern, intellectually and to some extent spiritually, emancipated woman setting off to seek her own future. All this is told against a background which is much more than simply a background, since it is organic to the changes within the characters, among much else emblematic of rural England finally giving way to urban England.

In *Women in Love* we enter fully into the lives of the third generation, especially of Ursula and her sister Gudrun, whom we have met only slightly in the earlier book. Now the two sisters provide the fulcrum of the book, two of the children of the fecund Anna, but each — though in very different ways — educated out of her family, in some senses released. One need only read the opening pages, where the sisters talk about what they expect from life. No earlier generation of the Brangwens could have had a conversation of such poise, self-assurance, self-choosing penetration, such self-definition. A striking comparison occurs in the first chapter of George Eliot's *Middlemarch*, where again two sisters, Dorothea and Celia Brooke, have a brilliantly realised, lucid, intelligent and honest conversation. One might also mention here Margaret and Helen Schlegel's relationship in Forster's *Howards End*; or even go back to some of the sisters' conversations in *Pride and Prejudice*. From those comparisons one sees both how novelists can join hands across half a century, and also how tone and manner change at least as much as does the range of what it is permitted to say, as the decades pass.

The greater penetration into relationships which *Women in Love* contains, as compared with *The Rainbow*, is best seen in the relationships of the sisters with the two men, Birkin with Ursula and Gerald with Gudrun. Here Lawrence made his greatest advances in depth. One result is that *Women in Love*'s chronological pace is much slower than that of *The Rainbow*. It deals with one generation only. It carries forward first of all that examination of the internal effects of industrialisation on the British psyche so effectively set off in the earlier book. The picture is now even more sombre, partly because of the effects of the First World War. Gerald is hard with a very twentieth-century hardness. One recalls his father, especially from *The Rainbow*, the father from whom Gerald took over the mines which he means to (as he might be likely to say now) 'drag screaming into the next century', to 'rationalise' or 'make viable' or to 'be up there with the best in the Second Industrial Revolution'. He would almost certainly have a degree in industrial management today.

The mining district has become, even more than it was in *The Rainbow*, not simply a dirty, depressed, miserable, damp, hopeless, living and working area but a symbolic expression of the psychological destruction it creates. It is a sign of what industrialisation does, inwardly, to the people caught up in it at all levels, whether as workers or managers. It is this which Birkin and Ursula, when they declare that they are opting out in the name of liberation, are rejecting.

That is one advance in Lawrence's art in this book: the great command of social change and its effects. Another is in his increased sureness in analysing the inward ebb and flow of relationships or in one personality. More of that later; and also about the advance in his examination of subjects it was at the time improper even to hint at: homosexuality, including homosexuality between predominantly heterosexual men, and lesbianism, even in women also predominantly heterosexual. All this recalls and helps validate one of Lawrence's fine *obiter dicta*: 'The novel, properly read, can reveal the most secret places of life.'

It may be as well to look first, as an entrance to this long and sometimes difficult novel, at Lawrence's use of symbols, one of the mainsprings of his art. Sometimes the symbols can seem forced. This has often been said against the symbol of the rainbow at the very end of *The Rainbow* itself. That is certainly rather overblown; one is too evidently being invited to see the symbolic closing. I am a little uneasy too about the so-obvious symbolic implications of Gerald's tussle with the horse at the level-crossing in the present book. Lawrence, one might say, had a soft spot for horses as the symbols of naked power, physicality, thrusting sexuality; they recur in his work and sometimes seem largely willed.

At their best, when they mesh properly, his symbols dramatise and body out subtle internal states. At such moments they take us as if by surprise, into depths we would not be likely to penetrate in simply descriptive, 'surface' prose. Very often the symbols arise from, are vested in, something small and tender, and suggest a responsiveness to those qualities in the characters, though probably not known to them: young pheasants, thrushes' eggs, crocuses opening, new windflowers under a hedge – all vulnerable, fragile and beautiful things which call to tenderness and vulnerability in us and in our feelings for others. By contrast, and as we have seen in part when horses appear, Lawrence's symbols can body out some of the deep animal forces in us. There are many of these instances in *Women in Love*. One of the most effective is in chapter eighteen, where the rabbit Bismarck lashes out at Gudrun and is finally mastered by Gerald. Those few pages are, first, a superb description of the power and force of a fully grown male rabbit. There is nothing cuddly or flopsy-bunny about Bismarck. They also, but in the right implicit but unmistakeable way, reveal elements in Gudrun's character which have been hidden even from her. But Gerald sees; she is exposed: 'He saw, with subtle recognition, her sullen passion of cruelty'. He, too, is soon just as revealed. As he 'masters' the rabbit 'his face was gleaming with a smile'. Profound impulses in both have been forcefully disclosed; something deep down in each has responded to the other:

> 'You wouldn't think there was all that force in a rabbit,' he said, looking at Gudrun. And he saw her eyes black as night in her pallid face, she looked almost unearthly. The scream of the rabbit, after the violent tussle, seemed to have torn the veil of her consciousness. He looked at her, and the whitish, electric gleam in his face intensified.
>
> 'I don't really like him,' Winifred was crooning, 'I don't care for him as I do for Loozie. He's hateful really.'
>
> A smile twisted Gudrun's face as she recovered. She knew she was revealed.

One could go on, through symbol after symbol. I will mention only one more at this point, because of its double character: the incident where Birkin stones the moon; or, to be precise, stones the moon's face reflected in a pond (chapter nineteen). Frank Kermode has written about this scene economically and effectively:

In this mood of 'contemptuous ridicule' for humanity she [Ursula] comes upon Birkin throwing dead flowers and stones into a pool, and uttering 'Cybele – curse her! The accursed Syria Dea!' Not surprisingly, she finds this ridiculous. But Lawrence is giving Birkin, in this silly situation, many essential things to say. Characteristically, therefore, he makes Birkin absurd at the outset, brings in his doctrinal critic, and then tackles the enormous task of leaping from absurdity to power. At once he writes the superb passage about the reflected moon, 'a white body of fire writhing and striving' as the stones shatter the surface of the water. Doctrine loses itself in pagan symbolism – the presence of the castrating moon-goddess may be shaken but not finally dispersed – and that, in turn, is lost in the virtuosity of the description of the interflow of light and dark on the water.

Such a passage illustrates more than Lawrence's complex handling of symbols at his best. It shows how his attitude towards his own work, and towards himself and his 'philosophies', contained – and this is not uncommon – its own antibodies. There are writers on Lawrence who take his philosophising and his symbols 'straight', as it were. Professor Kermode hints that Lawrence did not always do so himself. The symbols he locates in Birkin's attack on the moon-goddess occur in a passage in which he also recognises and invites us to recognise that Birkin is being rather foolish and self-dramatising. Nevertheless, the power of the symbol remains; indeed, one might argue that it is given greater force by not being presented in an over-solemn way, but by contrast. A character is overreacting; but the heart of what he is saying emerges as powerful and important. So it was much of the time with Lawrence himself, as we may particularly see in the often self-ironic comedy of his poetry. He had a powerful prophetic side, but also a rooted, Midlands, working-class distrust of anything airy-fairy. He was likely to become strongly down to earth and even on occasions to take the mickey out of himself.

So we come to the heart and core of the book: the interweaving of Ursula and Gudrun's search for 'real' intimate relationships, though of very different kinds. It is a search which is accompanied by a great many articulate exchanges with all those with whom they have to do, but especially with each other. We meet them at the start of this book doing just that, working and talking. Here, both the sisters are as if waiting for full life to start, to some extent still baffled and held back (again to use favourite phrases of Lawrence). The girls are also honest and clear-sighted, again like those intelligent provincial women Lawrence was lucky enough to have known during his own growing-up.

So they move out into the tortured landscape of their mining district and watch the wedding of Gerald Crich's sister; and quite soon we will know that Gudrun will choose Gerald and he her, in a sort of corrupt death-choice by each. We know also that Ursula will begin a long and tortuous movement towards an apparently lasting relationship with Birkin. At this point Birkin is moving away from his relationship with Hermione. It is an inevitable break. She is an aristocratic intellectual, but by now he has taken her emotional measure. She is 'all will' and has 'a deficiency of being'. I have heard one critic speak at great length about the classical symbolism of the fact that it is a paperweight of lapis lazuli with which, when it is clear that the affair is over, Hermione hits Birkin. I do not myself feel the need to look for more than the plain and power-ful meaning which these lines effectively give.

Birkin himself can find no god nor take any comfort in politics nor, least of all, in the politics of egalitarianism. But he must have meaning in his life and that meaning must centre in an honest and full relationship with a woman. He is, as we meet him, at a crucial moment of change in his life. Much of what he is rejecting can be seen in the passages about his trip to London in chapters six and seven and in those about the bohemians at the Pompidour Café (the Café Royal in London). Many of the characters pilloried there and elsewhere in this book were acquain-tances of Lawrence, such as Bertrand Russell and Lady Ottoline Morrell; but that is a secondary matter. These early London scenes seem carica-ture, thin in comparison with most of the book and thus fictionally unconvincing.

There is a good deal of agony and stress to be endured before Birkin can declare his love for Ursula. That comes in the gentle and intense conclusion to chapter thirteen: "'Let love be enough then. I love you then – I love you. I'm bored by the rest." "Yes," she murmured . . .'. It is at this point, just two or three pages further on, that Lawrence also pulls off one of his small master strokes. He suddenly lets us see, dressed in their best for the water party, Ursula and Gudrun's father and mother. They look innocent and unknowing, not in any way sophisticated. We have been living for almost two hundred pages with the intellectual and emotional convolutions of the two modern, emancipated daughters. That contrast is heightened enormously by the unexpected walking across the scene – as though a cameo by a Sunday painter had been inserted into the middle of a Picasso – of this couple left over from the, by comparison, innocent period of *The Rainbow*, a couple whose intense relationships we had followed closely in that book, but whose relationships were much more 'in the blood' than those of their daughters, and almost wholly inarticulate. Now, in middle age and clumsily dressed in their Sunday best, they look to the self-aware girls both comical and touching: 'the shy, unworldly couple of their parents going on ahead'. It is a masterly stroke, to increase depth by difference. And a salutary rejoinder to those who think Lawrence is only a scandalous writer with no sense of the quiet shining ordinariness of some lives.

Lawrence does not leave it there. Almost a hundred pages yet further on, and by now past the halfway point of the book, he creates the same startling, explosive contrast by letting Birkin – the tense, thin-skinned, articulate, nervy school inspector who is wooing Ursula – meet face to face her father Will: fleshy, compact of energy, sensuous within himself. The contrast is extreme and reveals a great deal about both men. It also knits, again, the two books, and the generations which move through them:

> Birkin entered and sat down. He looked at the bright, reddish face of the other man, at the narrow brow and the very bright eyes, and at the rather sensual lips that unrolled wide and expansive under the black, cropped moustache. How curious it was that this was a human being! What Brangwen thought himself to be, now meaningless it was, confronted with the reality of him. Birkin could see only a strange, inexplicable, almost passionless collection of passions and desires and suppressions and traditions and mechanical ideas, all cast unfused and disunited into this slender, bright-faced man of nearly fifty, who was as unresolved now as he was at twenty, and as uncreated. How could he be the parent of Ursula, when he was not created himself?

That passage, while showing the incomprehensibility of one generation for another, also shows the present limits of Birkin's tortured self-consciousness; there is about him still a kind of ignorance, a lack of the most common kind of common sense.

So the affairs of the two sisters interweave, their major moments of change marked, as is usual in Lawrence, by symbolic or thematic or exemplary scenes. As shown, for instance, in the force and implications of the scene in the chapter 'Water Party' where Gudrun dances dangerously in front of the group of cattle. Ursula is frightened, but nothing will dissuade Gudrun from running straight into that risk, from somehow getting in tune with the animalness of the beasts. She is riven by 'a terrible shiver of fear and pleasure'. Meanwhile Ursula sings thinly; and it is thus the two men find them. Not long after this Ursula and Birkin make love for the first time, a hard, ungentle, fierce love-making which had to be gone through but which each knows has been the exercise of a kind of separateness, not a fulfilled experience.

The battle goes on for all four of them but most weightily in Ursula and Birkin's attempt to find a relationship which is true to all aspects of themselves (Gudrun and Gerald's is doomed from the start). Even by two-thirds of the way into the book they are still fighting to achieve it; as in the conversation in the chapter 'Woman to Woman' between Ursula and Hermione where Ursula explains why she will not agree to marry Birkin – because what he wants from her is submission and she will not give that. Enormous, articulate storms have to be lived through between them, such as that appalling quarrel in the chapter 'Excuse' where she hurls abuse at him:

> 'You! You truth-lover! You purity-monger! It stinks, your truth and your purity. It stinks of the offal you feed on, you scavenger dog, you eater of corpses. You are foul, foul – and you must know it. Your purity, your candour, your goodness – yes, thank you, we've had some. What you are is a foul, deathly thing ...'.
>
> A clearer look had come over Birkin's face. He knew she was in the main right. He knew he was perverse, so spiritual on the one hand, and in some strange way, degraded on the other. But was she herself any better?

The price of getting through to an honest relationship, physical and mental, is never easy for Lawrence's couples. They needed to have far more emotional stamina than most of us can muster. We know how terrible the fights between Lawrence and Frieda could be, though also histrionic. One visitor noted that after throwing plates at each other, they sat at the piano and played together. Lawrence could be punishingly frank in his impulse towards the 'truth'. We also know their fights could be followed by a marvellously resolved peace. So is it here with Ursula and Birkin, in the scene only six or seven pages on from that awful row, when they make love in a transported way: 'It was a perfect passing-away for both of them, and at the same time the most intolerable accession into being, the marvellous fullness of immediate gratification, overwhelming, outflooding from the source of the deepest life-force ...'. And so, again like Lawrence and Frieda, Ursula and Birkin decide to resign from the world of routine work so as to find their own truth in their own way; if they can.

Meanwhile the relationship between Gudrun and Gerald is pursuing its own dark and tortuous course, a terrible tearing at each other and then a blind submission. As we saw in the incident with the cattle, there is something savage and elemental in Gudrun to which she is drawn to give full scope. We saw it also in the incident with Bismarck the rabbit. At a more obvious level it makes her sexually attracted to coalminers she passes in the street. This urge above all is what brings her and Gerald together: 'they both felt the subterranean desire to let go, to fling away everything and lapse into a sheer unrestraint, brutal and licentious ... a black licentiousness'. They come together in the chapter entitled, suitably, 'Death and Love', when after old Mr. Crich's death Gerald walks through the night to Gudrun's home, seeks her out blindly, in a state of awful dependence, finds her room and is taken into her bed for a love-making which, for all its elements of tenderness, also has in it the seeds of all that which will finally destroy the relationship.

Beneath these elaborately explored heterosexual relationships there is also something of homosexuality, notably in Birkin. Lawrence discusses this in his prologue to the book – an essay particularly worth reading for the light it throws on how some novels come to be written. The American critic George Ford rightly noted how fond Lawrence was of describing men's loins. The fight between Gerald and Birkin in the chapter 'Gladiatorial' has clear homosexual overtones, and the vest last lines of the book contain a conversation between Ursula and Birkin in which he insists, against her assertion that to wish so is 'an obstinacy, a theory, a perversity', that he was right to have wanted two kinds of love, that with a woman and that with a man.

All this interlocking swirl of relationships comes together in those last chapters of the book, on the Austrian holiday. Loerke, the Jewish artist – corrupt, egotistic, in love with the art of death – becomes the focus of Gerald's mad jealously, the means by which Gerald's powerful drive to impose his will on all around him (we have already seen him doing that with horses and with the miners he employs), all his *wilfulness*, the hard force of his unyielding mental consciousness, bursts out in the most crude form when he hits Loerke. Whereupon Gudrun hits him. He tries to strangle her and then just gives up. He goes out into the snow and becomes the victim of a hard, cold, white world, the symbol of his own icy, Northern will.

As to the connections between Ursula and Birkin at the close, one remembers the title of the group of poems Lawrence wrote after the first period of his life with Frieda: 'Look, we have come through'. For Ursula and Birkin one might change that to: 'Look, we may have come through'. Even that would not be accepted by some critics, who find the ending unstable, and Birkin's unease in a simple heterosexual relationship more threatening than the ultimately unfulfilled indications that Ursula and Birkin have at last reached an enduring relationship which, though it must have its ups and downs, will not again be fundamentally threatened. Too much, we are invited to think, has been burned out by way of false foundations for the connections to collapse; what has endured is well founded. I join those who are not wholly convinced of this.

It is time to recapitulate the greatness of the book's achievement. It traces, with a sustained depth no other novel in English matches, the inward ebb and flow, the flux of close relations, their polarisings, the revulsions followed by the attractions and the passion, the alternating hate and love, the force of will and the need to surrender within the same personality, the urge to know and to articulate, and the urge to merge with and give release to deep animal feelings, the urge to procreate and the urge towards death. In the four or five thousand words I have written I have been able to do no more than draw a sketch of all these movements. That is why it is not exaggerated to claim that *Women in Love* is the peak of Lawrence's work in fiction and one of the peaks of the English novel. It is not repeatable and not a good model for others. It is, rather, a quarry. Any would-be novelist must have read it and cannot fail to be affected by it at some level; but this should be in indirect ways if talent is to find its own route. One recognises the greatness of the book, admires it and – if one wants to write fiction oneself – goes round it. The critics, though, will be mining happily on its slopes for decades to come. It is a *tour de force* and that by a man who could see death not far off. Simply to put yourself to this long and elaborate analysis, this setting in motion, over time and space, of such complicated inner relationships, to get it all down, is physically, intellectually and emotionally a huge task. Lawrence could have stayed within the recognised and recognisable form of the chronicle novel as he had seen it at its best in such writers as

George Eliot and Thomas Hardy. Instead, he pushed himself on relentlessly into new ranges for that kind of novel; and in the process transformed it. Like all great works, it changed the possibilities of the form from which it took off; the novel would never be quite the same again. And it may change us, its readers. Our sense of the submerged inwardness of our personalities can also never be the same again. It can change us to the degree that we have attended to the book. It can change the way we see ourselves, our connections with others, our society, time and the generations, family and place and space. For all the insecurity which some find in its ending, *Women in Love* fully lives up to one of Lawrence's own definitions of prose fiction: 'the one bright book of life'. He sometimes intervened and talked at his readers. When he had done so, he usually knew and admitted it. He respected the novel too much to want to cheat on and with it; he regarded the writing of fiction as a difficult moral exercise. Which is why he said some of the best things ever said about the difficulty and beauty of the form: 'If you try to nail anything down in the novel, either it kills the novel, or the novel gets up and walks away with the nail.... When the novelist puts his thumb in the scale, to pull down the balance to his own predilection, that is immortality.'

Farnham, 1982/2000

LADY CHATTERLEY AND THE CENSORS

WHEN PENGUIN BOOKS announced in 1960 that they would, on 26 August, publish an unexpurgated edition of D. H. Lawrence's *Lady Chatterley's Lover*, the Director of Public Prosecutions appears to have decided that an offence would probably be thereby committed, and told the police to buy copies.

This would usually have involved the police in a journey to Charing Cross Road since that street, in the official imagination, was the haunt of 'dirty' booksellers. That in turn could have meant that the chosen bookseller would have been prosecuted for selling 'an obscene libel'. The solicitors for Penguin thereupon told the police there was no need to buy copies, since simply to be given one would, in law, constitute publication; they could have some for nothing. A police inspector called on Penguin and was given twelve copies. An offence had been committed.

The Director of Public Prosecutions was acting true to form. During the second half of the fifties there had been several prosecutions for obscenity. There was a feeling in the air that the dreadful Permissive Society was about to arrive or had already emerged. The country had to be protected from filth.

The Society of Authors had by now become more and more concerned about the threat to serious literature posed by the existing law on obscenity, and increasingly by the enhanced disposition to invoke that law. With help from several eminent literary figures it set up a committee to propose civilised amendments to the existing law. Their bill took five years to draft, defend and finally be transformed into a new act

– the Obscene Publications Act of 1959 – which entered the statute book.

En route, the Government tried to emasculate it; that they did not succeed was in good measure due to a Labour Member of Parliament, Roy (now Lord) Jenkins. He more or less forced the Government to refer the bill to a Select Committee of the House of Commons; that, in March of 1958, reported in favour of it. The Government still pursued its aim of having a tougher measure, but, after a sizeable further battle, the new measure was passed. It became popularly known as the Jenkins Act.

It made several important changes to its predecessor, of which the most significant to the subsequent *Chatterley* case were:

1. A book should be judged as a whole. This was to prevent prosecuting counsel from wrenching out 'filthy bits' and using them to imply overall obscenity.
2. Even if a book might be likely to tend to deprave some people, publication might be allowed as being for the public good 'on the ground that it is in the interests of science, literature, art, or learning, or of other objects of general concern'.
3. The testimony of experts for or against a book's literary merit was allowed. They would replace 'the man on the Clapham omnibus' – the ordinary citizen regarded as the arbiter not of literary merit but of obscenity, which had been hitherto overriding, unqualified, 'objective' (an exceptionally obtuse use of this word).

Before the *Chatterley* case, there was one prosecution under the new Act but it was of little significance since the book did not seriously raise the question of literary merit, as *Lady Chatterley's Lover* certainly did. It may be that the office of the Director of Public Prosecutions had thought Lawrence's book would provide a thorough test of, particularly, those three of the new Act's provisions – as to literary merit, the role of experts and the approach to the book as a whole. Yet to accept that may be to assume that the office was more liberal than it had so far seemed. The *Chatterley* trial did provide that test, though in a very garbled way and certainly not, at the end, in the way the Director of Public Prosecutions may have hoped.

The trial began on 20 October 1960 in Court No. 1 of the Old Bailey in the City of London. Judge Byrne presided; the defence team was led by

Gerald (later Lord) Gardner, Jeremy (also later Lord) Hutchinson and Mr Richard du Cann. The prosecution was led by the Senior Treasury Counsel, Mr Mervyn Griffith-Jones.

Penguin's solicitors had written to three hundred people thought likely to be willing, and known to be qualified, to give expert opinion for the defence. In the event, thirty-five were called and as many more held themselves ready to be, but were not needed. Many others wrote letters of support, and of these most were willing to act.

Not one of those who agreed to be witnesses for the defence would have imagined that that trial would come to occupy so histrionic a place in the British imagination, and for so many years. There have been several books, at least two television re-creations, a play and a hilarious, pirated, long-playing record from Singapore. All these were about the trial itself, not about the book; there are certain to be more.

Clearly, the event touched on sensitive English nerves: about the limits and justifications for censorship, about sex, about literature and – bound up with all those – about social class. It became a setting for these issues to be publicly laid out and played out in one place to a degree not seen before. In that sense it focused certain changes in mid-twentieth-century Britain as nothing else did; or it seemed to do so – some of the conclusions drawn from it were mistaken, overdrawn.

Two elements came together: the new law on obscenity; and the impulses of a remarkable publishing maverick. We have noted that English publishing law on obscenity had for long been excessively narrow and astringent. Lawrence's work had more than once fallen foul of that law. Joyce's *Ulysses* had been predictably banned also. University students often brought it in from Paris, in plain wrappers. By contrast, a New York court could and did allow expert testimony to literary merit. So, after an admirably well-informed and balanced hearing there, *Ulysses* was freed. Some people in Britain would have had none of that if that book had come before them. They continued to mistrust and hoped to weaken the 1959 law.

Allen Lane had founded the remarkable cheap paperback imprint, Penguin Books, a quarter of a century before. He had in the few years before the new Act been bringing out in large printings as many of Lawrence's novels as possible; but not *Lady Chatterley*. He would have recognised that under existing legislation the unexpurgated version would certainly have been banned. The 'Jenkins Act' must have seemed to give him his opportunity. It was a gamble and a dangerous one; prison might lie ahead for him if the gamble failed. But Lane was a gambler, a risk-taker and an anti-establishment figure. He printed 200,000 copies of the book, at three shillings and sixpence (17.5p) each, and distributed them to booksellers but with an embargo until 26 August. Once the police had collected copies he waited for the Director of Public Prosecutions to act; which he did quite quickly. The stage was set.

There was to be one more delay before the trial could begin. The defence asked that the twelve jurors be allowed to read the book immediately before taking their places. A room with comfortable chairs was eventually found. Since the rules for reading had to match those for a naval convoy, the slowest member of the jury determined how long they would be closeted. Three days. Clearly one member was an unsophisticated reader. The trial could now properly open.

By 1960 I knew Allen Lane moderately well. He had enthusiastically published my *The Uses of Literacy* in 1958 and from time to time talked about his plans to me. I was not altogether surprised when the solicitors for the defence asked me to join the witnesses. Slightly surprised, though; there were better expert witnesses on Lawrence's work than I to be found. I suspect the motives of the defence team were more subtle. They might well have expected (they were right if so) an extremely hostile prosecution led by people who would take every opportunity to dismiss the defence witnesses as loose, promiscuous, bohemian, metropolitan types whose private and sexual lives were probably no better than they should be. That type of witness, it was no doubt thought, was to be avoided.

The line-up of defence witnesses was therefore eclectic, not strongly metropolitan, sometimes almost humdrum. There were some Lawrence experts, but even they tended to be provincials; there was a Church of England priest, a psychiatrist, a young Catholic undergraduate girl, some elderly lady university dons impregnable in tweeds and sensible shoes, some earnest *Guardian*-reading types, and so on. I imagine I was cast as a very very slightly sub-Lawrentian figure: ex-working class, provincial, literary but unflashy. In those days one of the preferred items of uniform for provincial lecturers was the V-neck pullover. It later become for some of us too identifiably conventional-ordinary to be retained. Years later, the BBC made a television film of the trial, in which an actor played me

– in a V-necked pullover. I suggested to the producer that he had fallen for a stereotype. I wouldn't, I asserted, have worn such an obvious item. He produced a photograph of me taken at the time – in a V-necked pullover. Habits were strong and collective.

I did not and do no think *Lady Chatterley* Lawrence's best novel, but I much admire parts of it. The fashion after the trial was to say that, though one was glad the book had been freed, it was nevertheless 'boring'. That was a predictable 'smart' opinion, often made by people who had no more than skimmed the book. The landscapes and the portrait of Mrs Bolton alone should have been enough to reject that flashy dismissal.

From the start, the case attracted almost overwhelming press and broadcasting attention. It would have done so no matter how it was conducted. But the prosecuting counsel startled everyone by asking the jury near the beginning: 'Would you wish your wives and servants to read this book?' A wave of amused bewilderment went through those millions in the country who were paying attention. It was the first clear indication that the prosecution was to be led by someone astonishingly out of touch with post-war changes in the culture, fast-bound in his almost closed legal world, a world where males still ruled, were expected to have servants and to guide their reading and that of their wife.

Griffith-Jones also revealed himself as a direct descendant of Dickens' Sergeant Buz-Fuz; a bullying, hectoring figure, his method designed to intimidate. British cock-snooking at authority, a favourite response, reacted at once with a tailor-made joke: How does Griffith-Jones decide that there should be a prosecution? He puts his feet upon on the desk, starts reading and, if he has an erection, shouts: 'Obscene! Prosecute!' Early on the second day of the trial I received a telephone call at Leicester University asking me to go down to the Old Bailey as soon as possible. I arrived in mid-afternoon.

Here I must for the time being concentrate on my own part in the defence, not because I wish to but because it has sometimes been claimed to be one of the 'turning points' of the trial. I believe that to be an exaggeration but will try to show how the impression came about.

On arriving that afternoon I was advised by the defence solicitor something to this effect: 'Hold the fort ... dig in hard if possible.' The case for the defence was at that stage not going well. I was called to the witness box a short time before the court was to rise for the day. In the few minutes left, Jeremy Hutchinson began to examine me. He asked me if I agreed with the prosecution, that the book was 'vicious'. I said, 'No', and added that it was 'virtuous, if not puritanical'. A few minutes later the court rose.

I wandered into the street aware that I had given a very large hostage to the prosecution. How could a book which they were firmly convinced was vicious be puritanical? Griffith-Jones would certainly attack that the following morning.

He did, with considerable sneering relish. He professed himself as, so it now seemed, up to that point ignorant about the meaning of 'puritanical'. Perhaps I would enlighten him? I did so, rather economically; in four brief sentences. This seemed to throw him slightly off-balance, since he left his line of straightforward if brutal cross-examination and descended to quite low-level sarcasm, to the effect that he was 'obliged for my lecture'. That weak rejoinder was a further indication of his hidebound snobberies; it was said in a tone of voice which one felt sure he would not have used to a don from Oxbridge.

It became a long session in the witness box, one of the longest in the records of No. 1 Court I was told, but found that hard to believe. The judge had ruled that none of the witnesses could sit in the court until after they had given evidence. Perhaps he thought these clever-clever experts would learn in advance from each other. I took the opportunity of staying on after my examination, and had a remarkable experience.

The fifth witness after me was called forward by the usher: 'Edwin Morgan Forster'. A small, rather stooped figure in a very clean mackintosh went up into the witness box. The judge seemed not to recognise the name but politely asked Forster if he would, being elderly, like a chair. He declined.

The defence must have decided, in their stocktaking the previous evening, to take a big risk next day. They told Forster that a previous witness had described Lawrence as a puritanical writer; would he tell the court what he thought of that? I held my breath. Forster looked upwards in thought and then said, in his well-modulated King's College, Cambridge, voice: 'I think the description is a correct one, though I understand that at first people would think it paradoxical.' I nearly leapt from my seat with relief and pleasure.

The procession of defence witnesses, some very successful, some troubled by the force of the attack, continued. Others were, it was rumoured, in the wings. At one point the defence team seemed to be showing some slight concern. I asked one of the Penguin people why. 'The prosecution have just pulled Eliot's *After Strange Gods* from under their desk.' Were they going to invoke Eliot's criticisms of Lawrence in that book? No matter – Eliot had told Penguin that if they did so, he was to be phoned at his office in Russell Square, would come to the Old Bailey at once and defend Lawrence. Eliot was phoned and waited in the corridor outside the court, but was not called; *After Strange Gods* had been put back under the desk.

It was not a surprise that F. R. Leavis had refused to appear for the defence. He was known to think ill of the book, which surprised few, especially those of us who were admirers of that great Cambridge figure.

It was, on a first thought, more surprising that the prosecution called no witnesses. Plenty were available, including one eminent publisher and bookseller, who had said he felt tainted after reading the book. It was rumoured that John Sparrow, the brilliant but mischievous warden of All Souls' College, Oxford, would be appearing. Among much else, Sparrow enjoyed acting as the scourge of what he like to think of as the liberal-minded heterosexual Establishment; Sparrow was homosexual.

It was thought that the prosecution, noting that the defence had not been at all wild and bohemian but measured and quietly 'liberal-minded', had decided that by contrast witnesses on the other side might have seemed narrow-minded, congenital censors; that therefore it had been thought best to have no witnesses but to play the plain-man card (if not that of the man on the Clapham omnibus; Griffith-Jones did almost invoke that legendary figure). We learned later that the prosecution had tried hard to find witnesses for their side but without success. It had early become obvious that a shocked approach would suit the judge well, whatever the 1959 Act might say. The judge had implied that one could recruit 'experts' on anything – out went one main plank of the new Act – and added, again against the sense of the Act, that a jury did not need outside assistance to define 'obscenity'; it was an 'objective' matter. Similarly, Griffith-Jones cheekily and against the spirit of the Act extracted 'dirty bits' with which he hoped to shock the jury. It had become clear that he and the judge had a complicit relationship, by the way they between them dismissed the three main elements of the new Act. It was no doubt an unconscious complicity, more a matter of a shared cultural myopia than a sort of conspiracy.

Sometime later, in *Encounter*, Sparrow enjoyed himself hugely in an article designed to show what innocents or tricksters the defence witnesses were. He argued, rather convincingly, that one chapter in the book described the buggery of Lady Chatterley by her lover Mellors. I certainly belonged to the 'innocent' side, not having read the passage in that way. Whether other defence witnesses had so recognised it I do not know. If Griffith-Jones had been aware of it, why did he not use it? He would not have hesitated, given the nastiness of his approach in general. That puzzle remains. Of course, in a more open time such as the present a defence witness might have responded: 'Yes. Buggery. It is not uncommon.' Even nowadays, that would not have been easily received by some jurors and might have sunk the defence.

There was for me a curious coda to the Sparrow intervention. All Souls' College has an annual series of public lectures, named after its founder in 1438, Archbishop Chichele. Shortly after the Chatterley trial Sparrow invited me to give them. The warden has to present the speaker on each occasion and this involves him walking to the rostrum in full academic fig with the speaker, also enrobed, in tow up the centre aisle of the Schools, the University's great hall. I could almost have sworn that beneath Sparrow's gown one could detect a tail, lashing to left and right with perverse pleasure.

The trial drew to its end. If the prosecution had won, there would have been a strong case for an appeal, for the judge's summing-up to the jury was transparently biased. He was a classic example of the entirely convention-encased member of the judiciary; a devout Northern Irish Catholic. I was told that his strongly supporting wife had knitted a little bag to hold his copy of the book, presumably to disguise its awfulness from other eyes. He seemed not, to put the assumption mildly, to have been a reader of fiction, let alone of serious fiction; *Country Life* might have been more to his taste. He was not an aggressively wrong-headed man in the manner of Griffith-Jones. While the jury were out considering their verdict, he despatched some other cases, this time of the sort he was used to, typical criminal cases. He was reported as doing that with a firm humanity; he was at home, judging the plainly erring in ways he understood.

With *Lady Chatterley's Lover* he was entirely out of his cultural, intellectual, imaginative depths. He was outraged that anyone could claim literary merit for a book which explicitly described sexual acts and which used That Word. Clearly these experts were a sorry lot. For example, by misunderstanding what I had said, he implied by a rhetorical question in his summing-up to the jury that I was hardly fit to teach students. Would responsible parents like to think of their children being taught by such a man? For two minutes or so I found that rather hurtful; then I thought: will some members of the English judiciary ever break out of their kennels? The judge and Griffith-Jones were a well-matched pair. Both seemed to think they were trying not so much a book as Lady Chatterley herself, for letting down her class; and Mellors for getting above himself (and by getting on top of her).

The jury eventually returned and duly acquitted Penguin Books. The defence asked for costs in their favour. After all, the costly case had been initiated by the Crown and had failed. The judge replied dryly that no costs would be awarded to Penguin. It may be that he had reflected that Penguin would now make a lot of money from the sales of their book; they did – two million were sold in a year. But that would have been an irrelevant consideration. The ruling had an air of petulance. I have since been told by a lawyer that this is a proper and built-in protection for the Crown's freedom of action. I do not accept this justification; especially since the prosecution throughout went against the provisions of the new and relevant Act.

I thought during the trial and many times afterwards of Lawrence's judgement on Mrs Bolton, the nurse to the crippled Clifford Chatterley, and her endless gossip: 'One may hear the most private affairs of other people, but only in a spirit of respect for the struggling, battered thing which any human soul is, and in a spirit of fine, discriminative sympathy ... it is the way our sympathy flows and recoils that really determines our lives.' That splendid humane observation puts the disabled judgements of the judge and the prosecuting counsel in their place; as it does that of others who read Lawrence partially and shallowly.

A few weeks after the trial, on 14 December, there was an epilogue, a well-attended debate in the House of Lords. Life peerages had been introduced only in 1958, so in 1960 hereditary peers were in even more of a majority than they are today. The backwoodsmen from the county shires turned out in unusual numbers; even their names were hardly known to many people. Lord Teviot put down the motion: 'To ban for all time writings of this nature, particularly those of the author of this book'. 'My Lords, what are we coming to,' he twice rhetorically asked, after the manner of a nervous aunt. 'Not liberty, but licence' inevitably followed. 'It emanates from the warped mind of the author ... pure invention [straight out of authors' heads]. It never actually happened.' Which led at least one more relaxed lord to reflect that this 'actuality test' of literary merit would lead to the banning of most novels, they being invented by their authors. Another lord took the opportunity to object to the showing of pugnacious current-affairs programmes on television; they might bring the Authorities into disrepute. It was all like looking at a slow-motion film of medieval life.

The trial and its concomitants were 'very English' affairs, especially in the remarkable heat they aroused across society. They gave rise to what has been called 'the cultural debate of the century', and to some extent that is true. It was also said to have been a main agent for cultural change. That is less likely to be true; a main reflector would be more accurate. But why did it rouse such heat?

I believe, and this may at first seem to be attributing to a minor element a major role, that the main source was that one word 'fuck'; or perhaps it would be more accurate to call it the relatively small fuse which set off a sizeable explosion. The reaction to it on the bench, in the Crown Prosecutor's Office, in parts of the press and the public, illustrated the truth that even 'sophisticated' societies seem to need magic words for things they fear. The naked word 'fuck' was such a one to the English. It was part of Lawrence's rather earnest intention that he wished to clear and cleanse it, to recover it as a plain Anglo-Saxon word, for its proper use. 'Simply, one fucks,' I said from the witness-box, thus ensuring that the judge thought I was a foul-mouthed libertine. Lawrence's aim was misguided and hopeless. The word was and is used obsessively among many English workmen, so that they would find it hard to utter a sentence of more than two clauses without inserting it, probably into each clause. That too was told to the court, but the forces of law and order could not take the message. I think it likely that if that single word had been removed from the text, no prosecution would have followed. Indeed, an edition thus expurgated – like a filleted fish – had been published and not proposed for banning. There are some explicit love scenes in which the word does not appear; they might, with a little cleansing, having remained without too much disturbing the public pros-ecutor. These scenes are rather gentle and loving; which reminds us yet again that one early proposed title for the book was *Tenderness*.

Second among the effects was the shock the book gave to the established view of British society and culture. There runs through some parts of British life the fear of anarchy, of revolutionary disturbances by the workers (Tennyson expressed it memorably, if not in his best verse). Couple that with overt puritan suspicions about sex, though the English upper classes are hardly sexually puritanical in acts or speech; neither are working-class people, in deeds if not in explicit speech. That word 'fuck', so overused by many workers, is a mere expletive, an intensifier, divorced from actual descriptiveness; they have many other words for the act itself, none of them elegant or admirable.

It begins to seem that the central home of sexual fear is to be found in the respectable working and lower-middle classes, and that they are convinced that rough working-class people are sexually rapacious; here, they probably join hands with many in the middle class. Perhaps that is why it can be thought dangerous to let 'ordinary' people have access, through a cheap paperback, to explicit and uninhibited descriptions of sex and to the use of That Word in print. That might give the mob ideas. There is a favourite joke which mocks this attitude. Queen Victoria, it is said, had just enjoyed sex for the first time. 'Do the poor do this, Albert?' 'Yes, my dear.' 'Gracious me. It's too good for them!' Griffith-Jones's portentous question about the advisability of wives and servants reading such a book belongs to that tradition; as does a fear that a book which cost only three shillings and sixpence (37.5p) might fall into the wrong hands. The surprise is that such an attitude should have surfaced after the middle of the twentieth century. It is a slow-moving culture, ours, and one whose publicly prominent members are often impercipient to the changes long going on within it.

Was there a long-term result of that remarkable week? A sort of release? Not really. Many books exploited the new freedom and used words and descriptions previously forbidden. Most had no literary merit. Some were prosecuted, but on those occasions it was the defence which found it difficult to recruit expert witnesses. That job was left to out-and-out rejectors of any sort of censorship rather than to literary people. Gradually, the public prosecutor's interest even in those kinds of book seems to have fallen away so that you could within a few years find quite explicitly 'filthy' books on sale in even the most cautious of chain book-stalls; though usually put on the higher shelves with the 'girlie' magazines. Almost all books such as these could properly be called 'boring'. Perhaps the censors felt it more worthwhile to prosecute hardcore pornographic illustrated magazines, on the reasonable grounds that they have a more immediate impact than books of print. Those have to be read, and to read and recreate scenes in your head is much harder than simply to look at them. That is why the film *A Clockwork Orange* raises more weighty questions than *Lady Chatterley* should have raised. But perhaps that is too subtle an approach for the public prosecutor's department.

The truly literary reason why the acquittal of *Lady Chatterley* had only a mild effect on literature is much more interesting, and of long standing. To create an erotic effect, and there can of course be good literary reasons for that aim, it is not necessary to describe explicitly the writhing of bodies, or to use explicit language about the physical details or to include grunts and groans. Obliquity is much more effective. Here I always cite Chekhov, who said something to the effect that you do not need to try to describe exactly how two people make love on a canal bank; you should describe the moonlight glinting on a broken bottle floating in a canal, on the bank of which a couple are making love. In *Madame Bovarty*, when Charles sees Emma for the first time, she is under an umbrella, since it is softly – and one assumes warmly – raining, drop by drop. He looks at her, captivated; she passes her tongue slowly across her lips. That is all that is needed to suggest erotic attraction. Hardy used much the same skills to suggest Tess's physical attractions. The acquittal of *Lady Chatterley* proved nothing about literary limits and potentialities. Similarly, the nudity and sexual gymnastics in some television 'adaptations' of *Madame Bovary* add nothing. They remove subtle insights into the birth and nature of eroticism.

Over the years, aspects of the trial have kept surfacing in odd connections. The man who holds the key to 'The Bottoms', of *Sons and Lovers*, one of the Lawrence houses in Eastwood, used to tell visitors that Eastwood folk did not much care for him; *Lady Chatterley* is after all a dirty book which had been taken to court. He added with distaste that on the day the book was freed the miners at the local pit came to the surface when their shift ended and ran across the fields to the local newsagents for copies, then searched for the dirty bits. No emancipating result there, either.

One or two other related effects were personal. Soon after the trial E. M. Forster asked me to dinner at the Reform Club and we talked of the trial, mostly ironically and comically; that was an unexpected bonus and coda. Almost twenty years later, a retired judge invited me to a formal dinner at his Inn of Court. Mervyn Griffith-Jones was by then dead. But as I was introduced, one of them seemed vaguely to remember the name: 'Hoggart? Ah, yes [as if searching] ... Mervyn.' He seemed to be with difficulty recalling the time when one of their kind drew the short straw and had been required to go into alien territory. Gerald Gardiner and Jeremy Hutchinson were rare birds in that professional aviary.

So: very little direct effect from the trial. Perhaps some changes in attitudes in some quarters. It was certainly, as I said much earlier, taken as symbolically important, a representative moment, at the time. Did it move cultural opinion; or did it rather mark in a striking way the fact that cultural opinion had already moved, before the case was even tried, ahead of the public prosecutor, the Lord Chamberlain and their kind? Probably the latter.

There is evidence in this direction from the first day the court assembled and the jurors were sent out to read the book. After they had finished their reading, they took a straw vote. At that moment, before the trial had begun, nine of the twelve are said to have wondered what all the fuss was about; why, that is, anyone was bothering to prosecute. Not only literary people but general opinion also seemed to have changed.

So perhaps it was all a waste of time? But perhaps not, not a wholly unreal joust; because it revealed precisely that gap between popular opinion and some firm beliefs about class, literature, the need for censorship and all their intertwinings – that tenacious mixture of assumptions which were obviously still firmly in play in some areas even in 1960. In that sense the trial may have served a useful purpose; as a typical moment, though one founded on false assumptions. As that, it revealed more than any of us would have expected at the start, and was in parts gloriously comical. It still captures some part of our imaginations. As we enter a new millennium, just forty years on from the trial, we are almost certain to hear again about *Lady Chatterley*. Perhaps an actor will again represent me; in a V-necked pullover.

Farnham, 1998

PART THREE

POLITICS AND LITERATURE

Like George Orwell, Lawrence is one of the authors whom in adolescence I 'made my own'. I hope some grounds for that become clear in the following pages.

The four essays were all commissioned; each of whom has been to some degree amended for this appearance, but they all remain substantially as they originally were.

I was at first dubious about writing something which might seem like 'A Guide to Lawrence's Country'. An exploratory visit there I found still surprisingly moving. It also made me think more about the different kinds of relations between authors and their backgrounds.

Had I not been prompted in another direction I would among the novels have chosen Sons and Lovers. *But I wrote about that many years ago, and there was a special challenge and pleasure in writing about* The Rainbow *and* Women in Love *as a proper and magnificent pair.*

Writing the essay on the Lady Chatterley *trial reminded me of a curious incident. Immediately after the trial Allen Lane asked me to write a prefatory essay of about five or six thousand words for the first reprinting of the book. It was a rather pompous, moralistic essay which I greatly laboured over but of which I am not proud. It must have appeared in something like one and a half million copies. Allen did not mention a fee, nor did I; I did not want to profit from the case. Some weeks later I received a cheque for thirty pounds, a small amount even for that time. That was a sort of relief. I gave it to a charity.*

Soon after the trial one critic said something to the effect that all defence witnesses should have been prosecuted. For promoting obscenity, I imagine. That was wrong-headed. Most, if not all, of us thought the book well worth publishing for its literary merit and did not find it degrading; we were glad to speak against censorship in that instance. Perhaps some of us over-egged the pudding in our statements; the prosecutor and the judge probably pushed us that way, since the prosecutor was remarkably brutal and the judge unpleasantly myopic. An explanation for weakness, not an excuse.

THE ROAD TO WIGAN PIER

*M*y favourite authors, and that is not a guide to greatness but more a matter of personalities as they come off the page, include Chaucer, Donne, Sterne, Matthew Arnold, Clough, Hardy, Lawrence, Forster, Auden, Larkin – and Orwell.

Forster was a most attentive host, Auden a somewhat tricky guest. Judging from the painful account of a well-intentioned meeting between Orwell and L. H. Myers, I suspect that a meeting with Orwell would have needed careful negotiating.

If we meet in the afterlife, I might amuse him with an account of the 1984 conference on his work, in Strasbourg, organised by the Council of Europe. It was clotted with Orwell 'experts' from all five continents, some talking an abstract language, others using graphs and charts to reveal hitherto unsuspected aspects of his fiction, all of which would have had him out of the door in seconds.

The climax came near the end when T. F. Fyvel, whom I had been ferrying around the city as carefully as if carrying a prize exhibit, stood up and began: 'I imagine I am the only person here who saw Orwell plain; indeed, I knew him very well indeed especially in his Tribune days.' He did not reveal very much, but after that opening they were queuing up to touch the hem of his garment. I hope Orwell would have given at least a dry laugh at that.

BROKEN-BACKED, ERRATIC, sometimes sloppy, often perverse, *The Road to Wigan Pier* has nevertheless gripped most readers and infuriated some since it first appeared three-quarters of a century ago. It is a very English book by a very English character:

an eccentric, public-school type who lambasts public schools and all they stand for (or stood for in his day, some might quickly say). Not a typical old Etonian but, like Cyril Connolly and many another, an oddity of the sort Eton spins off. That most establishment of public schools has long created its own antibodies. The antibody Orwell was a writer of exceptional immediacy, freshness and vigour, opinionated and bold, by turns very angry and very tender. One is forced to reach for such handfuls of epithets to capture some of *Wigan Pier*'s paradoxes.

Orwell's earlier work, notably *Down and Out in Paris and London,* had given a hint of what he might do if set down in the unemployment-ridden industrial North of the thirties. So the left-wing publisher Victor Gollancz would have had some idea of what to expect when, in January 1936, he commissioned Orwell to contribute to the line of 'condition of England' books which runs from Cobbett, Mrs Gaskell, Disraeli, Carlyle and others to our time. Later, Gollancz decided to include the book in his Left Book Club series. Orwell's biographer, Bernard Crick, records that Gollancz wished to publish only the less contentious first half. But Orwell's representatives – his wife Eileen and his agent (Orwell had by then gone to fight in Spain) – refused to allow the text to be cut, so Gollancz felt constrained to write a foreword. Particularly in its second half, his commission had – to use an often misused phrase in its exact sense – given him more than he had bargained for. 'A highly provocative piece', he said stuffily, as he twisted and turned to protect his readers' and his club's ideological purity from this rude Old Etonian.

There would be little point in referring to that foreword today if it were not an exemplary minor document of English left-wing intellectualism at the time and a striking example of much Orwell was attacking. Gollancz could accept many things in Orwell's description of working-class life; yet, for example, he tut-tuts nervously when Orwell says that working-class people are believed by middle-class people to smell – which indeed they did, as I can verify from personal experience on Leeds tramcars on rainy days, going to and from one of the poorer districts. Gollancz found it difficult to accept that sort of directness about a class he knew chiefly through his intellect. He would have been less shocked if Orwell had said the Hampstead intelligentsia were wife-swappers. Gollancz was on safer ground, though he got there for the wrong reasons, when he criticised Orwell's self-indulgence in vituperation; but that applies mainly to the book's second half.

Few books are so dramatically split. The first half is a graphically unforgettable depiction of the very texture of poverty-stricken, Northern working-class life in the mid-thirties. Not mainly of the 'respectable' working-class, certainly. Orwell had been shocked by what he had seen during two months in Wigan, Barnsley and Sheffield, and was not disposed to add face-saving qualifications. He knew that not everyone lived in filthy conditions, but filth was a true indicator of the cost of capitalist industrialisation in one of its worst forms. One remains captured by the picture, glimpsed from the train as Orwell went back south, of the tired young woman hopelessly trying to unblock a pipe: 'She knew well enough what was happening to her – understood as well as I did how dreadful a destiny it was to be kneeling there in the bitter cold, on the slimy stones of a slum backyard, poking a stick up a foul drainpipe.' An unsympathetic reader might comment that Orwell read a remarkable amount about the women's inner feelings from having a glimpse of her, from the back or sideways, and from a moving train. That is true; but the passage is characteristic of the sort of bold assumption of inner sympathy which Orwell practised, and let his readers take or leave.

The second half of the book is argumentative rather than descriptive, an uneven critique of English socialism, and especially the socialism of the earnest middle class. Occasionally it has the slapdash and slapstick hilarity of a man who would feel impelled to jump up and utter rude words in a Quaker meeting; just as often it punctures with precision infantile left-wing intellectualism. It is easy to see why the book created and can still create so sharp an impact: so much adverse notice on one hand, so much cheerful fellow-feeling on the other. Above all, it is a study of poverty and, underlying that, of the strength of class divisions. Orwell notes with contempt how in 1937 it was fashionable to claim that class divisions were fading in Britain. Twenty years later I published a book which made similar claims and was told by some reviewers that I was grievously mistaken, stubbornly and probably stupidly out of date; that class feeling was virtually dead. Forty years on and the same things are being said; a self-deluding automatic response, always to be expected. Class distinctions do not die; they change their spots, find new titles and ways of expressing themselves. Orwell's stance in this matter is still up to date. Each decade the fortunate or the blind shiftily declare we have buried class; each decade the coffin stays empty, or virtually empty – half an arm might by now just be showing. Perhaps, say the optimists, we should simply accept it as a universal fact of social life; Orwell and many another of us would not adopt that cheap solace; the cost in unnecessary human unhappiness is too high.

Orwell's precision about the nature of class distinctions is a surprising pleasure. Look only at his description of his own social origins in the 'lower-upper-middles', and the endless shifts to which they are put to keep up appearances so as not to sink 'into the working class where we belong'. The last phrase is perversely loose; his kind would not sink into or ever belong to the working class, but he knew that tossed-off statement would startle those of his readers among them. His precise kind, if they are dislodged, drift to the inter-class, the home of the unbelonging; hence their deep unease. Still, few writers have so forcefully and nakedly described the near panic which that threat of sinking can induce at this insecure social level, when one begins to lose acknowledged social status and money, are no longer securely above the lower-middle class, to whom rather than to the working class they might well fall. They occupy a near-imaginary level indicated only, or almost entirely, by their accents; a thin thread keeping them from the Fall. He ends that passage with one of his comical, distorted but echoing images: 'probably when we get there it will not be so dreadful as we feared, for after all we have nothing to lose but our aitches'.

Much of Orwell's work, especially *The Road to Wigan Pier* and some of the early novels, is therefore about a struggle towards a liberation, liberation from the constrictions of class. Those affect us all, since each class and sub-class has its own sustaining network of styles: its codes, its received wisdom and even more its received prejudices. When Orwell hits the target directly, as he so often does, this can give the reader a sense of relief, freedom. Yet he is always, underneath, fraternal, seeking a more communal, undivided England. By his own physical and mental journeyings he earned as we have already noted the right to say, as few of us have or would dare to utter, that England is after all 'a family'.

This set of attitudes accounts also for the pendular swings in his writing: from anger, as he swipes at another hawser of class, to deep and sympathetic sentiment when his imagination opens to new insights, new fellow-feelings, as those hawsers uncharacteristically lose their grip, at least for the time being. For many readers the fellow-feeling is harder to accept than the anger, especially when he does not regret but celebrates aspects of working-class life. He makes some characteristically wild generalisations even about the working class, such as when he asserts that 'during the past dozen years the English working-class have grown servile with a rather horrifying rapidity'. This produces the odd question of whether Orwell might have welcomed some newer and not servile 'working-class' attitudes of the turn of the century; or not – given that some by-products would certainly not have attracted him.

His praise of other aspects of working-class life has been inevitably labelled sentimental or praised as a fine insight of the kind he could command, as few observers, standing back to risk a generalisation, could; I belong to that second group, the praisers. The moment comes in the lyrical passage at the end of Part I in *Wigan Pier*, where he describes the humane warmth of a working-class living room when the father is in steady work and the family in good heart. It is not, he concludes, the technical triumphs of modern civilisation, nor great artistic achievements, nor the grandest public monuments, which he treasures about Britain. Instead, it is 'the memory of working-class interiors, that reminds me that our age has not been altogether a bad one to live in'. One may add, from the essay on the 'naughty' seaside postcards of Donald McGill: 'The corner of the human heart they spoke for might manifest itself in worse forms.'

To call that passage on the living room 'sentimental' is almost always meant to be pejorative; those lines are in fact full of a genuine sentiment and that is different. People who find it difficult to face this, who are deeply uneasy before expressions of warmth and affection, take refuge in habitually adding the 'al' to 'sentiment' so as to dismiss it. The passage reflects, rather, Orwell's courage of his own convictions, his own important discoveries, the strength to admit that his heart has been opened in a most unexpected place; not at Eton, not in Burma, not in his own conventional professional family background. Orwell himself was an adept at antagonistic judgements; here he is almost surprising himself by discovering that these people are in their own way 'in the truth' at least as much as any who are socially above them.

The paradoxes within Orwell himself and so in his writings pile up as we read. He can be exceptionally gentle but also wildly harsh. He had intense pity for the poor and down-and-out, and at the same time a middle-class – a more than middle-class; a deeply personal – squeamishness about close contact with them. He can be hugely charitable but also bitterly rejecting; he reaches out to be brotherly but is essentially lonely.

He can be unusually clear-headed but also wrong-headed and pig-headed. He can display common sense of such a high order that it becomes an uncommon form of high intelligence; he can also display the ingrained prejudices of his class. It is not surprising that, though he spent so much time immersing himself in the life of 'the lowest of the low' in the cities of the twentieth century, he would have liked to have been an eighteenth-century country parson, watching his walnuts grow and exhibiting the traditional English decencies.

Whatever the intellectual interest of his ideas and opinions, much the most fruitful and enjoyable way into an understanding of Orwell is through his handling of language. Through the sloppinesses first, since they indicate almost as much about the temper of his mind as do the strengths. He loves extreme adjectives, adverbs and nouns, and does not mind how much he repeats them; redundancy is one of his favourite stylistic tactics. Top of the list is 'dreadful', closely followed by 'frightful'; then by 'appalling', 'disgusting', 'hideous'; then 'unspeakably', 'horribly', 'obscenely', and finally 'horror'. They are idiomatic and they hammer at you repetitively. But they are excessive; if you use them to describe a filthy boarding house you haven't many left for the Holocaust.

So do his demonstrative pointings and jabbings, determined to make his readers see straight: 'You see this ...'; 'You see that ...'. The 'yous' march on, together with the 'this's', especially in such formulation as: 'You see this business of ...'. It is all very direct, colloquial and arm-grabbing; and mutually involving. Orwell assumes a great range of common knowledge with the reader in such favoured locutions as: 'in *that* peculiar watchful, loving way that invalids have ...', or, 'For dinner there were generally *those* three-penny steak puddings which are sold ready-made in tins' [my italics]. We are all assumed to have shared such experiences and it all makes for the peculiar intimacy of the writing. He was a good hater and sometimes his style became melodramatic beyond reason: '... all that dreary tribe of high-minded women and sandal-wearers and bearded fruit-juice drinkers who come flocking towards the smell of "progress" like blue-bottles to a dead cat'. Amusing in a way, but, as he might have just possibly have admitted today, 'way over the top'.

For all their force and the irritation they can cause at times, these are minor elements in comparison with the virtues of Orwell's prose. Above all, it is usually a model of clarity and simplicity. I deliberately opened *Wigan Pier* at random and stabbed a sentence equally at random. It runs:

'Probably you have to go down several coalmines before you can get much grasp of the processes that are going on around you.' It is not elegant; it needs a little tightening; but it is entirely clear. Only six words of the twenty-four have more than one syllable and only one of those is an abstract noun. 'Good prose is like a window-pane,' he said, and most of the time lived up to that axiom. He will not be a guide for everyone, but, for some of us, he – and Samuel Butler, who died the year before Orwell was born – are models for contemporary prose-writing. Butler's platonic lady friend, Miss Savage, told him that the prose of *The Way of all Flesh* 'reads like cream'; not quite an Orwellian phrase but one he would, if slightly reluctantly, have appreciated.

Orwell is, first, a voice by which he draws us straight towards him and meets us. Other writers have 'voices' but those may be matters of manner, of style rather than substance. Style can be an offshoot of manner, and Orwell is not mannered; manner is an offshoot of 'show', the way we present ourselves to best advantage. In these senses Orwell had neither manner nor style. His voice came immediately from his inner character, his convictions, from the things of substance he had to say. Orwell's voice is direct, demonstrative, uncompromising, rarely abstract.

His prose expresses what is seen by an eye of unusual clarity and perceptiveness. That fashionable phrase for an aspect of smart political and journalistic language today – 'soundbites' – meaning verbal tropes invented by 'spin doctors' and meant to stick in the memory, that sort of messing about with plain language would have met Orwell's contempt. But we might say, half jocularly, that he was himself a master of 'eye-bites'; a gift he shares with Graham Greene.

He has an eye for the significant and telling image In the Brookers' boarding house he notices that when dust lingers and gathers it coagulates greasily (which was no doubt to him 'frightful'). He notices such a startling detail as that in pit offices they have a rubber stamp applied to the men's pay slips to indicate death stoppages, making one realise how common, how 'matter of fact', are deaths down pits. Or he starts, again characteristically: 'I was struck by …' and goes on to muse about how status affects your whole approach to a pension. Or, more intellectually, he says: 'Here you come upon the important fact that every revolutionary opinion draws part of its strength from a secret conviction that nothing can be changed.' It is too absolute a statement but it pulls you up very sharply and makes you think again.

Orwell was a public conscience, a conscience with an exceptionally well-developed sense of smell. He makes us realise how much that neglected and lowly rated sense can inform our whole being. Read only the end of chapter nine in *Wigan Pier* where he has to force himself to enter a common lodging house: 'like going down into some dreadful subterranean place – a sewer full of rats, for instance – and into a frowzy firelit kitchen underground'. A drunken, dangerous-looking young steve-dore lurches over; but only to fling his arms round Orwell and offer him a cup of tea: 'I had a cup of tea. It was a kind of baptism.' Orwell's Christian childhood was forever reasserting itself, but had to be proved again in each experience.

In *Wigan Pier* the best example of this sense of duty captured in the sense of smell appears towards the end of the first chapter, in the perora-tion on what British imperialism has meant for so many: '... and this is where it all led – to labyrinthine slums and dark back kitchens with sickly, ageing people creeping round and round them like black beetles. It is a kind of duty to see and smell such places now and again, especially smell them lest you should forget that they exist; though perhaps it is better not to stay there too long.' 'A kind of duty ... to smell such places'. He had a very fastidious nose; but, in spite of that dry admission that one shouldn't stay too long in smelly places, one not at all genteelly fastidi-ous, not class-infected and not drawing back from the vulgarity of 'common people'. Orwell's nose was above all a moral nose, a Protestant nose, a nose which forced him to smell out sin and salvation, the nose of an old English moralist.

I would be, I think, a poor spirit that was not, in the end, impressed and chastened by such writing and – inextricably – by such a writer. One is bound to wonder what he would have chosen to see, to smell and to use his voice against today. The trivialisation of so much in the press, including the broadsheets, their flight from opinions in favour of opin-ionation, their showbiz and youth obsession, their neglect of discrimination? Or the decline of the National Health Service, which was founded just before he died, but which after half a century is dividing into two, one for the poor, the other for the well-to-do? Or the wide-spread deterioration of language (and, as a side issues, the idiot-aspect of political correctness): the prodigious rise of the advertising and PR world? 'Cool Britannia'? There could be a lot more but that is enough to be going on with.

On the other hand, Orwell would have been glad that some of the more important agencies in defence of human rights, most established since his death, were founded in Britain: PEN, Amnesty International, Charter 88, Article 19, Index on Censorship. A moral voice, then; at its frequent best clean, economical, direct, fraternal; in its impulses one in the line of his great social democratic forerunners, the three Ts; Temple, Tawney and Titmus. For Orwell, the last, fitting word might best be heard from the Catalan poet, Salvador Espriu: 'I shall have lived in order to preserve the meaning of certain words for you.'

Farnham, 1989/2000

THE STATE VERSUS LITERATURE

I gave this paper to a meeting of writers. By some it was not well received. They objected mainly to my saying that writers were not owed a living and should not be pensioners of the state. One stood up and, more in anger than sorrow, said that he had never expected to hear the author of The Uses of Literacy *refusing to defend the rights of writers.*

In recommending, for some but certainly not all, that teaching could be a good source of basic income for potential writers, I also registered some disaffection among my listeners. I remembered then one of Shaw's sillier obiter dicta*: that those who can, do; those who can't, teach.*

I thought of those mentioned in the text and of others, all of whom combined the two roles; with some stress, certainly, but also some gain. D. H. Lawrence got out fairly quickly; he, even more than most, had to; but not before he had registered the goodness of good teaching.

Trying to explain and to inspire is one of the best things we can practise; but yet, as with most activities, not to practise beyond the point which feeds but does not drain our particular spirit. Then is the time to go somewhere else.

In that sense, I taught for far too long and as a result lost some books I might have written. The regret is deep but not overwhelming.

VERY ROUGHLY, WE can say that most modern societies show one of three main approaches to literature, as, we saw earlier, they do to 'cultural' matters generally: the fearful, the over-loving and the neglectful. The USSR, its satellites and societies like them, are fearful because though many of their apparatchiks may know little about literature, they suspect imaginative works and see them as, potentially at least, highly explosive loose cannon. So they keep books on a rein, and if one escapes and looks dangerous, they stamp on it. My experience at UNESCO, which is, among much else, the cultural arm of the UN, suggests that a majority of member states are like that, some violently.

On the other hand, very rich societies, societies which have everything, tend to see literature as yet another commodity, a matter of fashion and style, a sort of expensive psychic shampoo containing a secret ingredient. Within their own terms and definitions they are overattentive, and some writers, but not the more difficult and not necessarily the best, can easily become wealthy celebrities.

Neglectful societies, of which ours is a partial example (being wealthy, it also has a place among the over-loving), do not within their central culture fear or stamp on literature, because they do not regard is as very important; not something which could conceivably imperil the state, but rather something marginal and irrelevant to their real lives. If there is an edge of fear, that comes from the suspicion that it may be at least slightly subversive of the capitalist/democratic values they hold dearest. They also suspect that the purlieus of literature are inhabited by people who are probably disreputable. In short, not being extremely rich, they do not want literature as the equivalent of the mink-lined backscratcher, an ultimate commodity; yet they do not feel it is important enough to need serious tackling.

In Britain we are not likely to be writing by candlelight as we might have been if we had lived on the other side of the Iron Curtain, wondering whether there will be a peremptory knock at the door in the early hours. Nor is there any need at all to starve in a garret unless you insist that you must continue with your writing of great but so-far unacknowledged poetry, give up paid work to pursue it and can find neither a loving working-wife or parent or patron, and have no solid private means. Less hardy types may sell out and seek an adequate living writing advertising copy until recognised; or, at the extreme, some teach.

Most writers who have some slight degree of success suffer in societies such as ours – middle-range, moderate-mother societies, we might call them – suffer from overexposure, too many reviews and invitations to broadcast and so less and less time given to the next book, not always because of financial need but because the immediate is always the enemy of the good and because writing is a lonely occupation. More suffer from such habits than look round at the pinched faces of their children and say to themselves: 'Look what the demands of my genius, coupled with public neglect, have brought us to!'

Here is another trio: three warnings we might give ourselves as we start thinking about 'the state and literature'. They vary greatly in importance but each has its point.

First: avoid false international comparisons. They tend to be those which suit our claims, of course, though others could be found which would not be so pleasant or encouraging. You know the kind of thing: 'The city of Frankfurt spends more on its opera than the Arts Council's opera vote for the whole of this country.' I have invented the comparison but its general line is sound. Assume it to be true. It could be a further likely assumption that Frankfurt has many more armed police and gas canisters than the entire British police services. Such jackdaw comparisons work by selective cultural raiding. German cities do spend hugely on 'culture' and there are clear historical and civic reasons for that. We do wrong to take a bit that suits us out of any other social body, set it against our chosen and to us regrettable British habit – opera being regarded as only for toffs and snobs – and so make a false comparison, ignoring any odd parts which don't fit. 'The Soviet Union spends much more than we do per head on public libraries.' Yes; but do you also want the British state to take over other Soviet attitudes towards what books may be made available in those libraries? Is Solzhenitsyn available? A friend asked this direct question of Mme Furtseva at a UNESCO conference where she, the Minister for Culture, was lauding public-library provision in the Soviet Union. She then demanded that he be withdrawn from the UK delegation; and was ignored.

The second of these early warnings is that none of us, writers or others, are owed a living. We have no inalienable right to state support just because we are writers. We do not have to write and should be glad of that. Writing is one of the few gratuitous acts we can perform, thank God. If enough money doesn't come from writing, we can, most of us, look for ancillary work. More about that too, later. I mention this now, though I am still surprised that it needs saying, because not long ago I heard a 'radical' playwright asked why he thought the state should pay him to write, why a direct subvention should be available. He replied:

'Because it is my job and I should be paid for it as the carpenters and scene-shifters are.' The analogy is ridiculous, small-minded self-justification. We need carpenters and scene-shifters and bus drivers and doctors; and I can argue as fiercely as the next man that we need artists, too, but that is another use of the word 'need'. For the good of our souls we need artists; so the taps are stopped from dripping, we need, in another sense, plumbers. We do give some financial aid to artists in Britain and I have supported that. I wish I did not have to, all in all; it is better not to be a pensioner, to be free. Moreover, if his plays are successful, a dramatist will have gratifying and continuing royalties; it seems a fair gamble. Carpenters have no royalties (here, incidentally, dramatists seem usually better rewarded than, say, poets or 'serious' novelists – incidentally, for the latter the newest get-out title is 'literary novelists').

As you will have gathered, I think that in a society such as ours most of us should be content, at least in the early years, to be part-time writers; or, if we feel that we must write full time, should be prepared to strike the best balance we can between our 'real' writing and occasional work which pays the rent and grocer's bills. It is not, for all but the exceptionally driven though not necessarily exceptionally gifted, an overwhelmingly difficult moral decision and no one else can or should make it for us. My mental amber lights flash when someone shows a tendency to begin sentences: 'Speaking as a writer ...'. It is too self-conscious, too self-awarded a medal, slightly smug. Imagine it in, say, T. S. Eliot's mouth. To be a writer is a condition to which we aspire, not a 'profession'. To be described as a 'published author' is less troublesome because it is commonly used to designate a recognised profession and is a catch-all to cover anyone who publishes any kind of thing, from authors of DIY handbooks onwards.

Many good writers write in the margins of their time: Philip Larkin, this century's equivalent of Spinoza's lens-grinder, was a university librarian; Charles Causley was a schoolteacher for decades (very draining unless you have a gift for it); David Lodge was a university teacher, also for decades, as was Raymond Williams; P. H. Newby had a long, demanding and distinguished career which took him near the top of the BBC hierarchy, and wrote his novels at weekends. There are many reasons why some people choose that way, especially if they have a dependent family and do not wish to force insecurity on them. Some like the order and formalities of institutional life against which to brace themselves as they face the uncharted waste of their next book; some would hate having to make up their income by writing to order pieces they have no interest in, and would equally hate having to be nice to people they do not really like just so as to be given the next commission. On the other hand, anyone is at liberty to set out on that open sea and take their chances. That can be admirable. What I am doubtful about is their right to grumble as though it is someone else's fault, a lapse in the dues owed to them, if they lose the gamble. It is sad to think that Marghanita Laski, who was pleased to be asked to chair the Arts Council's Literature Panel, declared after a few months that she had never worked on a body in which those members who were writers were in general so uncharitable and self-righteous in their demands; she rightly regretted 'the literary pressure group's total lack of philanthropy'. The Drama Panel, which I chaired for a while, was not as unpleasant as that; most of the actors and actresses especially were fair-minded; but some of the directors saw their membership not as an invitation to try to make dispassionate judgement in support of their art but as an opportunity for relentlessly pushing their own case. To be invited to 'declare an interest' in an item under discussion, and then to leave or stay and keep silent on that issue, seemed outrageous to some of them.

The third warning is less important but still worth adding. Briefly, and in support of what has just been said, it is: 'Don't let's be beastly to the Arts Council'. The Council has become for all sides of these arguments too convenient a scapegoat or whipping boy. The Arts Council is not elitist or aloof. If anything, it is nervously all-embracing, and certainly confused – council members and officers alike. That may sound superior but is not; it is simply to recognise yet another element in the general confusion in the debate about the arts and society today.

It is time to ask, as unemotionally as possible: why should there be any state support for the arts? I said earlier that I wish there did not have to be, so far as writers are concerned. In going further we come at once to a clear distinction: that between the large performing and the individual arts. Symphonic music, opera, ballet, large-scale theatre all need many people to present, and a lot of money to mount. If they have no public subventions they will either wither away in favour of chamber arts or will have to be priced so as to be accessible only to the wealthy, or American tourists. Which points back to the most basic, the bedrock, question of all: are they worth preserving anyway; and with public money? This raises the matter of a conviction which obviously cannot be objectively proved. Personally, as I also say when discussing broadcasting's fields of interest, I believe all those arts should be preserved and developed, that they are essential elements in a truly civil society. That very many people do not apparently think so is chiefly a result of class connections over centuries, educational inadequacies and, nowadays, populist attitudes. I do not imagine that, if the more objective among those hindrances were greatly lessened, a majority of the population would at once flock to those arts; I believe that greatly increased numbers would. So here we arrive at the fork in the road. If you do not accept those basic premises: about the value of those arts in themselves and to society, and about the much larger potential audiences, then you need read no further, since we can have nothing more to say to each other.

If you provisionally accept those two convictions, I suppose the next question is: if the state would find it difficult properly to support those arts, can commercial subventions seriously help? On the figures of such support so far, it is difficult to foresee a future in which industrial and commercial sponsorship could sustain these big arts and keep on sustaining them, even at the level they now have, and that is skimpy. With one or two exceptions, in particular where well-endowed and powerful individuals rather than large and primarily profit-conscious boards have the final say, that sort of sponsorship is inherently quixotic, short-term, safe if fashionable, short of breath. If we wish those arts to be well performed, to have some assurance of continuity, freedom to make experiments and so mistakes, to charge no more than reasonable admission prices, then substantial state support is unavoidable.

This brings us back to literature. Drama apart, literature is different from the other arts and for two main reasons, one practical, the other philosophical. Literature is a hedge-occupation; in principle, it needs no mounting. It does, you may reply, need promoting today with all the energies of agents, PR people, publishers, the mass media. That is an argument which starts from a false foundation: that books are a part of commodity culture and all it involves. Do you really believe, one has then to ask, that all the increasing hype of literary salesmanship, from an appearance on the smallest chat show to the Booker bonanza, do you think all that has much seriously to do with the continuing health of literature?

Second, literature is the most directly critical of the arts, since it uses words and names names. So it would be best for it to keep as far as possible away from state support. Here is an interesting comparison. Drama is a public performing art and receives sizeable public subventions, especially to the Royal National Theatre and the Royal Shakespeare Company. The absurd Lord Chamberlain and his lavatorial preoccupations has gone. We still have hassles such as those over the play *The Romans in Britain*, from Mrs Whitehouse and some members of the Greater London Council, who questioned whether public money should properly be spent on such productions. Of course, books can come under that spotlight, as the *Lady Chatterley* trial illustrated. But one secondary reason why that case attracted so much attention is that it was unusual; staged drama is much more vulnerable to the attentions of the would-be censors.

Books are not so much in that particular public eye and we should be careful not to edge them too far towards it, as might happen if literature became heavily subsidised by the state. Ideally, what one might like to say to governments apropos their approach to literature would be something such as this: 'We will be glad to have a little money from you for carefully defined purposes, but we do not ask you generally to try to improve our lot, to make us dependants. We accept that lot as the price of writing freely. We do not wish our lot to be made harder by pressures to make us toe a conventional line.' We have always to preserve our freedom to say that things are as they are; we are the children of Galileo: 'Nevertheless, it still moves.' Not at all easy, that, in many places. Here, the warnings are slightly silk-lined. Norman St John Stevas, once Secretary of State for the Arts, caught the tone. He was objecting to a startling exhibition supported by the Arts Council. It may have been rather silly and was very obviously out to shock the easily shockable. Still: one was sad to hear the minister advise: 'If you do things like that, it makes it more difficult to get money for the arts.' No doubt he meant well and was thinking of the popular press's routinely outraged reaction to art of that kind. But he was implicitly advising polite, democratic self-censorship. The Arts Council might have decided and said that that exhibition was foolish and ungifted, but only because it believed this, not by pre-defining itself from ill-meant and ill-judged public criticism.

'Carefully defined purposes' in giving help to authors? Such as? First, the main thrust should be directed at readers and services for them, starting with the libraries; in the belief that as readership improves so will the rewards for writers, and that anything which deflects writers from the need for direct patronage is a good thing; and because many public librarians today have only a wobbly understanding of their institutions' own high purposes. Second, there might be carefully allotted grants for writers, but only rarely recurrent grants. No regular bursary holders, no yielding to the most insistent candidates and their friends in high places. ('Princess Margaret is very interested in my work ...', or '... is on our Board'), no frequent personal callings-upon or telephone calls, or letters to members of the Arts Council's Literature Panel or to the Literature Director; and a very careful look at any previous work and what may seem the promise of that proposed. Some writers and their supporters object violently to any considerations such as these last; they know their work is important. Good, but it should also be capable of standing up to sensible scrutiny.

When we left Paris, I was due to go into a demanding full-time job. But I needed a few months to prepare the first draft of a book on five years' experience in the UN; without that the book would have been much delayed and the freshness of memory largely lost. My prospective employers, Goldsmiths' College, agreed to wait and Leverhulme, prompted by Asa Briggs, gave me a fellowship which brought with it a small and quiet room at the University of Sussex and use of the library there, plus a quite small but very useful amount for new incidental expenses (chiefly of renting an attic in Lewes during the week); that was what it stretched to and very useful it was. This was in late 1975; I started full-time work at Goldsmiths' in January of 1976, with a first draft in my bag. The book appeared three and a half years later. Without that quiet, uninterrupted space it would have taken at least three more years before it was ready.

Third suggestion, and the trickiest. The system should at least try to have room for really special cases, the James Joyces, those who simply cannot bear to do other than write and may be extraordinarily talented; but have not so far found a rich patron. That is not a job for any committee. Rather, it is worth risking that the recipient be chosen by one person only, who is riding a strong hunch and has no ulterior purpose or relationship. Once every two or three years and for a longish trial period (say, to a maximum of three years and not renewable?). I doubt if that idea will ever be taken up, unless the new National Endowment helps meet the need. Best meanwhile to go on looking for a rich and patient patron.

Fourth, there should be steady attention to the availability of good, older literature, so much of which is now out of print, and to translations of foreign literature, about which most of us know little. Compared to the Dutch, inheritors of a major language such as ours become lazy. Herman Bang's fine novel from Denmark, *Tina*, has appeared in translation here, an act of courage which I hope will be rewarded; it appeared in French many decades ago. Last, some literary journals should be supported and for some years at a stretch unless, after the first five years, there is a strong case against doing so, on literary grounds or because of hopeless management.

It may be said that, though my order may differ from that of others, many of these things have from time to time been fostered by the Arts Council's Literature Panel, and that is true. The panel has been in existence for long enough to have thought of most things. But my list and my order are based on criteria which should be regularly argued about; they did not arrive as responses to the piling-up of successive odd thoughts, and shovings and pushings from various places. The panel's difficulty is that it is again and again being pressed to take up its roots as fashion and panel members change, and as they continue to insist that their favourite really is a Very Special Case for support, in spite of members quarrelling, coalescing into cliques, and generally giving the appearance of such discord as to make it easy for any politician or senior civil servant to dismiss literature's claims on public funds as too often inspired by bad tempered log-rolling. The Literature Panel has so far had no reliable literary compass.

Behind all this discord is the biggest current worry of all; the fear of choosing, of selecting some things and rejecting others. Think of the two thousand new novels published each year, and of the difficulty of choosing between them. Some will be very good indeed; some atrocious and perhaps riding on the wave of an atrocious brief fashion. One would hardly know this from the way they are treated in that part of the press which cares to review novels. To avoid making vertical divisions of quality, of risking seeming to 'guide' anyone, new horizontal generic divisions are regularly created: 'the literary novel', 'the popular novel', as well of course as the crime novel and the sci-fi novel. Then there may be 'the working-class novels' or 'the Aga Sagas' or 'the Islington novels'. Or the novels by age: 'the teenage novel', 'the 8–10 years old novel', and no doubt 'the senior citizens' novel'; and 'the holiday novel'. Anything to avoid that vertical classification; and so to remain able to fit virtually everything in. Capacity, catholicism, hospitality, inclusiveness override. One literature director of a Regional Arts Board told me angrily she would never make 'elitist' distinctions; she went on to blame the Arts Council for not making enough money available so that she could distribute it among many many more novelists. That was their 'right'. One felt like replying that there ought to be a prize to discourage some novelists from writing yet more fiction; but perhaps trying another form. That will be regarded as a heinous, because snobbish, remark. Sometime ago I read an essay in a journal devoted to community arts. It argued that the frescoes in the Arena chapel at Padua should not be regarded as the achievement of a particular genius, Giotto, but were the result of team-work to which all concerned, including those who held the ladders, were contributing artists. One could hardly go further than that. We tend to live in our own enclosed and self-justifying worlds, talking only to one another.

In the literary world's engagements with the state, what is needed above all is less parti-pris thinking; then we may move things. It can happen. Take the Public Lending Right. That was long overdue and was only created because a few writers fought a long and tough and exceptionally well-managed campaign. It does not greatly help struggling writers, since, in the nature of the arrangements, the rich become slightly richer by it. It must award by the number of borrowings; so Barbara Cartland received the maximum allowed, and no doubt sincerely believed that to be just. The logic is impeccable; it seems impossible to build in a qualitative factor, and is probably undesirable in view of the fights it would encourage. Yet PLR is, so far as it goes, a triumph.

Then there is VAT. Are we going to resist the imposition of that on books in the absolute and high-minded way in which university academics resisted limitless tenure? 'A good book is the precious life-blood of a master spirit'; yes. Do we really want to invoke Milton, at this level of high principle, so as to protect all those tens of thousands of books a year? And at the risk of seeing VAT levied by an impatient government on all books, including those scholarly books which *are* essential to the advancement of knowledge, and many others? Or are we willing, if the threat became closer, to try to make some sensible discriminations? I do not know the answers to these questions, but they need asking more often.

Finally: the greatest threat to good writing today does not come from governmental pressure. It comes, for most of us, from distractions, from the tempting invitations to become public figures and probably well-paid ones; it comes, in short, from the mass-media machines which so remorselessly need fresh copy day after day; it comes from human spirits often under pressure; it comes from our own weaknesses. The long effort at good writing is most often betrayed, to echo Meredith, by what is false within.

London, 1986/2000

FREEDOM TO PUBLISH: EVEN
HATEFUL STUFF

T owards the end of this speech to the triennial conference of the International Publishers Association, I remembered a letter by Thomas Mann, and impulsively referred to it as one of the greatest twentieth-century statements on freedom of speech. It was written in response to a letter Mann had received from the Senate of the University of Bonn which, in obedience to the wishes/orders of the Hitler regime, revoked his honorary degree of that university. I added that it was and is a superbly dignified expression of the power of that tradition, at a time when the country's rulers were denying it.

I was shocked to hear that after I had spoken, a very few German publishers (not, I hope, of books in the humanities) had approached the conference chairman and objected to that reference to Mann, as 'a criticism of Germany'. Praise, rather, if they had been able to listen adequately and so hear properly that tribute to a great German, great European, great human being. I had not realised that any reasonably educated persons could be so obtuse.

IRST, A RAPID roll call for 1988 of a few recent British governmental interventions in the work of the mass media of communication: in the misguided objections to some of the reporting of the Falklands campaign; in television programmes such as *Real Lives* and *Secret Society*; towards books such as *Spycatcher* and towards Amnesty International's decision to enquire into the Gibraltar shootings.

And now we have the creation of the Broadcasting Standards Council, a quite superfluous watchdog, to be trained – like guidedogs for the blind, though with more difficulty – to snuffle out those scenes of sex-and-violence which broadcasting's statutory governing bodies are thought too lax to notice. This may in part look like throwing a sop to quieten Cerberus, but that would be a mistake; this is making blind Cerberus itself a sop for the moral majority, which, carefully scrutinised, may not be a majority at all; and on what grounds is such a majority automatically to be taken as a sound moral arbiter?

These are the hallmarks of a government which is at one and the same time free-for-all and illiberal, in favour of the widest commercial freedom to make individual fortunes against freedom of expression when it offends their particular and peculiar *lares et penates*. Unbridled competition but no sex, please; we're British. The paradox is that they therefore need to hire more and bigger gamekeepers, such as the BSC above, to control more and more predatory poachers. As a result, the habitual social consensus here, and its tolerance-enduring muscles, are now under exceptional strain.

This year sees the fortieth anniversary of the United Nations Declaration on Human Rights, sometimes honoured, often ignored, but still a cause of guilty feelings and occasional better behaviour, even among those who most flout it. In the last twenty years we have seen, in Western Europe alone, three dictatorships disappear; and, in Europe again, the Court of Human Rights at Strasbourg is slowly but surely gaining in recognised importance. The World Report on the Practice of Human Rights by that admirable new organisation, Article 19, make chastening reading, all in all. But Article 19 exists and is only one sign of an increasing concern for human rights in many parts of the globe, even in those where such a concern is most dangerous.

UNESCO, when it was founded just after the war, put the free flow of information at the forefront of its principles; and did not merely promote a well-intentioned myth. The benchmarks were there from the start: freedom to hold one's own opinions and to try to arrive at them honestly; freedom to express them publicly; and freedom to listen to what others think and believe.

There is no golden age just around the corner. The urge to censor, to shut up others who disagree with you, is as natural and as nagging to humans as the urge to be free of anxiety or to have sex. Even if we wished it, we will never be rid of either. There are five main forms, all much in evidence today.

The most obvious, common and crudest is governmental censorship. Less obvious, but endemic in capitalist societies, is censorship by commercial pressure. Third is the ineradicable petty-bourgeois or half-timbered type, the censorship demanded by the Traditional Guardians of Morality, most of them on the right. Quite evident nowadays is also censorship called for by a small group politically on the far left. The far left has traditionally been as puritanical as the far right but has naturally not felt itself the Guardian of Traditional Morality. It is, by contrast, fond of conspiracy theories; especially those assumed to be directed towards themselves. It has found more of a voice over the last quarter-century in particular and has shown willingness to adopt an ideology of justified repression. Fifth and last is the most convoluted and so most interesting type: self-censorship.

Some colleagues and I in UNESCO once played a dour game. Of our one hundred and fifty-odd member states, how many lived up to the Declaration on Human Rights, especially as to the free flow of ideas? Ten per cent. Perhaps the rules were too tough, but the game made a point. Almost every state practises some form of censorship, along a line from the bullet to draconian laws to unspoken, backstairs squeezing-out of unwelcome opinions. Most politicians are not by nature extremely liberal-minded; their drive to manage – which easily becomes the urge to manipulate – feeds on itself. That is one price of democracy; though by no means unique to democracies, it is almost as common there as in blatant autocracies. The price is that some of our elected legislators right across from right to left are bound to be inadequately literate, culturally and intellectually. Their other interests are often, or soon become, narrow. Few have much hinterland. Professional deformation frequently sets in.

Most politicians declare themselves in favour of freedom, until its practice becomes awkward and difficult. Then they invoke national security, or outrage to accepted morals. But, all too obviously, freedom means nothing if it does not mean freedom for those who think otherwise than we do. Hard thinking is more often than not disturbing and most of us do not like to hear it, least of all politicians, once they are caught up in the sheer business and busyness of day-to-day political life.

When they are in power, politicians are transmuted into statesmen, and so are able to invoke patriotism as the grounds for their 'necessary' infringements of freedom. A very senior English legal officer, not long retired, recently attacked television enquiries into what looked like miscarriages of justice on the grounds that 'they undermine public confidence in the administration of justice'. What if they demonstrate that that administration is faulty and needs undermining? There spoke the authentic voice of the authoritarian state, but one blithely confident that it was enunciating 'reasonable' democratic sentiments. The defence of the State or of the status quo (however bad that status quo may be) soon and virtually always becomes a primary 'moral' principle, not a second-order rule.

Hence two epigrams much favoured by politicians: 'The business of government is to govern', which is code for 'our business is to stay in power by hook or by crook'; and 'You can't make an omelette without breaking eggs', which is, again, a coded justification for doing whatever seems necessary, at whatever cost to others, to stay in power. On one level it is self-evident; on another level it prompts the question: 'Even with rotten eggs?'

Of the new nations, few allow freedom of speech and we are told, with some justification, that this is because their public institutions are still very fragile. One wonders how long that fragility will last, and so feels no more uneasy with those governments which say either that individual free speech is a western liberty which is impracticable for them in any foreseeable future, given the present inadequate provision of education and the lack of a lived-in sense of practical tolerance; or is a shibboleth they simply do not share.

A fairly common reaction in this general debate asserts that since almost all states practise some form of censorship, there is really very little to choose between them. Certainly, our first duty is to resist censorship in our own countries. But to fail to distinguish between that covert censorship which might block me from getting a certain job (as in the quiet private word – 'he's not sound!' – but here that sort of poisoned chalice always leaks), or blocks me from publishing a critical piece in a certain paper (there are usually others to go to), to fail to distinguish between that and being thrown into jail or declared mentally unstable – that is a luxury we cannot afford to give ourselves. It betrays all those who work underground so as to tell the true state of things, in countries where all public speech is interested, not disinterested.

A second contemporary misjudgement: the fact that writers suffer such indignities is at least a sign that authoritarian countries take the arts, and especially literature, seriously, whereas open societies have many covert ways of neutralising any serious effects they might have. Having been called to help, through the UN, when a professor was imprisoned with hard labour for making a translation into his native tongue of *Das Kapital*; and having had a member of my own field-staff slung up by the heels for criticising the President of his host country (silly of him, since he had made the standard UN promise not to intervene with the internal political affairs of any country to which he was posted – but he could have been simply expelled. They were of course trying to discover who were his native accomplices) – having known those and other atrocities, I find no comfort in the thought that the torturers were at any rate expressing a 'serious' attitude to the importance of freedom of speech. 'This just shows how seriously we regard writing' – as that bullet goes into the back of the writer's head.

By contrast, commercial pressures, the second kind of censorship, habitually affect and afflict open, mass-persuasion societies. There so easily seem to be economic justifications for cutting this or that corner or not turning over this or that stone, especially in periods such as the present, when economic forces have come to seem more and more self-validating. In such countries this kind of interference with freedom works more by omission than commission. Best not to say that, do that, imply this; otherwise trade might suffer, our 'image' be tarnished. A journalist relative of mine, hearing a military band greet the British Foreign Secretary as his plane landed in a distant country, observed in his dispatch that a Lancashire Boys' Brigade band can play better. The Foreign Secretary sent a message down the plane saying that, since he was trying to stimulate trade, such jokes were undesirable. The message was, of course, ignored.

The Traditional Guardians of Morality, that third group of censors, also support the status quo; or, more accurately, an imagined past when people were better behaved, and did not 'mistake liberty for licence' in behaviour or language. In Britain such people are more likely to exhibit small-mindedness than incipient totalitarianism. They are the Foot-Soldiers of Suburban Morality. They are sure that they are in a majority, yet they also fear 'mob rule'. They are sex-and-language obsessed. This low-level moralistic backlash is strong in several advanced countries today. The fear of the sexual potency of words was most strikingly illustrated, as we saw in an earlier essay, in the *Lady Chatterley's Lover* trial more than a quarter of a century ago. Such people fear most that most cutting of literary tools, irony. It is inherently slippery, whereas the pattern of their reactions is straight and simple: one, I am startled, shocked, offended; two, so this must be obscene; and three, must be banned.

It is easy to see why broadcasting attracts more of the attention of these people than do books. When you decide to read a book, you make a choice and often spend some of your own money. But broadcasting, it is felt, and especially television, enters your home like a pushy salesman inserting a very fast foot between the jamb and your front door. You are not, it is unconvincingly argued, one of a self-selected audience but are indiscriminately sprayed at with hardly a by-your-leave. At the extreme, such people seem to think that everything that is available on the screen at any time must always be totally acceptable to them, to their narrow range of taste, and that no element of programming of which the approve must ever be changed; or they are not receiving what they are owed, especially since they have paid the licence fee.

Pictures, as is noted in the essay on *Lady Chatterley* here, are felt to be more powerful than words, especially towards those less well educated rather than to those who advocate and practise censorship; for others. One needs that proviso. In their effects words are probably more powerful than pictures to those who can read effectively; they reach more comprehensively into the psyche. Since many, perhaps most, people have not acquired that level of ability, it is argued, for them pictures are more effective. An unpleasant thought, but true. Hence the recent law on the censoring of videos. I agreed to serve on the Video Appeals Committee of the British Board of Film Classification, on the principle that if we leave it all to the Habitual Guardians, the new Act will have an even more regressive effect. I wonder increasingly whether I can remain on the committee in good faith. I would not choose to spend my Sunday morning in a pub watching women wrestling in mud; I do not think I wish to be my brother's keeper in such a matter; on others I might be willing to try, especially if they concerned children, but our rules go wider than that.

It is yet another paradox that those most ready to rap their brother's knuckles, for his own good, can show a more general lack of charity; they are rather nearer the rascal beadle. The most vocal of them congenitally lack a sense of fellow-feeling, are too anxious to straighten jackets. General opinion is better than that. Recent studies by the Broadcasting Research Unit have revealed that most people are more tolerant, more live-and-let-live, than the self-recruited moral majority. I suspect that would be true in most prosperous democracies. There, may be one gain at least.

As to type four, censorship from the far left, one wonders how much the impression that it has greatly increased is due to the considerable attention it receives from some of the press, tabloids or broadsheets (as compared to that given to activities on the far right). Certainly it exists. The breaking-up by left-wing students of meetings of which they do not approve, on the grounds that they both reject 'repressive tolerance' and are devoted to a higher morality than the unqualified right to freedom of speech, is the more depressing because some of us would like to be sure of better behaviour from the left than from the right in these democratic matters.

At the worst, such people, when they come to authority – in local government, say, as councillors or executives, or as trade union officials – are self-righteous and programmatic, ready to stifle unwelcome opinions out of their sense of political virtue, 'correctness'. They like to assume that literature can or should be 'correct' in the attitudes it displays, as measured by external tests of correct opinions. There is no need to list many of the numerous idiocies; two will do – a headteacher refusing to approve of a school visit to a performance of *Romeo and Juliet* because it reduces women, is 'sexist'; and a local authority objecting to the singing of 'Baa Baa Black Sheep' on the incredible grounds that it might insult black people; insensitivity can go little further. Such silly things have happened, and are not to be shaken off by the embarrassed resistance of some more sensible supporters of political correctness to the very mention of them. They always leap to object as though any criticism of the madder margins of correctness is a dismissal of the whole enterprise.

The British Publishers' Association has made some brave attempts to tackle this problem, not always with sufficient support from individual publishers. The Association's prose is often nervous, as of someone walking over hot coals in stockinged feet. They urge their members to be 'sensitive to racist or sexist implications' and to avoid giving offence needlessly or by default. Well, yes; but that is vague. It would have been stronger if accompanied by instances of foolish and therefore unacceptable takings-of-offence. George Orwell observed that some views are so batty that they have to be briskly rejected not through prejudice but out of good judgement. Of course, those rejected will then accuse you of prejudiced censorship.

To be fair, the Association's pamphlet does go on to make impeccable general statements of principle. It ends with a strong condemnation of the kind of book selection in schools or libraries which threatens the free flow of ideas. Resisting some demands of anti-racists and anti-sexists, it asserts that book choices must not be distorted by social objectives, characters must do as the story requires, bits must not be taken out of context, and partisan works have a right to be stocked. Lots of room for 'giving offence' there, thank goodness. But they also, to give one example of the confusion which can soon set in, urge writers to avoid portraying ethnic groups as having collective characteristics, for example greed or ignorance (perhaps modesty and intelligence would pass?). 'Such portrayal will be seen as racist,' they say. Indeed it will, justifiably or not. But until there is sound evidence that no such characteristics exist, we can do no harm by musing on the facts that, for example, some ethnic groups seem very musical, others imbued with the collective rather than individual spirit, and that some show more initiative than others. Then we might go on to ask whether such collective characteristics, if they are found, arise from cultural or genetic influences. The answers in all instances may prove negative; but we will have looked at these interesting questions as objectively as possible, not out of unconsidered prejudice.

The line between proselytising and telling the truth as you seen it is a fine one, but to cross it in the wrong direction marks the beginning of the end for free speech and for literature. In any event, most seasoned readers can be left to detect when the shirt-tail of the authors' prejudices are showing. As Samuel Butler said, every man's work, whether he will or not, is always a portrait of himself. Heaven help us if an author can't be a thoroughly unpleasant person with thoroughly unappetising views. They may be able to open our eyes to some truths through their art, if not in their personal lives. If those truths are sometimes witnesses to the inhumanity of man, there can be no assurance that any or all of us will be prompted by them to do otherwise; that is not the way things work. A thorough villain may read them and revel in them.

I said earlier that the fifth kind, self-censorship, is the most interesting because most convoluted and morally complex. It is much easier for us to censor someone else, or to censor the censoring of someone else by others, than to catch ourselves in the act of self-censorship. Self-censorship runs from the outward-looking to the deeply internal. There are many forms: evasive censorship (very common in the drafting of UN documents); censorship by default or omission; censorship because of the fear of costly litigation; that anticipatory censorship which is a form of being more royalist than the king; and ego-protecting censorship.

Many of those types are inspired by the wish not to annoy the authorities or the financial backers or the audience-out-there. They are hugely practised in totalitarian states but, like persistent bad drains, haunt open societies also. We may all – authors, publishers and booksellers – practise both self-censorship and commercial self-censorship; or that *mélange* which is really the second form but calls itself the first, and so sits easily; as in those books, so often rewarding to both authors and publishers, which expose the ills of capitalist society in a way which gives readers a frisson but does not pierce below the skin.

The most intriguing forms of self-censorship are the most internal. An attempt at autobiography is, in this, the most testing of all forms. Not to hurt the living, or be unfair to the dead (especially if we still feel some resentment towards them, or obligation), not to shake one's image of oneself as you suddenly and surprisingly discover a weakness. You come to hate prescriptive censorship by outsiders all the more because the 'straight' job is so difficult; sitting at that table alone trying to be honest, pushing aside all the face-saving personae which your urge to retain self-respect offers you. Direct censorship from outside can be very nasty, and also reduces your freedom to go to hell in your own way. In self-censorship that freedom, that right, that demand, are in front of you all the time.

If – since – some of these five types of censorship are to some degree present in all societies all the time, how are the open capitalist societies confronting them these days? Feebly. A reluctance to judge except in the most heinous cases so pervades these societies that the will to resist has been sapped and a glazing comes over the eyes if a commitment is called for below that level of obvious scandal; it is as though the will has become porous. Yet in some parts of the world more and more aggressive claims are made for the pre-eminence of collective cultural traditions over the rights of the individual and of freedom of opinion and speech.

See, for example, the most often quoted example, the defence of involuntary female circumcision. Or recall the long debate on freedom of reporting in UNESCO, which led one British journalist to say that if the proposed code of conduct for his profession were adopted it would no longer be safe for foreign correspondents to work in more than half the countries of the globe. By and large in that debate, the West gave the impression of being smug about the shortcomings of its own reporting in the Third World and at the same time not sufficiently strong in its support of its own cornerstone, the freedom to report as objectively as possible. As usual, these weaknesses are captured in the defensive language of the age.

It is time to reassert one of the greatest single ideas offered by humans to humanity, the idea of individual human rights. It is the foundation for our claims to freedom of speech: 'Here I stand. I can do no other'. Of British formulations, I like best John Barbour's, six centuries ago: 'A! Fredome is a noble thing/Fredome mayse man to haiff liking.' Barbour is saying that freedom is a noble thing because it allows us to make our own choices, to have our own likings, to make our own minds up (even if it leads to ghettoblasters on every square yard of every beach, and worse). The urge for freedom may often start in bloody-mindedness rather than in 'Set my people free!' But they merge. There is an inescapable moral dimension to the true practice of freedom. And so often, Milton puts his finger on it: 'No one can love freedom heartily but good men. The rest love not freedom but licence.' Set in its context, as there, that has a weight which brings us up short and sharp.

There are some signs of a reaction. Across Western Europe, for example, there is a tendency, especially among young people, to be disenchanted with nationalism, political parties, restrictive religions, in favour of causes which flow across national, political and religious boundaries; as with environmentalists, to name only one. To hear (up to 1989) convictions such as these from an East European dissident belonging to a small culture is to be made to think again about much we take for granted in the West.

Well-educated people can be the enemies of freedom, especially where power or profit are involved. Yet censorship in general feeds on illiteracy and reinforces it because it closes air holes. We owe it to others to assume that they need as much freedom as we do, and so must help them to have as much opportunity as we have of using that freedom intelligently. Much nonsense is talked about books being ousted by a purely audio-visual culture. Books will survive all that because they are an irreplaceable way of speaking to ourselves and then to others; speaking in depth, one to one, and then one to many, to large numbers of the ones. Now more than ever there is a need for literature which is not interested in the political or commercial sense, nor uninterested because simply meeting an obvious need, but disinterested in exploring the terms of our lives. Above all, literature can help recreate, inwardly, that shared sense of being human without which our world would truly be a wilderness, a chaos.

London, 1988/2000

REVIEWERS AND REVIEWING

I cannot remember what prompted me to get this piece off my chest. I do not feel greatly aggrieved about reviewing today; curious, rather, and certainly in many ways dissatisfied. Also concerned, because I think the characteristics I describe do indicate that there is too much poor work in what should be an important field. I am not tempted to go out of my way to join those book-launch haunters. In a way, I almost wish I were; to eavesdrop and come closer to the atmosphere and underlying attitudes.

But that doesn't greatly matter. That proprietors and editors should give literary editors greater freedom to think well about their jobs; that some regular reviewers should be given a better deal by their literary editors; that readers too should be given better, even if less fashionably up-to-the-minute, fare — these things should matter.

'Prolonged, indiscriminate reviewing of books involves constantly inventing reactions towards books about which one has no spontaneous feelings whatever.'

George Orwell

IT OUGHT TO go without saying but perhaps does not; so, to forestall even minor outrage, let it be said at the start that some reviewers are admirable: responsible, fair, intelligent, lively. Others can lack one or the other or more of those qualities. Depending on how the mood strikes them and what they think their editor expects, and how hard the fight for space is, English reviewers can be irresponsible, unfair and too rushed to make an intelligent examination and report on the books they review. As to the broadsheets, more and more try to be smart and trendy rather than, say, wittily responsible. All this is not new: 'Of all the cants in this canting world – though the cants of hypocrites may be the worst – the cant of criticism [reviewing] is the most tormenting' (*Tristram Shandy*).

It is easy to make a check-list of the more common faults, some of which but not all I have directly experienced. In general, and I say this with so far as I can tell complete honesty, I have very few personal grumbles.

Casualness. A busy national reviewer, hearing that a less practised colleague has spent several days reading a long book, asks with surprise: 'But you don't read any book for review all the way through, do you?' Few except the author of the book in question will recognise this practice, since shoddy workmanship can be disguised in a number of ways. The author may notice it when he finds himself accused of omitting an important element in the argument to which he has given five or six pages.

Simple showing-off. 'How clever I am, actually cleverer than the author of this book.' Acting the Young Turk until long after youth has flown and one's Turkish practices have become routine. Trying to catch the literary editor's eye – and the readers' – with one's boldness and naughtiness. For freelance reviewers especially it is essential to catch the editor's attention frequently. That need has to be balanced against the urge to rush things, to save time for attention to one's own long novel, which is developing more and more slowly. Rushed, but eye-catching; a brittle compound. Since they encourage this bad habit, Auden thought bad books the most tempting: 'One cannot review a bad book without showing off'.

It is dreary work, often, and one has sympathy; but who pays? Usually the author. Perhaps it is marginally more respectable than writing advertising copy. It is a cottage industry, generally ill-paid except for the high-flyers; literary stockinging. Orwell wrote movingly of its horrors: 'The prospect of having to read them [the latest batch of ill-assorted books] and even the smell of the paper, affects him like the smell of eating cold ground-rice pudding flavoured with castor oil. The majority of reviewers give an inadequate account of the book that is dealt with ....

That kind of thing [having a much bigger team of reviewers so that more are knowledgeable across a wider range of subjects] is very difficult to organise. In practice the editor always finds himself reverting to his team of hacks – his "regulars", as he calls them.'

The reviewer's latest opinions may, he hopes, become a quotable commodity in fashionable places where books are chattered about. Almost two centuries ago, Hazlitt noted this habit: 'The more you startle a reader, the more he will be able to startle others with a succession of smart intellectual shocks. The most admired of our Reviews is saturated with this sort of intellectual matter . . . . The intrinsic merits of an author are a question of very subordinate consideration to . . . supplying the town with a sufficient number of grave or brilliant topics for the consumption of the next three months.' The more things change . . . Except that today 'intellectual' shocks tend to have given way to the 'smart'; and the time span for the turnover is much less than three months.

The ill-informed. It is assumed that a regular reviewer will accept virtually any book offered, no matter how little he may know of the subject. Refusing may make the editor less likely to telephone next month; and at a pinch a lively *ad hominem* piece can be produced. The person who sends the book back with regrets for his own ignorance is an oddity. The one who goes further and recommends 'X' for the particular job, one whose name does not spring immediately to the editor's lips but who is very knowledgeable, writes well and delivers work on time – such a passer-on of other names is an innocent. Almost always, then, the editor again reverts to those regulars. Time is pressing on, some risks are too great, old so-and-so can be relied on to turn out a serviceable piece; and our readers know him or her.

Selective distortion. This device can serve well the reviewer whose grasp of the subject of a book is shaky; it can also be used where the reviewer is knowledgeable but does not wish to engage in an argument he finds is undermining his own warmer convictions. He picks out a single and not necessarily large element in an argument, one that may be weaker than most other parts, a relatively weak link in what may be a strong chain. The reviewer makes a considerable fuss about this weaker point while almost ignoring the longer and stronger parts.

He thus creates the 'washover' or 'hammering' effect; an out-of-proportion attention to one small and less successful part implicitly suggests he has made a cogent criticism of the book as a whole. Selective nit-picking is thus elevated into pseudo-comprehensive criticism. The reviewer seems to have shown that he knows more on the subject than the writer and has comprehensibly damaged his argument; which he has not.

Plagiarism, parasitism and plain thieving. This has many forms, some internal to a review, others external and with a longer life. The internal type adopts the form of repeating, apparently in the reviewer's own words, the arguments of the book but without acknowledgement that these are the author's words not the reviewer's; it is appropriation, unacknowledged – jackdaw's work. Readers of the review, among the majority who do not often go on to read most of the books reviewed (most reviews are self-sufficient entities, closed forms), will be impressed by the reviewer's knowledge, insight, fluency; they do not know that what is written is a form of professional plagiarism. The book's argument is neither honestly presented nor intelligently taken further.

A similar practice occurs in some face-to-face interviews, where any *bon mot* of the interviewee can be included without attribution and so by implication may be assumed to be that of the interviewer.

External plagiarism is harder to pin down and, to be charitable, may be unconscious even to the plagiarist; something has lodged in the memory but without its label. Someone writes an early book on a new author who goes on to gain considerable repute. In it, elements of that writer's work, his linguistic and intellectual manners, are for the first time examined and given identifying marks, verbal tags.

Rather in the way stolen goods rise to the surface in different places for years afterwards, elements such as these begin to appear in yet other reviewers' judgements on the by now well-known writer. In the early years, though not always even then, the original identifier of some characteristics in the writer's work will be named. As the years pass, attributions fall away, especially among critics who have not read the original study; they pick up the points at one remove, and either decide not to brother to acknowledge their source at this distance or do not know the source. At this point such discoveries have lost their identity, have come to seem an anonymous part of the common store of knowledge: 'As we all know, X is a subtle practitioner of that obscure . . .'. This may be a small, but only a small, consolation to the purloined person, who will cast a wry glance at the better habits of astronomers in their naming of new stars, no matter how small.

Free copy. This is a variant of the practice with particular items described above, a more general form of theft; what may be called the 'it is, of course, a feature of the present age' type. A book appears which tries to analyse and name elements of change in British life – social, political, cultural – and which identifies those changes rather effectively. At least five such books appeared in a single year recently. Within only a few months, almost all acknowledgements of the original authors' namings for such changes are dropped. They become features of the present age, features that 'we all recognise'. Or, even more, the general invocation, the slightly lubricating 'we all recognise', is foregone. The identifying phrase has simply entered, unheralded, the bloodstream of the reviewing and even the critical language. Some survive long, justly. Carlyle's 'cash nexus' entered the relevant debate not long after it first appeared; it is still current but, understandably as time has passed, not always with its source specified or known. By now that hardly matters. It is linked, at a much lower level, with 'the chairs on the *Titanic*'. Who invented that? Imitation being one kind of flattery, he may be mildly pleased, or wish he could now bury the boring image.

Ageism. This picking-up and rolling-along, this adopting of second-hand opinions, extends particularly to judgements on writers whose work has been generally noticed and admired for many years. Then a change of course appears. Favourite characteristics having been noted, it now begins to be said that this writer is 'stereotyping', 'repeating himself', to be too fond of this or that linguistic trope, to be tired, to be now writing clumsily. This is especially brought into play if there has been a fairly large gap since the elderly author's last publication.

Authors may have all those faults, but there is sometimes little consonance between the naming of those qualities and proof of a chronological line of decline. Generally, it is not difficult to find quotations which might seem to bear out a preordained minor thesis. But I enjoyed once hearing a speaker follow through a line of five or six quotations from my own books, which proved, he said, that I had progressively undergone some rather large intellectual change over the years. The difficulty was that to make his point he had used five or six quotations in entirely jumbled chronological order; so they proved nothing.

The same negligence may cause an author to be routinely praised for years, until it is time for him or her to be 'given a going over'. The inspiration for destruction may come from a reviewer who has sniffed the air and decided that so-and-so's time has come and that this will give him the opportunity to display how effective a demolisher he can be.

Or the decision may come from the editorial desk. One journalist came to interview me in Paris and wrote a favourable piece. The editor asked for it to be redone – 'We wanted a put-down'; the writer refused.

'There is one gratification an old author can afford a certain class of critics: that, namely, of comparing him as he is with what he was. It is a pleasure to mediocrity to have its superiors brought within range' (*Over the Teacups*, Oliver Wendell Holmes).

This is the derogatory use of 'ageism'. Like Lear, an author may then feel he needs to apologise for being a very foolish, fond old man. He should not. If he thought it worth the time, he could, as a test, publish a small but well-regarded piece from thirty years back, undated. If one or two reviewers neither recognised nor liked it, it would probably be described by at least one of them as 'old man's writing'.

Passed on to others, in the form of what appear to be literary judgements, are reviewers' uneasinesses, irritations, anger. Descriptions which don't suit the reviewer's political positions are made into literary weaknesses; descriptions of satisfactions in family life must be called 'uxorious' by those who, for whatever reasons, find them always hard to take. The personality of the author may simply be found unattractive, or there may be half-conscious class or status snobbery.

Lazily received opinion. We can all be confident in calling on received opinion. *Lady Chatterley's Lover* has many weaknesses, especially those common to prescriptive novels. I argued earlier that it also contains some of Lawrence's best writing. Nowadays, it is a matter of form to dismiss the book as almost worthless and, in the predictable word used by people most of whom, it is plain, have not read more than a few pages of the book, or not for a very long time, it is 'boring'. Back-stroking of conventional taste.

Politically correct convictions. These are relatively few in reputable journals and sometimes they are silly. Some politically correct critics, when they turn to Lawrence in particular, find it hard to see him straight. In a broadcast discussion one attacked him violently because, in a tender love scene, he had written 'then he penetrated her' – 'a clear case of male aggression'. The temptation to invent acceptable alternatives was fairly strong.

Fashionableness above all. Many of these activities are products of the overarching communications revolution. It can make space for almost anyone and any opinion, especially those which do no more than echo what are assumed to be 'the tastes of Joe Bloggs' [today's media substitute for the man on the Clapham omnibus]. The short list of nominees in many of the annual British book prizes illustrates, at higher than the Joe Bloggs level, a narrowness and provinciality. The recent *justifications* for not choosing Vikram Seth's imaginative, witty, perceptive *A Suitable Boy* for one of the annual main prizes seem to illustrate this.

Abuse by telephone. A further sub-branch of parasitism is to be found among weekly columnists with intellectual interests and duties. They decide to write about a social or similar movement which is just gaining circulation. They have not the time to read all about it, this being Thursday or even Friday afternoon. They telephone a number of people who are said to be expert on the subject and, with some flattery, proceed to pick their brains. In the background can just be heard the hum of a recorder. The thanks at the end are effusive but do little to take away the 'expert's' feeling that he has foolishly allowed himself to be used again, for the third time that month. His chagrin is increased when, though admittedly with a touch of anticipatory, proprietorial pride, he opens the relevant newspaper only to find that his best thoughts have been reduced to a mangled state or, if presented accurately, have not been attributed and so seem to have emerged from the apparently formidably well-stocked mind of the 'intellectual journalist'. Plagiarism as telephonic brain-picking.

Over-egging the pudding. The reverse of the destructive review is one which, whether inspired by friendly log-rolling or because the reviewer has been genuinely impressed, makes excessive claims. This is particularly common in this tidy tiny island, the home of the literary Happy Family. Just as there is little so stale as yesterday's newspapers, so there is little so ludicrous as overfavourable reviews quoted in succession on the rear of a paperback published a year or two after the hardback edition.

Still, few reviewers would care to begin: 'This is the latest in a long line of novels by non-novelists I have read this year, and as unimpressive as almost all the rest.' The hatchet would have to be sharper than that if the readers are to be sufficiently titillated. That kind of review would rightly raise the question: 'Why bother even mentioning it, then?' Excessive praise and excessive denigration have the same hidden aim: to appear to justify the decision to choose to review this book rather than that, out of the hundreds which appear each week.

Obliquely, this raises another point: the attitudes of some current literary editors. Most used to have weight, substantial literary and historical knowledge and judgement. The reader was aware of a well-nourished and intelligent process of selection in the decisions as to what to review. Some of that type do still exist. Among journals, the outstanding example today is the *London Review of Books*; but, much as one enjoys it, it stays, as it has the right to do, within its own highly intellectual niche, does not reach for 'the common reader'. In this, it does not do as well as the *New York Review of Books* (many of whose writers are British!).

Nowadays, too many literary editors have their eyes on the bestseller lists, are caught up in the books-as-commodities roundabout, the latest ephemeral fashions and book-cocktail-party celebrities. Of course, they are under considerable pressure to go in those directions. They are the servants of sales or of eye-catching fashion, not of judgement.

A friend adds one of his own considerable dislikes: the printing of the reviewer's name larger than that of the author. Presumably another instance of the ingrown personality cult, but a pity for the diminished authors.

You can scan the books pages and be led to ask: 'Why on earth did they think that lightweight thing – those lightweight things – worth space; especially novels by footloose young women or blacks or outed homosexuals or demoralised members of pop groups? They will be forgotten within a year at the most, whereas this other book – weightier, more thoroughly considered – will be ignored as "too heavy", not the kind of thing which will amuse "our readers". How do they know?' But occasionally there is a sort of corrective coming up from behind: in a book almost totally ignored by even the broadsheets' book pages but, by word of mouth, becoming its own kind of success, with its own kind of audience; perhaps not a truly bestseller audience but certainly solid and worthwhile, of genuinely good book-readers.

An odd phenomenon. This is the 'Don't mix categories' rule, especially as it is applied by academics. Most academics uphold it and do their best to discourage infringements. If one stays within one's own discipline, promotion will follow. There is more than professional caution here; there can be deep unease at a straddling of two worlds. It can be interesting and

illuminating to move across, say, social-scientific analysis and autobiographical reflection. One who does this will worry both some social
scientists and some autobiographical writers. They have to be politely
ignored. Train-hopping, at the right junctions, needs no justification;
there are more gateways to the truth than one. We do not have a claim
precedence for our own first discipline over another; we have to remain
open to, willing to accept the value of, moving between the two, difficult
though that can be.

The uses of repetition. The tendency to pick up and pass on inadequately
considered limiting opinions is endemic to reviewing; especially since it
may seem to indicate the reviewer's independence of mind. Such opinions soon become part of the available critical baggage, apparently
unassailable.

I am occasionally accused of repeating myself in some important
particulars and that, it is assumed, is manifestly a weakness. It is not;
circumstances alter cases. If you have come upon what seems to you a key
idea about, say, the way society has been moving for several decades, you
would be at fault if you decided not to return to that idea, simply for the
sake of change and from the fear of being charged with repeating yourself. That is not the same sort of habit as the repetition of smart tropes,
linguistic or intellectual.

You know in advance that many people will resist the uncomfortable
argument, it being too much against the thrust of their profitable or
personal-professional interests; so they will do their best to shrug it off.
Instead, they bring the charge of repetition, which we all know is inexcusable in the world which must market successive novelties of style and
substance. Best, it is felt, to be among those who pray 'not, please, to
resemble the beasts who repeat themselves'.

'Humankind cannot bear too much reality.' So I for one will go on
talking, though in various forms, about the rise and spread of relativism
and its miserable N.C.O., populism, throughout the whole texture of a
would-be democratic but actually near-naked-capitalist society, which
strengthens itself by anaesthetising independent judgement.

I believe, rightly or wrongly (and am not the first to say so), that that
is a very important idea and one that should be repeated again and again;
until more begin to face, not evade, it and its implications.

As I said at the start but had best repeat: there still are reviewers who
try hard to read a whole book with care, who look at it straight before

beginning to write. They do not parade their personalities, write for effect or put demands from the editor, or even the carelessly assumed tastes of the readers, before justice to the author. They will exist, but their world has become bleaker and their numbers fewer.

Farnham, 1997/2000

Postscript

As I was finishing the revision of this essay, I saw my own name among the book pages in the latest issue of a weekly intellectual journal. That page contained a good example of *stereotyping by false comparisons*. The book being praised (rightly – I too admire it and have praised it myself in several places) was an account of a harsh childhood in South London. The reviewer went on to say that those working-class people 'refused to conform to the cosy stereotypes of Richard Hoggart's *The Uses of Literacy*. Odd, that, since the description of my own childhood in that book was of a place constantly riven by fierce quarrels. Not, perhaps, as dramatic as the South London home, but sad enough.

I went on to say that more typical homes in Hunslet could be happy places: warm, yes, and cosy, as Orwell discovered with surprise. They were therefore more 'typical' than mine or the South London home. But 'stereotypes'? No. 'Stereotyping' is what a sloppy *author* commits when failing to see the difference between that and the 'typical'.

PART FOUR

LEVELS OF EDUCATION

POLITICS, ANTI-POLITICS AND THE UNPOLITICAL: THE UNIVERSITIES IN THE SECOND HALF OF THE TWENTIETH CENTURY

Obviously, I wondered whether to include here this fifteen-year-old essay. So much as happened to the universities since then that some people would claim that they and their purposes are now almost unrecognisable.

My main justification is that, whatever the number and scope of the changes, the main purposes of universities remain the same, but are not being sufficiently acknowledged nowadays, by government and by many within the universities. And so they need restating.

The financial squeezes on universities are greater than ever. The need to look for funds outside state provision has greatly increased. Under the Universities Grants Committee about 90 per cent of funds came from that body; under the Higher Education Funding Council (with a greatly increased number of institutions to be resourced), the proportions are more likely to be 50 per cent HEFC and 50 per cent outside funds, which have to be found, against competition.

Salaries are relatively lower than they were; tenure has gone; scales for profes-sors no longer apply. Money is allocated under several heads, of which research performance is especially important; universities are breaking out and offering up to £75,000 a year and a chair to someone who looks likely to boost their research record.

The payment of fees by students themselves is likely, it is felt, to make them more demanding, out for what they see as value for money. That sounds democratic, but are all or many students good judges, while they are going through it, of what constitute the true tests of value in a high-level and difficult course? They may be able to judge who is a good teacher, or what might lead them to a well-paid job, but those are only two parts of the complex assessment of quality.

Extra-mural departments have lost their protected funds from the Department of Education and Employment; they are now totally competing in a colder climate. The head of Ofsted, the body which supervises the performance of schools, announces that he does not see the point of extra-mural departments. Here, as in some other places, he does not know enough of that whereof he speaks, and is punching above his weight. [Mr Woodhead resigned as head of Ofsted in 2000.]

Some departments at some universities – philosophy, for example, and physics – have been closed as unproductive, surplus to need on a national level. That may be fair and reasonable viewed nationally, but can be a loss to the idea of a university as precisely 'universal', and self-governing. The senate at each university has to agree to each closure; self-governing, under some duress.

No wonder most universities now have sizeable departments of public relations. Some of them need better supervision from the top; they sound as if they are promoting a new model of car.

At least the millennial year brought a discussion of the continuing social bias in admissions to universities. It was a most ill-conducted argument, but may improve; at least it has started.

Battered in all these ways, the universities have so far shown hardly any disposition to discuss their wider and deeper aims in the way I have argued. If the pressure eases, perhaps they will come round to that.

Meanwhile, they are, at their best and in spite of everything visited on them, some of the finest in the developed world: in the advancement of learning, in devoted teaching and in returning true value for money.

T HE CORPORATE LIVES of universities, like those of all large and complex human institutions, move in great phases. Individual universities shift and turn, chiefly according to the pressures put on them by particular personalities and groups – a powerful vice-chancellor or president, a dominant and coherent group of disciplines, an ambitious head of department. Universities as a body in any one country also respond, rather more slowly, to the pressures put on them by particular departments; or, less directly and even more slowly, by their societies, the flow of change in their surrounding cultures. To such public forces, working at exceptional pressure, universities over most of the world have been responding, in sometimes different and sometimes similar ways, and with more or less success, since the early sixties.

So this is an apt time for stocktaking. Of outside forces bearing on the universities across this period – 'outside' in the sense of not being primarily concerned with the advancement of learning and the training of the next generation to carry on that work – of such forces, two have been paramount: the huge, publicly funded expansions in higher education which began in the early sixties in almost every developed and some underdeveloped countries; and, from the mid-sixties, the widespread and sometimes violent student demands for change in both the universities' relations to their societies and in their own internal governments. Today, both activities have all but expired. The expansive building, whether of departments or physical structures, is largely done. Most of the developed world is now spotted with new university or university-type campuses, often disconcertingly similar to one another. 'If today is Wednesday, this must be Murdoch, West Australia.' And the revolutionary fire has almost gone out; most campuses are fairly quiet.

Why did governments over much of the world discover at the same time, like natural creatures responding to a change in the ambient temperature, that higher education was such a good thing and greatly to be encouraged? For one reason, the ambient temperature was indeed favourable; all this was before the recession and when we had begun to feel that we had really climbed out of the stringencies of war and the immediate post-war years. 'You've never had it so good,' Prime Minister Macmillan had informed the British in 1957.

In addition: it was believed, felt, assumed that more higher education must lead to more economic growth at home and hence greater competitiveness abroad. Some of us believed, also, that more higher education could lead to a more civilised society. Both beliefs may be over the very long term correct; neither is simple nor yet proved. The first might presumably be measured with difficulty. It would call for more public directing of their work than British universities have been used to (though they have begun to accept more 'guidance' than ever before). The second is by its nature much more difficult than to accept than the first, being a matter of subjective values on which there would probably be little agreement, even among the trained minds at universities. Although it could be argued that at bottom all subjects taught at

147

universities involve assumptions about values, not all academics would agree on which values their disciplines assume or whether the question does have any meaning for them. Even in the humanities, especially literature, study of them as they explore human experience in depth may not necessarily mean that we absorb the lessons of those explorations into our daily conduct. Experience is not that simple. To many, that belief seems more like a will-o'-the-wisp, 'out of this world'.

So, we almost all expanded; we admitted many more students. In the United Kingdom most of us did so while at the best still managing to retain fairly small group teaching and to advance knowledge at a good international level. We may not do well in applying that knowledge to the production of internationally saleable goods, but we have picked up a good share of Nobel prizes for our primary contributions to knowledge.

In the UK, however, we did not, especially in the first decade and a half, greatly notice that though we had many more students, the social base from which they were drawn had widened only a little. It was a slow process, through socio-economic groups A and B down to parts of C, but hardly to many of D and even fewer of E. A slow drip down the social pyramid, inevitably starting where people were already partially disposed to look up to university entrance for their children. The British universities' response to invitations to expand tended to be ready, willing, well disposed – and narrowly focused socially. At the outer limits, though some will deny this, expansion was bought second-hand and at one remove; by arranging for some local colleges of education to have their courses validated for degrees, sometimes at implicit and unacknowledged lower levels than those of the university itself.

Nor was expansion sufficiently often taken as an opportunity to think again about the nature of subject boundaries. More commonly, some departments, especially those in which expansion did not require long lead times for the provision of large new physical resources, expanded by simple accretion on the usual lines, not by fresh thinking about the nature of those lines. Staff numbers grew but, except in some of the new universities of the second half of the sixties (notably Sussex), members of staff were not often prompted to think afresh about the traditional forms and connections of their disciplines. Rather, they preferred to cut the existing subject-cakes into thinner and thinner slices. A proposal for an entirely new finals paper would meet opposition; existing papers were left as they were, though staff attention to them might change. A new young assistant lecturer, asked to give lectures on Shakespeare to the first year, used to agree. In 1969 I heard one such member of staff, asked to lecture on seventeenth-century literature to new students, resist with: 'I end at 1580.' Specialisation is essential in a scholar; but this is unnecessary restrictiveness. At such moments I remember Charles Frankel, the distinguished professor of philosophy at Columbia; he always used to take some first-year classes, as good for him and he hoped for the students.

All in all, though, much in the British response to expansion was sensible, and many university staff of all ages and types worked well beyond the formal bounds of duty to accommodate it. In their own terms this was an effective response; but much in the guiding principles was too restricted.

The second major pressure for change at universities at this period, that from student agitations, had the two main branches already mentioned. It was demanded, first, that universities become more and more aware of and active (usually in the assumed right ways, of course) about their relations with society, and specifically with the 'military/industrial complex' and their own servicing of that complex. It demanded a far greater place for students in the universities' self-government than most universities had so far conceived or at the start felt likely to concede.

The first demand has had almost no result in most European countries except perhaps to shift some contracts to the safe, unbothered research centres run by the industries themselves. The second demand did affect some, chiefly mainland European, universities. But hardly for the good in most instances. Some idiotic procedures were set up for the election of rectors, and often resulted in the appointment of people who were certainly 'radical' but couldn't have run a fish-and-chip shop competently, or were judged to be safe and malleable but usually proved to be unable to judge firmly between the pressures of competing demands.

In many instances the student 'demand' for representation on all internal committees was met, often very generously. 'Participation with appeasement' it was called by some disenchanted academics. For some time now, many such committees find their student members are often absent. University committees tend to be long-winded, boring, harassed by the minutiae of restricted internal housekeeping. Many student members seem sooner or later to have reasonably concluded that they have better things to do, such as working for their degrees. Or a few regard the offer of membership of any such committee as a device to deflect them from their true political work, which is still seen as essentially 'contestatory', to be based on imperious strikes and sit-ins.

Full-time student officers, of whom the UK now has a substantial number, used to be tuning themselves for parliamentary candidatures of the left or right, or training as potential lawyers or, more recently, PR executives. Few have those horizons nowadays, except perhaps some at Oxbridge, where the unions are different kinds of bodies from those elsewhere. In these other places the unions' 'Executive Committees' now tend to be composed of members of the more extreme left-wing movements or the loopier fringe ideologies. Some seem to have decided, again as a political judgement, not to stand for full-time office themselves but to organise the election of a student president who will be a figurehead, being charismatic and concerned – and a soft touch. Then they clamp on the president, in the name of democracy, a control so rigid as not to be dissimilar from that of a totalitarian and ideologically doctrinaire nation state. As a result some student politics have become the activities of a fringe of a fringe, and most students ignore them. Presidents and their aides are elected on minute voting turn-outs. They represent student opinion less than their predecessors of 1968 did. Nevertheless, many vice-chancellors, being courteous or cunning people or both, give them the respect accorded to major trade union leaders elected by a majority popular vote. But if a sit-in seems like interfering with the work of the place, even the nicest vice-chancellor takes out an injunction and the corridors are sooner or later cleared.

Looking back over the last fifteen to twenty years, most European observers conclude that the upheavals of 1968 and after were not worthwhile; and it is hard to disagree. The evidence in the formidable compilation by Daalder and Shils, *Universities, Politicians and Bureaucrats*, almost all runs in this direction. The Italian universities, we are told, are severely damaged, and German universities now unofficially divided into two kinds: the steady and the politically raddled. 'The French universities,' Pierre Salmon of the University of Dijon says, 'acquired autonomy under unpropitious circumstances, and nothing has helped them to become fit for it.' I remember hearing Edgar Faure, as he looked out of his study window on to the Bois de Boulogne early in 1969, growing lyrical about the reforms he had fathered. Premature, Salmon again says:

'The final result of the whole undertaking was highly questionable' and 'the reform of 1968 [the *loi d'orintation*] is a pseudo-reform'.

In British universities in the fifties and sixties we used to grumble about the excessive power, conservatism and protectionism of the senate, which in those days meant, overwhelmingly, the professoriate. But that solid block looked porous by comparison with the power of the professors in most European countries; and, often, its even greater rigidity. Another memory surfaces from the work of the four-man OECD Commission of Enquiry into French education which ad interviewed M. Faure. We asked a senior professor what useful lessons, if any, might have been learned from the student uprisings. He rejected the question with rage, raised his voice very high and shrilled that his only interest was to protect '*mes cours, mes cours*'. He was a classical, old guard and diehard. But Daalder and Shils did not find experiments from the opposing side encouraging: 'Experiments with university "democracy" do not seem to have made European universities more adaptive than they were under exclusive professorial rule.'

Except in two or three universities (and some colleges of art), we did not have in the United Kingdom the larger upheavals of the European mainland and North America. I do not assume that this was because we are wiser than our cousins elsewhere. We are more phlegmatic, that is certain, and have a remarkable capacity to absorb, to roll with the blows, to ignore. Nor do we go in for Great Debates on Great Issues, or sit easily with abstractions. When the pressure for change becomes strong we usually adjust – a little. Committees are opened to students; some approaches are modified; we exercise those kinds of detailed, ad hoc, partial alterations. Or, against all precursors, a big change is made, such as the invention of the binary system for higher education. The new polytechnics, originally funded through their local education authorities rather than through that safe-and-sound and in many ways academically very well-informed buffer, the Universities Grants Committee, were set up to provide chiefly industry-related technological education, with much part-time and 'sandwich' work.

Exemplifying that educational near-law I described earlier, the polytechnics were soon but quietly regarded as a second division. Some responded by ignoring the differences from the ways of universities which they had been set up to promote, and settled into 'academic drift', gradually moving nearer the universities' styles. Some had departments equal to those in the universities, some had departments in subjects not known in the universities; some were academically excellent, others more dubious. Many soon had an admirable record in welcoming students who were older and from more diverse backgrounds than had been common before, and gave them a good education.

It is an irony of a characteristically British kind that that misguided scheme was put into effect by an Oxbridge-educated economist and Labour minister of education who declared, against all social and cultural sense, that the polytechnics in comparison with the universities would be 'different but equal'.

(The wand-waving of a Conservative Government in 1992, which at a stroke transformed the polytechnics into universities, was a cynical act of politicking. To create a university fully rounded in range and level takes decades. To do it so suddenly was to reinforce many in the established universities in their belief in their own superiority. Even those of us who are supporters of the former polytechnics believed there could have been a better, a more measured and gradual way. Meanwhile the new-new-universities are working hard to establish and validate their new status. Obviously some are making mistakes; others are gaining strength as each year passes.)

A much happier example of the surprising English response to change was to be found in the Open University. It was inspired by a Labour Government but was finally, after a near miss, founded by the Conservatives.

By now, in the mid-eighties, universities throughout the world are living in a colder climate. Most are no longer growing and some are even contracting. Unlike many of their European counterparts, British academics are not civil servants and so lack certain protections. They have what may be no less valuable: tenure – a job for life, the right not to be sacked except for 'gross moral turpitude'. Tenure tends to be achieved after probationary period of a few years but that is almost everywhere almost routine. Tenure is now under severe questioning from the Conservative Government. It is being defended on the very highest principles: as the only safeguard of academic freedom, of our right to follow knowledge without fear wherever it may lead; not from fear of being thrown into jail (though from the tone of some of the objections one would think that loomed constantly) but of losing our jobs. There is some odour of job-protecting humbug in these assertions. Academic freedom can be protected in other ways than by easy and early tenure. For that matter, too, some people who fiercely defend tenure in the cause of freedom cooperate willingly and without question with whatever the prevailing government and its orthodoxy call for in defining their research programmes.

In fighting against the threat of enforced redundancy for the first time in their history (there were, though, some forced redundancies among very small and financially unprotected university colleges during the last war), British academics have shown themselves as protectionist and self-regarding as members of the toughest trade unions. In fact, the reductions so far put through are small when compared with the wholesale redundancies being declared month after month throughout British industry, and academics' terms of severance are usually comfortable.

Governmental interest in tenure is only one instance of steadily increasing governmental intervention in the affairs of the universities. It began before the recent inflation and recession. It began in the sixties when the great injections of public money started. No government is likely to make such huge subventions without wanting more of a say than has been traditional in Britain as to how it is all going to be spent. When the slump did come and governments turned towards retrenchment, reducing public spending, then their scrutiny of and intervention in university affairs greatly increased. To judge from Daalder and Shils, that intervention is not as direct or as powerful in its effects in the United Kingdom as it is in the United States. Here, the existence of the Universities Grants Committee, its members drawn from major aspects of public life as well as from the universities themselves, still acts as an educated influence on all aspects of university financing and much else.

Another British–Continental Europe distinction: though, as has been noted, many European academics are civil servants, some of their governments have, when it suited them, legislated over the heads of those civil servants they had appointed to university posts. Ours did not do that, but nevertheless the screws tightened and the University Grants Committee began to seem like an executive arm of government required to manage the cuts, less a buffer body between the universities and government. The process continues because this Government practises a Conservatism of a new kind.

The old Conservatism was of the squirearchy, the City, Oxbridge, a very few distinctive clubs, Ascot, weekends in country houses, and the upper-class professions such as the law. The new Conservatism belongs to the home-owning outer suburbs, to suburbia or even exurbia, split-level or Queen Anne style; it reads the *Daily Telegraph*. It is drawn less from the major traditional professions than from the newer 'servicing' or communications professions or 'industries', such as advertising or public relations. It belongs less to traditional clubland than to the fashionable expense-account restaurants; it is practised in legerdemain with all the main credit cards. Its members are not very attractive, for all the manly smell of Brut.

It is thrusting, pragmatic, shrewd but not intellectual, cost-conscious, but not very imaginative. It dislikes quangos and other buffer bodies (I am talking here of old-style quangos, which typically addressed complex public issues and whose members were unpaid volunteers). Its view of public education at all levels is predominantly vocational, at the best technology and business-centred (though not of public-school education, whose advantages are more than merely vocational in the non-profes-sional sense; which is why they aim to send their children to those places. They correctly assume different qualities and gains, distinct social-network and professional advantages subsequently, for their children from the public schools). The new Conservatism suspects the social sciences, which it sees as uniquely 'ideological' and congenitally left wing. Its favourite horror novel in confirmation of that view is Malcolm Bradbury's *The History Man*. So it does not feel particularly tender towards the universities, except for Oxbridge and perhaps a couple of others, and cannot easily be persuaded to think more warmly of them over an odd lunch at the Athenaeum. Its members tend not to belong to the Athenaeum, let alone the Reform. They are more likely if they join a club at all to be members of the Royal Automobile Club, just down Pall Mall from the other two. That has extensive executive recreational facil-ities, such as a swimming pool. That old but immensely respected and desirable Conservative sanctuary, the Carlton, is for most still something to be aspired towards.

Yet, the thrust of the new Conservatism apart, one can say, not to mince words, that in some ways the universities were 'asking for it'. They had stood on their autonomy as though it was a fact of nature, not a historic convention which could always be challenged by a less than sympathetic government, especially if that government were under finan-cial pressure. They had been responsive to the call to expand but, as we have seen, did so almost entirely on their own existing terms. They had brushed aside suggestions that they might rethink. Shirley Williams, one of the most friendly of recent Secretaries of State for Education, had in the last Labour Government put before them a list of thirteen points about their role now that expansion was over. She is very good-natured but did not at all like the brush-off she met.

By the British community at large the universities are neither greatly loved nor greatly hated. Our universities have a different attitude towards education beyond the walls from that common in North America. American universities tend to offer a great range of subjects, many of them plainly utilitarian; they see themselves as a sort of bazaar open to all those outside.

British extra-mural departments have been both more formally academic, offering the subjects taught within the walls, and seeking to be 'enlightening'; they were in principle not utilitarian; they did not work for any sort of certificate. They offered the study of philosophy, literature, history 'for their own sake', for their capacity to make us understand better our lives, the lives around us and our society; 'to improve myself' was one commonly given reason for joining classes and still is. This simple and noble statement of principle is not understood by many people in the universities and in public life. So some take refuge in dismissive laughter about 'earnestness'.

Internal subject departments tend to ignore the extra-mural and slightly to look down on them. Yet the great virtue of the extra-mural departments has been their wholehearted commitment to liberal education; the kind of work which had R. H. Tawney as one of its revered progenitors.

That 'Great Tradition' is now and increasingly much weakened as more and more directors of extra-mural departments see their safeguard and salvation in 'in-service', 'refresher' and vocational courses of all types, training and retraining rather than liberal education, and liberal education becomes in some places light entertainment; one isn't expected to study hard except for a clearly functional end. For their liberal work the external departments receive 75 per cent of teaching costs from the Department of Education and Science, the rest from the universities' UGC funds. If that protection goes, and it is under threat, if the extra-mural departments have to compete for all their funds with the powerful internal departments, they will be at great risk.

Yet there is in society at large still enough general and generalised respect for learning, for titles such as 'Professor' and 'Dr', for 'letters after your name' to ensure that university people are accorded some reflex respect; it is nevertheless a respect for something felt to be remote – for 'them', for people higher up, not for 'us'. Change is slow but is coming. The daughter of the barber near here won a place at Leeds University; he told me that with pride but not as something quite exceptional.

The provision made for university staff and students is noticeably greater than that for staff and students in other branches of higher education. Their residential provision, for instance, is lusher. I am recurrently surprised by the grandness of many vice-chancellors' offices and residencies. What style they are accorded and accord and accept for themselves! And for their students: one vice-chancellor advised that curtains for students' rooms in university residences be of the very best. He mentioned prices which we could not have afforded for our own homes. There were two justifications: that good stuff lasted longer (true); and that to be acquainted with the best rather than the shoddy would be a good lesson for later life. True again, though that argument did not extend to colleges of education financed by local education authorities. And how much the argument seems today to have come from another world, another climate.

The new universities of the sixties tended to be established in two hundred acres of parkland, a few miles outside Baedeker cities – York, Canterbury, Norwich. These towns in themselves, most of them staid in their styles, found these influxes of several thousand youngsters with their hair down lucrative, fascinating and often unappetising. I once took a taxi from a town railway station to the new university just outside. It has well-equipped residencies, refectories, common rooms, bars and the like. When I gave the address the taxi-driver, a bloody-minded original, uttered in a tone which mixed puritanism with prurience, 'Ah, you want the state-supported brothel down the road.'

So far I have been taking a rapid, largely chronological look over changes in British and to a small extent European universities during the last quarter century. Inevitably, this has been chiefly about responses to pressures, pressures from within – student troubles – and pressures from without – governmental pressures – to expand, especially in certain directions, and now to cut back. Reactions, tactical reactions; these have been the movements.

Now: a more strategic view, a look over the larger, more continuing purposes of universities. Where should we go? It will be as well first to remind ourselves, the academic staff, of our remarkable good fortune. We are paid reasonably well [not so fifteen years later] – not as much as a successful accountant but well enough to live in fair comfort – and paid to do things we positively enjoy doing, such as talking about books. Paid to write about books, too, and to introduce the next generation to what we think are some of the most important and interesting aspects of the world; given long vacations to pursue those interests ourselves, with few routine or repetitive tasks and total freedom to follow issues wherever they may lead. I never cease being surprised that society is willing to pay me to live like this. And I try not to forget that these freedoms are to an important degree a by-product of our country's wealth and political system.

Some of us abuse these privileges and sit on our hands; some are self-indulgent. Here, I think especially of those who thoroughly and easily condemn their society for its capitalistic corruptions while living to the full the comfortable bourgeois lifestyle it offers them. Recently I saw a French professor of sociology at one of their older universities in action at a seminar. He was a wow with students; very 'radical' indeed. He wore a turtle-necked sweater, Levi's, scuffed 'trainers', hair to his waist held by a Red Indian-style bow – relics of '68, in which, I was told, he had played a prominent part. He was getting on for fifty years old and had put on plumpness since the heady days. I recalled then, with respect, meeting T. S. Eliot at seventy, still looking like a sober bank official, as he preferred to look.

The best university teachers work hard, each conscientiously or with enthusiasm, carry on writing and doing their research. Their attention to teaching and to other concerns of their students is an implicit criticism of those who will never, say, take freshman classes because their research calls, or advise and counsel individual students if asked, because their overriding interest is in '*mes cours, mes cours*' or 'my research, my research'.

We are all paid by the taxpayer, so what is so special about us, especially those in 'non-productive' disciplines, that the taxpayer should keep us thus comfortably pursuing our own interests? Practicalities apart, what really is the role, the justification, of a university especially at a time when there are few accepted frames for appraisal; a time when you certainly could not persuade a majority, in or outside the universities, to agree if you proposed that they should at least help their members to grasp certain basic human principles for guidance in the world outside. In some parts of the world universities are expected to subscribe to and support an ethical system externally decided for them. But not in the open, capitalist West. In the West, in general, the universities stick to their disciplines and let the consensus-forming tendencies of society outside do their work subcutaneously and largely unchallenged.

Today, many, especially politicians, are likely to claim first that the role of a university is to sustain and develop the economy, to keep us in the forefront of world technology, to help eradicate disease and so on. Some years later I was in a group which called on the then junior minister responsible, to urge that the Adult Literacy Unit be given more support. There was going to be some difficulty, we were told, in persuading 'the hard men' of the Treasury (these grey, faceless men are generally trotted out on such occasions) to release more money to help those who had not managed to become literate at school. They were not, we were told, likely to be greatly affected by high-minded arguments that a society as rich and sophisticated as ours should be ashamed to have almost two million functionally illiterate citizens. Nevertheless, the minister found our arguments persuasive. How to persuade the Treasury and the Cabinet? Couldn't we make the enterprise seem vocational? A retitled literacy programme was born: ALBSU – the Adult Literacy and Basic Skills Unit.

To some extent it is true that a university should be in part vocational; it is not the whole truth. A university should do more and be more than that. It is as well to remember, though, that for many people of different levels of wealth, power and education, the above aims are central and sufficient. The State has no call to pay for more than that to be attempted, they would insist. There is no irrefutable rebuttal to their position.

Let us remind ourselves of two types of institution which a university is not, and should not be. A university is not a higher technological institute or an institute of higher education or a further education college. All these may be very good places and often are; they can fulfil their roles well. But they do not fulfil 'the idea of a university', nor are they meant to do so. They are predominantly instructing institutions; to them, the advancement of knowledge at the frontiers is incidental, if it happens at all.

Nor is a university an advanced research institution only, though it should be that. There are many such solely focused, public and private, institutions in all parts of the world. They advance knowledge, certainly, if they are any good. But they are hermetic, often one-track and usually in their central being little aware of the larger society, its directions and the relations of their own work to it. The cuts year after year recently have had the effect of making some vice-chancellors sound more like executive managers of besieged research institutions than university statesmen. When money is tight, batten down the hatches and preserve what is – agreed – our irreducibly most important function, the advancement of knowledge; and finding the money with which to pursue it. At such times, the people chosen to head universities tend not to have at the front of their minds a larger, less objectively defensible view of the nature of a university. In warmer times, no doubt, they would have learned the language of Newman.

For a university should be before all else, and I borrow a favourite remark from Edward Boyle, one-time Secretary of State for Education and then, until his early death, vice-chancellor of the University of Leeds: 'A university should be a place in which teaching is conducted in the atmosphere of research.' He would not have objected if the sentence had been turned on its head. It has a rock-like simplicity such as is possessed by the definition of public service broadcasting laid down when radio began in Britain: 'It must inform, educate and entertain.' Either of those can be elaborated on, but as they stand they indicate the tap roots.

A good university *feels* different, organically different, from other institutions, some of which might seem superficially like it. Skins are thin here, so let me repeat: these other institutions are not 'worse', but have other purposes. In a university you sense around you people at the frontiers, perhaps abrasive and impatient of secondary considerations, pressing on – and, the best of them, carrying young people with them. Urging them to take nothing at second hand, not to be timid or face-saving, or self-aggrandising, introducing them to the revelation that few gratifications are as great as the feeling that you have at last reached at least an outer edge of your subject and from now on will be helping to mark out the territory. Such an institution should contain in its staff and students a high proportion of the best minds of their generation. These are, again, simple assertions but, especially at times such as these, bear repeating.

A university has three constituencies and three roles. Scarcely any thoughtful observer would doubt the validity of the first two constituencies or the first two roles. Many would question the third of each. The constituencies are: international ('the international community of scholars'); the national (helping the economy, making life better for us all, forming a national community of scholars, teachers and examiners); and the local (serving part-time adult students from as large a radius as is needed, to the point at which they meet other universities' territories). The three roles are: the advancement of knowledge through scholarship and research; the training of a new generation to take on that work (which is more than the passing-on of knowledge; that is an earlier part of the process and an essential preamble to the more difficult part); and, third, providing a centre which looks critically at the doings of the society and the culture. This is the role which student activists put first. The constituencies and the roles need not conflict with or between each other.

It would be agreeable to be able to say, about role one, that there should be no sensible dispute as to its value; that knowledge has to be kept up, and that includes 'useless' knowledge. Yet for many people, especially among our own new Conservatives, that is not a self-evident truth. To put the issue graphically: in the dispute between the office-block developers and the archaeologists about how long work should be delayed on a site which contains two thousand years of evidence of British history (say, the Billingsgate frontage to the River Thames), the natural inclination of the new Conservatives is towards the developers.

Certainly we have in the United Kingdom followed the pursuit of knowledge very well in many areas so that, as I have already suggested, our work in these places is internationally admired. Yet, and though as so often in these matters one cannot prove the imperative, all kinds of knowledge, many of them not cashable, have to be maintained, or we will have cut ourselves off from one of our dimensions, elements, from some of our past and from our understanding of our present. Nor are such high-minded, would-be functional, justifications finally the most important. A society which is not interested in its own past *for its own sake* – in its history, its arts, its artefacts – is a shallow society. Perhaps not a 'society' at all and certainly not a civilised society, but a collection of 'thriving earthworms'. We have come to a poor pass when a senior and no doubt 'civilised' civil servant can say: 'What earthly good can it do for us to spend money so that some chap can enjoy himself discovering the eating habits of the Celts'; or, 'I really don't see why we need to pay someone to tell us about what they like to call the "significance" of pop songs. Except to the advertisers, I suppose.' True instances, both of those. And here is Norman Tebbit, a cabinet minister: 'We've taken the money from the people who write about ancient Egyptian scripts and the pre-nuptial habits of the Upper Volta valley.' 'Oh God, oh Montreal!'

So, knowledge and teaching inextricably intertwined – teaching irri-gated by the sense that the teacher is at one forward boundary or another, bringing back the news, examining and questioning it with the students. Teaching not thus fed may be useful and effective in its own way and its level may be high. But it will be different in kind from that necessary to a university. There is on substitute for front-line people training emerging scholars of the same bent and brilliance, even though not all university students become scholars or research workers. But that activity permeates and defines the style, the professional moral tone of a university.

Among the six constituencies and roles, the universities in Britain do well in three and two halves. The best are international and national in their constituencies; they advance knowledge and train the next genera-tion of bright people to follow in their steps. But they are not sufficiently attentive to the part-time needs of their local areas; constituency number three is inadequately served. The scope of their training of the next generation is limited; they take those kinds of students the present system offers and do not ask enough questions about those who could have benefited from a university training but who, because of social constraints, have been filtered out of the system before university entry looked possible for them. Our universities gain only half a point under that second role heading. Finally, they score a virtual nought under role three, that of providing a critical centre on their society's doings and their culture's changes.

To the six subdivisions above, I am claiming, all universities in open societies should pay attention. Naturally, the emphases will vary from society to society and university to university. There is an intriguing set of differences here, illustrated by universities in the former colonies of France and Britain. Even today one sees in them the stamp of their orig-inating countries. The indigenous professoriates tend to look still to their *alma maters*, the Sorbonne or LSE or Oxbridge, rather than to the country next door, which may have French rather than English roots, or vice-versa, and therefore have a quite different style. The professors at the Francophone universities tend to remind you in their approach and personal manner of professors in France; those in Anglophone places give much the same English impression. A black woman doctor and minister of health in a former colony said, after some conversation about medical training in different places: 'I'm an Edinburgh man myself.'

So it is generally with the emphasis given to either face-to-face undergraduate teaching and personal research. There are obviously gains and losses on each side. Oddly enough, some Francophone African professors have, or had when last I visited them about ten years ago, less direct contact with other Francophone African scholars than they had under the French. The French had a central West African university, fully integrated into the national system, to serve their dependencies in that region. Those native Africans who became officials and politicians in different new states after independence were likely to know one another from common study at Dakar and then Paris. That is less likely nowadays, though on a conducted tour of West African universities from capital to capital one becomes used to seeing a succession of old university friends greeting each other warmly at each national airport. But the official lines still run more effectively from each Francophone university to Paris or from the Anglophone universities to London and Oxbridge, rather than across to other parts of Francophone or Anglophone West Africa. That will change at great speed as information technology develops; but the old colonial-cultural hold will continue to have some influence for a long time. Universities in the native English-speaking parts of the Commonwealth used to glance over their shoulders at Oxbridge or London. Other winds have been blowing for some time. If they seek models for some parts of their work, they are now tending to look much more selectively – to Harvard, MIT, Yale, CalTech, Columbia; and it is a long time since, say, a university such as McGill looked over its shoulder in that way; the reverse is just as likely to happen.

That was a short excursion up a loop line. It is time to come back to the main line and to look further into this business of constituencies and roles. If British universities have been less than successful in their attention to their local communities, if they have been less attentive than they might have been to the social composition of the students which the slow sifting processes of British society have handed them, if they have been less sensitive than they could have been to their own and their institutions' relations with society – so that they have let society use them for virtually, according to its own limited vision, what it will – if these constituencies and roles have been not altogether adequately served and fulfilled, what have been the universities' actual sociocultural roles and functions?

They have certainly had a function, functions, exercised absent-mindedly perhaps, but none the less powerfully. They have been enmeshed in the thrust of their society, whether they would or no. They have been sleepwalking into social change. In the last twenty-five years our universities have been busily and largely unquestioningly providing society with the new meritocrats or 'service class' it needs. This new class – or, better, 'status quo' – is less and less related to the old social classes as defined chiefly by origin of birth, type of educational opportunities and access to the major professions. Financially, the new group is at the comfortable upper end of society but tends not to define itself in traditional class terms. Its membership is steadily fed from below and still increasing. Most new professions pay less attention to birth than to brilliance. Some of the major old professions are still hard to enter if your face – that is, your background – does not fit. The new professions, especially those in modern communications and the expanded universities themselves, pay little attention to all that. You are a first-class mathematician or a clever maker of television programmes and you are accepted into that apparently 'classless' world; and will be well rewarded. This is another aspect of a theme which runs through many of these essays.

While, only half-consciously, feeding their members into this group, the universities have paid little attention not only to what they are doing socially in thus servicing a new stream in society but to the larger, knock-on effect of the yeasting process we are experiencing – to what is happening down below, to the other 85 to 90 per cent of society. But it can be firmly argued that the cost of selecting and hoisting the service group to their high level, well provided for in both its shared and its individual-specialist tastes, has been, through the immensely forceful and bland processes of commercial competition, to create a more solid mass of those outside and below. It is a mass less physically and visibly marked than the old social and sub-classes but more solidly held together by the tastes its member are so insistently urged to cultivate: the 'leisure industry's' offerings, the junk food, the packaged holidays in the packaged resorts, the overhyped TV shows, the indoor games that offer good profits and keep us near a bar or an arcade. For the minority there is that 'higher' level or at least more expensive and so more exclusive provision. But cultural change, unless it directly bears on their disciplines, interests a great many university teachers hardly at all.

Of this process the crown is Oxbridge. They have magnificent settings, still better than those of any of the new universities, some of which tried to make themselves into instant, visual, near simulacra of Oxbridge. Oxbridge facilities can give unparalleled opportunities for intellectual work out of the hurly-burly. They have some of the finest academic staff to be found anywhere in the world. Their libraries and laboratories are magnificent and industrialists still pour money into them for yet better laboratories, libraries and student residencies. You have made a fortune from selling groceries to working people; you send your son to Oxbridge (not necessarily because he is a budding scholar but because at that level of wealth one does that; it would be almost against nature and certainly against your cultural mores to do otherwise) and, having dined with the master, you offer a few million pounds for a new this or that. You refuse half a million to a very large college in an under-provided district from which your superstores make very large profits.

Some Oxbridge members are trying to improve a system still inexcusable on both academic and social grounds. The only possible grounds on which the present set-up could be excused would have to be drawn from Eliot's *Notes Towards the Definition of Culture*, from that part of his argument which suggests that a meritocratically stratified society would be so awful, so jealousy-ridden, back-biting, resentful, that we would do better to accept privilege-with-responsibilities. In that event, the Oxbridge colleges which are trying to reduce privilege should stop at once; and should try to negotiate an Eliotian contract against the thrust of a society in which 'the responsibilities of birth' seem increasingly old-fashioned and largely irrelevant.

To sum up: there are two main roles in which Britain universities perform inadequately. First, they do not do enough to relate their recruitment to the composition of society or to differences in opportunity. Leaving aside the claims of justice and fairness, they can be criticised for too easily assuming that the present selection processes somehow and magically override substantial built-in differences in opportunity and ensure that they receive the very best potential students and scholars in each generation at about the age of eighteen; and they almost ignore the need of adults of various ages who missed the boat earlier.

Second, even more marked and more of a pity: the universities do not sufficiently consider their relations to society in other than functional senses. This was the sound critical impulse behind much student protest, no matter how rebarbatively it was often expressed. It has been part of my argument throughout that we do not actually need universities so as to have good medical or engineering or pure science schools. They can function in research institutes, even in relatively monocellular institutes, though those might not encourage cross-breeding. These and other faculties do need to be inside universities if they are to ask, to be prompted to ask, questions about the existing social order, about how it proposes to use their skills, about the social situations which give some people, for example, adequate medical services and others not, about how to decide on the balance between cheaply available medical provision and vastly expensive and complex provision for extremely specialist work. Those in medicine and similar technological fields will be the obedient servants or victims of the existing social order, as they are in some countries, unless they decide not to be. Some scientists do not wish to ask such questions, are happy to accept the social order just as it is, whether that of the USA or Britain or the Soviet Union. So are some scholars in the humanities, though one feels that they especially are sinning against the light. Some refer to nineteenth-century debates and conveniently claim to be followers of Huxley's definition of a university rather than those of Arnold or Newman (or, after all, of Dr Leavis of Cambridge). Actually, Huxley had a wider view of a university's purposes than many people today realise. Certainly, his idea of a university has been less battered than that of some of us who make larger claims and wish to see the university as passing on a disposition to humane criticism, a respect for the intellectual and imaginative heritage. It is difficult but necessary to argue for standards in these things at any time, but particularly when many people leave universities, or stay and become members of staff, both cheerfully saying that there can be no criteria for such decisions.

An instances of the power of the creative imagination, some things are not comparable with some others. The latest pop song is not on a par with, is immeasurably less creative than, an aria of Mozart, and the latest and most numerically successful television soap opera is not except in the slightest way comparable to Shakespeare. The refusal to discriminate has often in the universities gone so far by now that, and I say this with feeling since I was one of those who twenty years ago helped to introduce contemporary cultural studies to British universities, if you lecture at some universities and suggest that one novel is better than another you will be asked why you are so elitist, so undemocratic.

This is not an arcane discussion. It matters fundamentally to the claim that universities should help provide a centre from which, in Arnoldian phraseology, a stream of critical thought can be brought to bear on societies. If graduates feel that everything is relative, they have no intellectual tools, no basis or foundation, with which to move disinterestedly within their culture. An engineer building bridges has irrefutable external judgements available, the effects of the law of gravity for one; indifferentism as to the claims of different building methods could lead to disaster. The humanist scholar has no such handy tests. It is easy to avoid making choices because you cannot objectively prove any of them. That way, you slide into assuming that all choices are of equal worth, that numbers alone can decide, that what most people like must be a test of quality. The only test.

It is a sign of the quality-fogginess of most open capitalist societies, and of the fogginess of their universities' practice of their roles within those societies, that many graduates do not feel that their education requires them to stand for or even to consider such distinctions in the marketplace, even on basic, honestly intellectual, if not on moral or religious, grounds. Without some such connections, university education will be little more than high-grade technological training.

Faced with the widespread failure by universities to accept this role, it is inevitable that a very few university teachers among those whose subjects do not have a manifestly useful role in society, or who do not need large laboratories or vast scholarly libraries, that such teachers may sometimes be led to think that it would be as well to become wandering scholars again, to use hedge-publishers and be content to reach only that small minority who explicitly and consciously want to question the drives of their society; as some writers in the Soviet Union bravely did. Faced with the fact that in totalitarian societies it is assumed that universities get on with adding to the sum of knowledge within the already given ideological framework, that the bosses need no help from university people in defining the frame, and that it is certainly not felt to be part of a university's role to question the ideology – faced with all this it becomes for some people a matter for *samizdat*, or the scientific underground, or nothing.

In spite of the shortcomings of our societies, that is not our situation, and we overdramatise if we claim otherwise. One reason why people in British universities should not go into the hedges and ditches and cut themselves off from tangling with governments, but should stand their ground, is that to some extent they can still engage with the movements of their society, that politicians do sometimes listen to them, that their books are occasionally read in centres of power, that they can take part in national committees and drafting bodies whose utterances are not always or wholly ignored. Not all their activities are permitted-but-ignored deviations. They can help to some extent to redefine discussions about any problems within their culture. If they insist that they do not want to do any of that but wish only to continue with their researches and their teaching, they must be free to do that. It is a pity if almost all of them give no thought to a wider role.

Working for five years for the United Nations, I saw many universities across the world and came above all to mistrust the generals who were presidents or prime ministers or ministers of information or directors-general of higher education. Across Eastern Europe, in Africa and Asia and Latin America one saw how truth was made tongue-tied by authority. So that those who, whatever the pressures on them, refused to do as the majority of their colleagues did and still believed that universities had a role beyond those likely to be defined for them by any general, such people knew every day often from cruel experience about the political significance of universities and the pursuit of knowledge. I spoke earlier about our great luck in being university people in the free West. Our greatest good fortune is just here: that we have freedom of enquiry and the consequent freedom to publish the results of that enquiry, even if they prove awkward to our funders and other authorities. Good work can go on in other places which are not so free, but only if it does not threaten the prevailing social philosophy. This is a crucial distinction and it is wilful not to recognise it. Things are not all rosy in the West; there are pressures, more hidden than those of the dictators and not so overtly brutal, but still powerful. The overriding distinction is that on the one side we are ordered to follow a particular line, whereas in the West we are more likely to be our own near-executioners. No one forces us to accept a lucrative technical contract without asking questions about the uses to which our findings will be put. No one forces us to be a well-paid consultant to a PR or advertising firm. No one forces us to write a trivial little piece for a fashionable magazine of opinion, or to shape our new play so as to attract the attention of the more powerful producers. If the word still has any meaning for most intellectuals and academics, these are the treacheries of the clerks in the West. They are different in kind from those critical engagements with the centres of power and influence in our society – usually unpaid, sometimes very demanding, ill-regarded – to which I pay tribute elsewhere in these pages when I argue that they should be engaged in by more university people.

We are not much called to dramatic confrontations with authority. To think that is our condition is to be as self-indulgent as our colleagues who continue with their studies with scarcely a thought about the world immediately outside. Our society looks well after us physically, gives us even now reasonably secure occupations, hardly ever directly attacks or makes demands on us. Its procedures, its prevailing atmosphere, tend rather to sap us, to suggest that even to university people no one thing is better than any other, or to suggest that the drive of the great, corporate, technological, mass-communications society is wholly self-justifying and that to think otherwise is an intellectual's overheated deviation, that technological advance is all important, that 'the life of the mind' is an out-of-date, old-fashioned phrase.

In the circumstances it is surprising that so many undergraduates still choose the humanities rather than the less ambiguous sciences, inspired by that increasingly odd-seeming idea that their pursuit – the greater understanding of these disciplines and their relationships outside themselves – somehow has meaning, is about more than reaching for a comfortable job, or for one which is fascinating entirely in and for itself. The pity is that we do so little to respond to that innocent but yet as-old-as-time enquiry, in ways that can be justified to many of us or to the idea of the university itself.

University of Victoria, British Columbia, 1984/2000

GAMEKEEPERS OR POACHERS:
A MATTER OF APPROACH

I come near here, but not quite, to apologising for the appearance of Miss Jubb. Obviously, she has been and is for me what today would be called an iconic figure. My grandmother, in spite of some reserve and a little deference, came to rely on her and even to like her.

I owe her a great debt; if she had not intervened with the board, when the question of my staying on at school after sixteen appeared, my subsequent life might have been very different.

For all I know, she might have been a Conservative voter, and morally very strait-laced; no matter – she had her guiding lights and in her professional life they were upright, honourable and in the end very flexible.

For that great range of people I call intermediaries (though 'lubricating joints' might have been more accurate and colourful, if a bit crude), in those professions which have so much expanded in recent decades, I think a training seminar on Miss Jubb's principles might be useful; even if in the end, and quite politely, the group decided that she would have had a much harder fight today than she had in the thirties, and as they certainly have.

IN ONE PLACE or another, I keep recalling Miss Jubb. She seems, though very much in a walk-on part, to have stood for much in my early life. And now she has appeared in a new slightly theatrical role, as a figure in a set of professional and cultural comparisons.

To recall briefly. For ten years or so Miss Jubb visited us regularly.

She was a Leeds Board of Guardians official and one of her duties was to ensure that children in the guardian's care were being properly looked after. I was an orphan, cared for by my paternal grandmother who received seven shillings and sixpence a week (37¹/₂p) for my board and lodging; it was Miss Jubb's duty to see that that seven and sixpence was properly spent.

She radiated controlled concern and the voice of proper, firm but kind authority. She asked direct questions such as 'What are you giving the "boy" for breakfast just now?' 'Has he had a cold this autumn?' 'How is he faring at school?'

A few weeks ago I looked in at a one-day conference at which trained social workers were teaching volunteers how to advise those in need on just what it is possible to claim from social security. It was a well-prepared meeting and in some ways very professional. But there was something odd to my uniformed ear in the tone of the whole operation. It took some time to identify what it was.

It was then that I remembered yet again Miss Jubb and came nearer grasping what was teasing me. Miss Jubb consciously and conscientiously represented the-powers-that-be, the public interest in an orphan, the 'proper' expenditure of public money, a code of morality assumed to be right and unassailable. She was doing her part in ensuring that that code and those responsibilities were lived up to, by both sides; by my grandma and by those above Miss Jubb herself whom, as well as fulfilling her statutory professional duties towards them, she reminded of the realities of their brief on the ground (and in one instance persuaded them to pay more for me each week so that I could stay on at grammar school).

What I was hearing from the social workers all those years later was a reverse of that attitude; these speakers were largely *identifying* with the clients, the customers, the 'cases', as against the public authorities, the providers of funds.

What follows are no more than notes on a theme which needs much fuller treatment. It is not a subject which can be captured in a phrase about 'the failure of the right' – or of the left. It affects people of all political persuasions and all parts of intellectual and artistic life. It is, at its starkest, about the relations between actions, attitudes and values in professions that use public funds for various purposes which are assumed to be socially valuable.

Over the years I have been involved with four such areas: broadcasting, arts policy, education and, to a much lesser extent, social work.
There are of course great differences between them. In one, the state is
through its intermediaries objectively and practically helping those in
need; in another, the intermediaries of broadcasting are trying to cater for
public taste as widely as possible and also, because of their public service
brief, seeking to widen that taste. That is not an objective all would share,
and value-laden, not objective. Intermediaries in the arts – what the
French call *animateurs* – are doing something similar to the broadcasters.
Teachers are in a double role: they have to fulfil the objective wishes of
society as to some of the main and inescapable purposes of education –
to meet society's needs for trained citizens – but are also inescapably
caught up with questions of value in their guidance of pupils.

All have clusters of characteristics in common. First, their professionals are agents, intermediaries and mediators. The broadcasters; the
artistic 'animateurs' or entrepreneurs or administrators; the teachers and
tutors; the case workers – all come between the listeners, the viewers,
the audiences, the public, the pupils, the students, the clients or 'cases',
on the one hand and society, authority, the establishments, the public
consensus, the society's image of itself, its frame of assumptions, on the
other.

Second, and as a consequence of this middle position, all the workers
in these professions are inevadably and directly involved with appraisals,
with questions about the relations of society and its assumed aims
towards individuals and their rights and aspirations. They are concerned
with questions about what their society really means, what its approved
organisations and acts stand for. What is good broadcasting, artistic
development, education, community care? What aims do they serve?
What is broadcasting's relation to the social consensus or to 'the average
person'? Why should the arts be spread, made available, more widely?
And, if they should be, which arts? What should be our fundamental
educational aims, beyond the passing on of simple technical skills? What
are the rights and responsibilities of open societies to those who fall by
the wayside? To what norms are 'aberrant' people to be urged to come
closer? How right-thinking is society in all these areas, anyway? The
intermediary has to find steady compasses within all this.

All such professions raise for those who work in them basic questions
of this kind: is our job to reinforce or to challenge the existing generally

agreed picture of society, the 'hegemony'? Should we help people to conform or to resist? Or to understand more – which might reinforce conformity or raise resistance. Everyone in these professions has to choose between being a gamekeeper or a poacher; or painfully to mark out another path. It is generally assumed that all will be primarily game-keepers; or why is society employing them? In reality, some break away and probably more do so than in the days of Miss Jubb.

For broadcasters, the situation usually finds its focus in the tired but resistant argument (one wonders how long it will continue to trot round the ring in its usually hackneyed forms) about whether one's duty is to give people 'what they ought to have' or 'to give them what they want'. As I note elsewhere in this book, the Pilkington Report of 1962 tried to nail that false antithesis. Those who claim to give the public what they already know they want usually mean what it is most profitable to them and the advertisers to offer. No one I know seeks to give the public what they ought to have in a doctrinaire or paternalistic sense; they may want to let people have the opportunity to see what other, so far unknown, things it is possible to have; to help widen and deepen choices because some choices are better than others and because we should all have the opportunity to recognise this fact. This definition, teased clear by Pilkington all those years ago, is still not much advanced in Britain. Too many, commercial broadcasters especially but also misguided others who have no urge to profit by leading people to close their ears, are still impaled on that artificial dichotomy. It seems to them that to urge people on in that way is undemocratic, mistakenly paternalistic and so imper-missible; they forswear that part of the public service idea in broadcasting; but most stay within the system.

A similar uncertainty affects funding for the arts. In any discussion about whether public money should be provided for the arts today one comes, sooner rather than later and from the intermediaries themselves, upon the claim that the existing 'high arts' are irremediably and irre-versibly bourgeois, that no effort can detach them from this social background and make them available to 'the body of the population', that they have nothing to say to 'ordinary people' and that therefore nobody should be encouraged to make that effort. Let the high arts be paid for in full by their self-selected audiences, or wither on the boughs. This is the left-hand view; the right hand claims that only an elite is capable of appreciating those arts anyway, an elite not only of the highly educated but also of the highly intelligent; to seek a wider appreciation is, not to put too fine a point on it, casting pearls before swine.

A related argument puts considerable stress on 'community' or 'grass-roots' or 'participant' arts on the grounds that, though they may not have the sophistication, technical expertise, intellectual and imaginative penetration of the high arts at their best, they have broken or bypassed the great forbidding wall of those traditional arts; that from this breakthrough a whole range of new arts might emerge; and that the people least equipped to judge the worth of those new forms are those used only to the traditional arts (such as, it is widely but mistakenly assumed, are members and staff of the Arts Council). Indeed, it is argued, such people cannot even know inwardly the experiences that are being communicated.

In response to this, a false dichotomy or contrast, one is forced to ask some extremely simple questions. Are the 'high arts' really to be explained, and explained away, almost wholly by their historical and class backgrounds? Are good political, ideological or social intentions necessarily enough in this area of the mind? Do we automatically come into touch with 'the people', let alone produce anything imaginatively worthwhile, by ideologically willing it? If you are paid to promote the understanding of the arts at the highest level over the centuries, are you in bad faith if you continue to hold your job while denying those very historical and artistic premises; by rewriting your own brief?

The fullest debate in this whole area has been about education, and its special focus has been on 'cultural deprivation'. About two decades ago the analysts of cultural deprivation claimed that many children from poor homes were culturally and linguistically deprived, and hence argued that various kinds of compensation were necessary for them. Some agreed; others reacted against.

The more politically minded among the objectors saw the argument for cultural deprivation as a sort of political trick. In their view, it blamed on deprived homes ills whose roots lay in the system; it foisted on the parents the inadequacies of teachers; and it refused to recognise that the 'system' merely sought to train children in society's public competencies only so far as to make them the slaves of the current Industrial Revolution, much as their ancestors were trained a century and more ago.

Others, more sociolinguistically interested, claimed that the cultural-deprivation view, insofar as it concerned itself with linguistic ability, often mistook competence in middle-class forms of speech for general linguistic competence; that working-class culture was much richer than had been recognised and certainly at least as rich as lower-middle-class culture; and working-class speech more subtly expressive than middle-class speech. The work of Labov in the USA reinforced this view.

There is force in all this; but again the questions recur. In what ways is working-class culture rich? In ways adequate for coping with the increasing public complexities of modern life? One can't seriously postulate a new kind of noble savage; such a one would be even more the victim of corrupt capitalist practices. Are teachers really willing, because they have rejected the social distortions of education, to let their pupils remain less equipped for coping publicly than even the certainly inadequate system sets as its target? One headteacher in East London answered 'yes'; until the Inner London Education Authority cried that enough was enough. The pupils were leaving school dangerously non-literate.

About social work I have had, as I said earlier, less experience than in the other areas above. About twenty years ago, when I was a member of the Albemarle Committee on the Youth Services, I remember being surprised by the degree to which in many places those services had up to then a Church of England, Boy Scouts, air and saw themselves as a form of compliant social conditioning (up to a certain level). The Albemarle Report asked, rather boldly it seemed then, for a better-considered set of assumptions, argued that moral influence was best exercised indirectly, by disinterested actions, not by particular forms of words. I gave a talk on the report in Oxford to a group of Church of England laymen and women. A life peer present telephoned the lady who had chaired the Committee to tell her that 'that man Hoggart is not sound'. Not a solid enough gamekeeper.

The area of social work is even more difficult than the others I have mentioned, for one important reason: its professionals are usually dealing with people already in distress. Their responsibility is all the heavier. The tone of poachers' conspiracy at that recent conference contrasted oddly with the concerned, rather grave tone of, say, Titmuss or Townsend. There is also recent evidence that a few social workers, because they are in reaction from 'bourgeois morality', are willing to allow, for instance, confused girls in care to take risks which could land them in even deeper straits; almost by definition they need guidance towards greater sophistication in relationships than they possess, and that inescapably involves questions of morality, not simply of prudence.

There is very often great goodwill behind decisions such as those. One relevant department at Goldsmiths' College agonised for a very long time before deciding that an unsatisfactory student should be dismissed from his course. He objected. The rules required us to set up a board to examine his complaint. It sat for almost a week with a lawyer in attendance, at great expense. It seemed to be getting nowhere; the man had good references from the places to which he had been sent for outside practice. Finally his tutors painfully revealed what should have been revealed before even a Board had been set up: he had written his own favourable reports. In their concern to see the point of view of the outsider, they had failed to fulfil their duty to society itself. What if that man had been allowed to pass and so to become a qualified professional? Perhaps his tutors would have gone on to argue that he might have learned a proper competence and probity in time. He might have done, or he might not; if the hope had not been borne out, what would have been the cost to those with whom he was deputed to work.

The same kind of goodwill appeared when a man with a criminal record, including bank robbery, applied to enter a course – on youth work, I think it was. The police had earlier arrested him on the charge of robbing yet another bank. He objected on the grounds that the arrest had been made because of his criminal record, not on any evidence. Few are as outraged as a villain for once falsely accused. The Home Secretary upheld his appeal. The man was offered a place on the Goldsmiths' course in the hope, I imagine, that his application showed a determination to begin an honest life. I thought it was on the part of the tutors more a gesture of well-intentioned hope than judicious; we needed more time and evidence. The problem was solved; the man never enrolled. He robbed a bank in North London before he could start the course. I imagine that his tutors might have argued that in spite of his new fall, his intentions at the time of application had been sincere ... And who knows what reform might have got underway if he had survived the course.

I do not doubt the devotion of most people in these professions. I am saying that dramatically simplified attitudes, near-identifications, are in some people causing too great a swing. I am not saying: 'Come back, Miss Jubb, all is forgiven'; not asking for such professionals to become simply the watchdogs of society, the gamekeepers of the consensus. I am saying that to move in one step from gamekeeping to poaching, to become a conspirator rather than a copper, is wrong-headed.

I recognise the virtue of the kinds of questioning which lie behind what I am calling poacher attitudes. They make it less easy for us simply to accept the cultural frames of reference we have been given; they remind us that, if we are professionals in an area where discriminations cannot but be involved, we have to take stock for ourselves. I know about the powerful thrust of any society to structure the world in the ways most convenient to it. I do not believe that that thrust always succeeds in 'open' societies. We still have a more than marginally free press, and a more than marginal freedom of speech. Broadcasting is not wholly to be defined as a mirror of established attitudes. Education, if we push it, can break clearer of the pressures of the system. Nor are all the aims of such a society discreditable. In furthering the arts, society is not seeking simply to provide soporifics or to make honest workers into well-behaved culture vultures; it to some extent believes in the fundamental value of the arts for free individuals. And it should recognise that some arts really are superior – imaginatively, intellectually, artistically – to some others.

In short, we should not oversimplify issues, nor while recognising the faults, the distortions, of society, fail to acknowledge its good sides; they exist and have a right to be counted; they can be among the pointers to a better state of affairs. In all these mediatory professional activities – broadcasting, the arts, education and social work – we should realise that some people do need direct help, that most may be capable of more than we always give them credit for, that in spite of social pressures to maintain the status quo, the system is not watertight and that those in such professions have the overwhelming duty to act so that the people they come into contact with professionally can better stand on their own feet, make more choices for themselves, become more publicly competent, have a better idea of the meaning of the good – that is, the worthwhile – life, break through the wrong constraints of the system and take better advantage of its opportunities. All this is part of the historic role of western intellectuals and responsible citizens. What we are hearing to the contrary today, from some people on both the left and right, indicates an uneasiness about living up to that role which strikes very deep.

Goldsmiths' College, 1978/2000

BETWEEN TWO WORLDS:
PUBLIC AND PRIVATE DISCOURSES

A friend suggests that I underestimate the amount of public work undertaken by academics. That may be so, or may be truer of scientists whose possible contribution is comparatively easily seen. The contributions of other disciplines are less sharply definable, especially to governments interested most in practical, vocational outcomes.

The biggest single group among members of a short-term government-established committee on which I served fairly recently worked in advertising or public relations; its subject was the promotion of good reading, and the talk mostly about targets, soundbites and impacts. That illustrates well the short-sighted shift. As does the fondness for 'focus groups'; which home in on one aspect of a problem so as to hand specific practical advice to the politicians, especially on how to present it to the public. There's neither room nor time for disinterested in-depth examinations there. Nor, it seems, inclination.

THE ACADEMIC WHO chooses from time to time to go into the marketplace or the corridors of power is sometimes regarded as an ambiguous figure; mildly suspect, though at times given grudging admiration from peers who do not leave the groves of academe; some others look on one who does as, at best, a misguided Arctic wanderer.

I recently let academic life and found myself taking stock. I realised then, more sharply than I had done before, that for almost thirty years I had been one of those shuttlers between two worlds. Not between

Arnold's wanderer's spiritual 'two worlds, one dead, the other powerless to be born', but between a rather closed and a more open world; each of them more full of the light of common day than of the spiritual. I began to think about what such movements may mean for those who engage in them, what they tell us about university institutions and what about public life, in Britain.

Why should anyone choose, be persuaded, to go outside the comfortable academic into the public life? There is no compulsion and no one should be thought wanting for refusing to do so. The heart and centre of university life, whatever else the university may do, is at all times the pursuit of pure knowledge and, through teaching, the passing-on of the ways in which that pursuit is furthered. Application also, yes; 'the relief of man's estate'. But above all the pursuit and transmission of knowledge. Whatever else is done, if knowledge is not furthered then the scientist and the humanistic scholar have not lived up to their titles.

To us, the word 'gratuitous' today may mean 'wanton', 'uncalled for' in a pejorative sense. Onions defines it as meaning 'freely given, spontaneous'. That academic enquiry should be in this latter sense gratuitous is just as true of students in some of those modern disciplines – for example, the social sciences – which seem to demand applications outside. Members of our present government are likely to brush aside as useless any study of which the social application is not immediately seen; by them, presumably. In the long run, though not immediately to be observed, such work may prove to have direct social utility. Yet that is not the point. We want to know not because there might be an eventual use; we want to know because we want to know; first and above all.

Even if, as we may with one part of our minds hope, there are practical and valuable spin-offs from pure research, it is usually best neither to go for those things directly nor to hurry them along. A scientist friend at Cambridge likes to list major technological gains which have been made, often later and by other people, as a result of advances in pure knowledge single-mindedly pursued by people who would not easily have accepted a contract or a consultancy from outside, with a fixed price tag, a fixed useful objective or a fixed time limit. That same friend also likes to laugh at the tendency of some governments to wish to hurry things up, sometimes against nature. 'Cancer research is moving too slowly. So let's put in ten times the amount of money we now put into it, point the work straight at the eradication of cancer and ask for results ten times faster.'

An American president is said to have hoped to effect exactly that. Naturally the scientists would be glad to have much more money; it can help things along. But most difficult things also demand their own time to mature and can't be hurried. My friend goes on to say that we still know little about the web of activities we call simply 'cancer'; to complain about the inherent slowness of some research in that or other areas is like complaining that nine months is too long to make a human baby, and proposing that nine women be paid well to work together to produce one in a month. There is one instance where scholarship can put useful brakes on the urgencies of politics.

So, no *requirement* to go outside the walls. Yet some academics do engage directly with public life and most are, I think, justified in doing so. In Britain, though this is an untested impression, the opportunity to take on public work seems to arise more frequently for academics than it does in some other countries. Our fifty-odd million people are crowded into a relatively small area. All roads lead to London: Whitehall, the BBC and the national headquarters of most quangos (again, I use the word 'quangos' in the old sense). Those are or have been much used and usually much respected in Britain, the quasi-autonomous-non-governmental organisations, the buffer committees, the arms'-length bodies. Their independence is often protected by Royal Charter rather than by Act of Parliament. That is the purest, most exemplary form; the Charter distances an institution from day-to-day governmental interference and changes of government; their members, though generally appointed by government, are not representatives of government and are free to make up their own minds. It is a mature concept and not much liked by governments. In the last few years there have been signs of more governmental encroachments and I expect we will see yet more of those. Such bodies have had their glorious moments: as when the BBC governors, over Suez, told Sir Anthony Eden, the Prime Minister, that they would not report the news as he wished, as a branch of government propaganda rather than as a news body seeking objectivity. Or as when the Arts Council publicly criticises government parsimony towards the arts; or as in the freedom of the British Council to send abroad those exponents of British arts which it and its advisers choose, not what the Foreign Office might find more palatable.

Quangos work by a set of unwritten conventions, of which a key one is that members are appointed because of their suitability for the task in hand – which is usually unpaid; though that principle is being breached now. A rough balance between persuasions, political, religious or whatever, is sought; that is, or was, all. I served for five or six years on the Arts Council and for about a score more years on various other quangos and in almost all that time did not know what the political inclinations of most colleagues were.

Latterly, Mrs Thatcher has been packing these bodies with pliant people of her own persuasion, thus fundamentally changing their nature. She does this, I think, not out of perversity or corruption but from her inability to see the intellectual probity and openness they can embody, to realise that they are a very useful device in a democracy and would of course be unthinkable in a totalitarian state. On the opposite flank, those on the far left react with predictable glee to the changes she has made: 'Ah, this is better. This is at least frank. The old arm's-length claim always was a sham. This is true to the reality.' That is wilful nonsense. The old system did work well more often than not and British public life was the better for it.

I have mentioned quangos and the like (say, Royal Commissions and departmental committees) because their existence, helped by our small surface area and hence accessible capital city, do much to explain why invitations to some academics to give service to national life are so numerous. Behind those elements and more important is the British tradition of voluntary service in the public interest. Not that you might guess this from the response of some academics to those of their colleagues who receive the call; surely they are about to 'sell out', if they start rushing off to London like that. One Oxford historian has written a shelf-ful of books and has also given a great deal to public service. He works quite exceptionally hard. Had he produced no more books but done no public service he would have met less criticism, much of it snide. As it is, the question circulates: 'Is he really sound? A true scholar?'

For him to chair a single major Commission on a matter of great public importance has meant that, however great his energy, one more book which might have been written has not been written. There is always a cost, and those who accept the challenge know that.

My own conclusion is that, for some but not for all, an involvement in public affairs is justifiable, may indeed be a duty (if one accepts such language); and that it may be most useful if it can draw on an academic's or scholar's training. But, first, why are some willing to do this work and some not? What drives those who accept? Since it would not be sensible to generalise about individual motives in such an area, I now have to some extent to assess my own motives.

Incidentally, it is surprising that some people in Britain, not usually academics and more in other professions than I would have thought likely, are prepared to suggest that their names might be 'put forward', as the phrase is, for service on some important committee, or for an honorary degree. Suggesting that a friend or friends might get together and suggest you for the honours list is also common. Yet most academics, most people, wait to be called like Cincinnatus from the plough.

Such a call is a duty but not a marked distinction. If someone asks, 'Didn't you play a part in that quite useful report on the incidence of child illnesses in triplets?', it would cause only a mildly pleasurable frisson. To have someone say: 'I enjoyed ["enjoyed" is the most accept-able word in casual academic praise, hardly "admired", let alone "agreed with"] your piece on George Meredith's style' gives a different and greater pleasure. The first activity may have cost more flesh and blood; the second seems more real, closer to your intellectual home, more warm-ingly personal/professional. Such a pair of reactions may indicate an uneasy sub-conscience; they may also indicate that we feel moved to do some things out of duty, others for love.

It all conflicts with, for example, finding time to write the book you feel, hope, only you can write; with the single-minded, solitary pursuit of your own road. Perhaps for some of us the creative urge is weak or afraid; we may not trust it really to have anything to say. The instant and demanding can be used as an escape from the pursuit of the slow but finally, we might feel just below the surface, more worthwhile use of our abilities. The call to public service can be distractingly insidious, as a call to 'do good' to and for others. Perhaps not the last infirmity of more or less yet would-be 'noble' minds, but the last-but-one infirmity. Like 'pity' as Graham Greene perceived it, this may be a virtue but essentially a second-order virtue, since pity can corrupt by getting between those we are trying to help and their funding of their own route to salvation. It corrupts also the exercisers of pity. That is rather a heavy gun to wheel out but not entirely irrelevant. Such activities may get between the prin-cipal actors and their own development, and the distracting interest of them may make that process all the easier to accept.

For me, one impulse seems to have been the wish to be wanted, and that seems to have been induced, simple self-analysis suggests, by being orphaned at an early age, by being small and by an early speech impediment. Like the comic who uses drollness and a sharp tongue, often against himself, to gain acceptance, one can use devotion and reliability, especially towards good causes.

Still, in British universities one doesn't have to go outside to assuage such urges. Since they are to a high degree self-governing, our universities always offer a very great deal of work of the steady, full, demanding but useful kind; and that can occupy all but the very gifted, or the totally committee-useless, or the ineradicably selfish. The equation is not, though, as neat as that. Some of the greatly gifted have a very strong sense of the importance of the self-government British universities enjoy and therefore regard it as a duty to honour that idea by serving on committees; on them the pressure can be exceptionally heavy. Others, whether or not so gifted, do not volunteer, or make a mess of their participation when they have been more or less drafted by their colleagues. For those in between, the shoulderers of burdens, the 'more work for the undertaker' principle comes into play.

Given that many academics, for whatever mixture of reasons and without having actually sought to do so, do agree to serve outside the walls, what can they best contribute? What they think in advance they can bring may prove to be mistaken, once they have sat round those long tables in London.

More important than anything else is the matter of what we should not do; and that is: not to change our spots, not to deceive ourselves into thinking that we have suddenly become sage statesmen or politicians or businessmen or fixers (though some do become thereafter one or other of those and are then likely to leave academic life). The figure of a professor, to whose head this public exposure has gone, self-consciously demonstrating that he or she knows a hawk from a handsaw, is not one of your doddering, ivory-tower dwellers, recognises the demands of 'reality' as he assumes that the businessman across the table or the politician to his left or right recognises them, knows about the need for compromises and corner-cutting, recognises that thug's idiom about the making of omelettes and so on – such a figure is never amusing and is probably getting into his sights a possible vice-chancellorship. Better for the academic member to be dry, a little difficult, 'out of touch with the real world', as he may be told now and again by one of the others round the table; better that than forgetting his high academic principles.

So we must each try to clarify, as academics and as particular kinds of academic, what we can best contribute to these public discussions. I exclude here, for example, a scientist who has been invited to join a committee specifically so that his particular scientific knowledge may feed the discussion; one on the effects of smoking, say; it is easy to think of others. The value of such contributions is plain and not seriously to be challenged (there have been instances where scientists who helped such committees have subsequently joined the tobacco industry's lobby; but those are aberrations). The precisely scientific contributions of scientists are plain and not seriously in dispute; and are, though essential, inherently not as intriguing as those I have in mind. Perhaps that puts the matter too simply. Some scientists who join committees with what seem to them clear and unassailable contributions to make find themselves gradually embroiled in a fog of political and other considerations within their compass is increasingly made to wobble.

Over a hundred years ago the two ancient English universities decided, within a few years of each other, to go 'outside the walls' as they charmingly put it when they began to establish extra-mural work for adults in different parts of England. I mention this now because that Great Tradition still exists (though under pressure in the present political climate). It was an admirable and unusual instance of universities looking outward for other than purely high-academic purposes, considering where they could best intervene socially, and deciding that their best intervention would be to offer to the wider non-academic world what they were best at – the inculcation of their highest academic and intellectual standards. That was their inclination, rather than direct service to the mid-nineteenth-century Industrial Revolution as consultants, contractors, think-tanks. There are, plainly, reasons why the universities of mid-nineteenth-century Britain did not much think in that commercial/ industrial way, and why the manufacturers did not look to them to do so. But they could have remained in their lovely cloisters. When they did go out in this disinterested way, they were sometimes practising a scholarly purity, devotion and energy which were not always evident within their own walls at that time.

The example is an important one. If we do go outside the walls into public affairs, we would do best, as I go on insisting, to keep our contribution central to our own academic and intellectual training; we should try to exhibit its virtues – rigour, objectivity and all the rest – in the round. This all the more because we will be going into a very expedient world, the world of the businessman who says: 'Whatever the environmental case against this, I've got my shareholders to think of', and the politicians who says: 'You may be bright in the abstract but my voters won't wear it.'

Incidentally, we still await a book which will analyse the language of 'reality' (e.g. compromise and expediency) in today's politics. It is a fascinating area, and I offer again, now as such a book's opening epigram, a phrase I have heard more than any other from British politicians, usually when they are seeking to justify one brutal short-circuit or another: that government's prime job is precisely to govern, which evades every conceivable question of principle. I do not wish to make excessive claims for academics. To repeat something said earlier, and likely to be said again here: I recognise that many academics, some of them very successful in their fields, have little or no interest in the discussion of general social or even individual human issues. Yeats's 'Bald heads forgetful of their sins' and Browning's Grammarian both have their justifications; but they would be no use on public committees. Conversely, there are some academics, not all of them in obviously relevant disciplines, who try to relate their work, their intellectual practice, to issues in society; they can be particularly useful. There is a small booklet, now lost and by an author I have not been able to trace, about the practice of public committees in Britain. He is too polite to say that the initial capacity of some members of such committees to think with knowledge, width and depth about the issues before them (let us say, again, about environmental questions which raise problems of human rights, individual and collective, as well as much else) – that this capacity is not often already well developed. But as the committee pursues its work, this author argues, some 'gladiators' capable of that kind of analysis emerge from their ranks and, as it were, fight out for the others the issues before them. It is a good image and I have seen it fulfilled. I like to think that academics will be able and willing to engage in such gladiatorial combats; in their own right ways.

It may at this point be useful to be personal once again and for a short while in this discussion of how one discovers what one can best contribute. I began working life as a university teacher of literature; outside the walls, to adults voluntarily giving up their evenings to the study. One could not, one did not wish to, escape two questions which

184

an internal university teacher to more or less captive eighteen to twenty-one-year-olds can ignore. What is the relevance of literary study or, more, literature itself to a busy adult who will make no professional gain from studying it? And how to best avoid, in seeking to show that interest and relevance, selling short the difficulty, the intractability and the disinterestedness of the best literary study?

These questions are always present to the extra-mural literature tutor, and led me gradually over almost twenty years to move out from literature into what became known as contemporary cultural studies. The value of literature of all ages was not being called into question. Rather, I was led to ask: if literature does mean and show all kinds of things about our common life at greatly different times, what could its techniques of imaginative analysis have to tell us about the bewildering forms of contemporary culture at all levels? Others were moving that way at that time. My own move was inspired by two other considerations: my growing conviction that the general understanding of working-class life in Britain was far too thin; and a long-standing impulse to make better sense of my own provincial working-class upbringing. Eventually, in the late fifties, a book came out of all that.

It is a common theme in these essays that debate about cultural matters, in a mixture of the Arnoldian and the anthropological senses, has been undernourished in Britain. The British have an interesting capacity to be open to criticism, to admit descriptions of shortcomings, to absorb and, often, submerge them. Not long after the above-mentioned book, *The Uses of Literacy*, appeared, the Government set up a national committee, mentioned in the preceding essay, to enquire into the needs of the Youth Service, by which provision is made at national and local level for the recreational, imaginative and intellectual needs of young people. Apparently, the proposed chairwoman of the committee had read my book and suggested I be asked to become a member.

Much of the evidence offered to the Committee today about young people reflected out-of-date and often curious assumptions. One local education authority insisted on an act of worship before each recreational evening's activities at its youth club. On the other hand, the submissions of evidence to the committee which argued for change were often examples of a kind of 'anything goes' openness, usually proposed on behalf of young people by middle-aged, middle-class people extremely anxious not to appear ever to hector anyone. Those members of the Committee who were selected to do most of the writing of the report did their best to steer between these two rocks. They were then, among many other reactions, treated as infidels by a bishop who fulminated in the House of Lords against their irreligiosity; and they were, naturally, accused of residual moralism by those who were anxious to prove to 'the young' (a pompous expression) that they were on their side. In fact, the report spoke rather better about these things than most of the existing literature. Happily, since this was at the start of the 'never had it so good' sixties, much in its recommendations was accepted and the Youth Service was, we felt, a little better for that.

My own next experience as an academic who was becoming involved in the British cultural debate came a year or two later, in the *Lady Chatterley's Lover* trial at the Old Bailey, which is discussed elsewhere in this collection. Among much else, that trial underlined the assumed tight relationships, by many in public life, between the ability to assume responsibility, and social class, education and distance from London or Oxbridge. Even today Sir Roy Shaw, who left a university professorship in the Midlands to run the Arts Council of Great Britain, tends in such circles to be referred to as 'a provincial educationalist'. Two birds with one stone.

The arguments – well, the little examined assumptions – continue and progress is slow. The Advisory Council for Adult and Continuing Education, set up by a Labour Government, established beyond doubt that there is a substantial demand from adults, far more than is being satisfied, for further education. The present Tory Government thanked the Council for its work, disbanded it and proceeded to dilute most of its recommendations beyond recognition. Two main impulses were evident in that decision: their narrow-minded concentration on utility in education at all levels; and their unshakeable suspicion that more education for 'ordinary' adults would often be politically biased education, if not outright left-wing indoctrination. A foolish junior minister plainly implied that to a meeting of the Advisory Council.

I am referring at this point in the argument to the general degree of cultural understanding in Britain. You rarely go far in such discussions before coming upon our educational system and its contribution to that understanding, its divisiveness and its unjustifiably assumed correlations with the different kinds of access and opportunity. These things do not greatly improve. Nor do the universities do enough to show that they understand these imbalances and are ready to make their own, proper, contributions to resolving them. They keep their eyes on protecting their own territories, especially today, when they are under pressure to turn themselves more and more towards industry. Matters would be even worse if the Open University did not exist.

So much for one way – by trying modestly to widen social and cultural understanding – in which an academic in the humanities may hope to intervene in policy-proposing committees. One of his or her other roles may look less important but is at bottom more fundamental than the first. It is to try to keep the language clean. Language, we say, should be the carrier of our thoughts, and we mean a clean and so far as we can manage this, a pure carrier; not a contaminated public river. Service on the Pilkington Committee on the Future of Broadcasting, with hours spent listening to the misuse of language by the profiteers, illuminated this.

One other main moment in that committee's life is worth recording, especially for the judgement it makes on the assertions, usually from conspiracy theorists from both left and right, that all such committees are chosen so that they will never reach a free, robust, collective opinion of their own, that they will always be compromising and pusillanimous.

By the time the Pilkington Committee had been meeting for a good few months, it had become clear that something was amiss with the conduct of the new commercial channel and that the evidence was pointing strongly towards radical solutions. So the chairman, as it happened a devout Congregationalist and industrialist of austere temperament who grew roses up in the North near his glass factory and went about his large-scale business dealings in London on a pedal bicycle, decided that we should all go away for a quiet weekend to discuss chiefly this overwhelming question: what should be done about commercial television, then only about half a dozen years old, but behaving very badly, putting profit from advertisements before public responsibility? We went to a modest and quiet hotel in Worthing or Hastings. The secretariat had prepared the meeting well and offered us a substantial range of optional solutions. We discussed for two days and were led – ineluctably is, I suspect, the right word – to a very radical solution indeed.

The chairman then said, in effect: 'Very well. I should remind you, though, that with this present government such a proposal has no hope of acceptance. A less radical proposal might be accepted. It is for the

Committee to choose. If you are greatly divided, I will of course give you my opinion.' It took very little time for us to choose the radical proposal, whatever the Government's likely attitude to it. We were not in the business of calculating political chances; we had been appointed to examine the condition of broadcasting and to propose what seemed the best solution to any problems, whatever might be the political and indeed the commercial forces against such a best solution. The chairman smiled, we moved to the next item of business; and that is how we had decided what to recommend. The Government duly rejected our main proposal: to separate the programme-making from advertising-revenue gathering. (A form of it surfaced as the original form of Channel 4, in which the gathering of advertisement revenue was separated from the making of programmes. Later that correct decision was, of course, removed by the Thatcher Government.)

Even so, the disinterested attack on the behaviour of commercial television was probably the best move we could have made. The Government were so shocked by the argument that root and branch reform was needed that, while throwing out our main proposals, they were led to make more reforms than they would have been likely to make had we toned down our criticisms. The reasons for making such strong criticisms were not, as I have said, because we misunderstood the tactical politics of the matter; they were a collective act of principle based on the evidence. The reactions of our opponents were in many instances deeply tactical; or, at a pinch, principled, if your main principle is to protect your and your friends' shareholdings, plus the unshakeable belief of some others that private financing is always better than public, whatever the evidence against in any particular case.

A decade after Pilkington I came out of university life for what eventually stretched to five and a half years, to serve as an assistant director-general at UNESCO in charge of the organisation's work in culture, the arts, philosophy, peace studies, population problems, the social sciences and some other odds and ends. I became part of a Byzantine enterprise which had over a quarter of a century produced – I leave aside its French – a fractured, abstract, evasive English in the light of which ambassadors could cable home, in most cases, something which looked at the worst harmless. To be able to write this kind of porridge is a gift not given to all. Consider only the six or seven or eight preambular paragraphs to a typical resolution for one of UNESCO's biennial

General Conferences; on peace, for example – the whole saying no more than that it would be A Good Thing if we were not producing weapons of mutual destruction. Or think of the clashing jargon of peace studies debates, with the West wanting among other aspects to look into the human psyche and the Soviet bloc insisting that psychologically-disturbed people should not be studied but simply be kept in mental homes because the threat to peace comes not from any characteristic in them from which we could learn about the roots of aggression in many of us, but rather from the western warmongers.

I kept saying that a spade was a spade and was not to be described as a hand-operated, metal-ended, earth-moving instrument, nor yet a bloody shovel. Some members of the Secretariat did not like this approach. It smacked too much of saying that the emperor had no clothes and left them feeling linguistically naked against aggressive member states. Some ambassadors and other representatives of member states also found my recommended plain speaking puzzling, indeed worrying. Then one or two decided it was a sort of double-take, a merely apparent straightforwardness, behind which a further duplicity was probably concealed, another example of the endless inventiveness of perfidious Albion. After all this, a further decade of English academic life on my return from UNESCO seemed likely to be almost easy-going. Naturally, it was not.

In our public debates about cultural change, and in the language in which we strive decently to clothe them but by which we usually end in smothering them, one overwhelming hidden attitude may occasionally be found: the fear of making discriminations, of separating, of accepting distinctions. To utter a critical remark about someone who happens to be black is to be automatically dubbed racist; to criticise anything in the language of a feminist pamphlet, however ill-judged that language may seem, is to be a male chauvinist; to say that not everyone's attempts at painting or writing or acting or making music show equal or potential gifts is to be a highbrow, an elitist, and probably a highbrow-bourgeois-elitist all at once.

The idea that some gifts fall unequally on the just and the unjust is simply not acceptable and yields to an idea of 'community' which will accept no differences. To hold that view while asserting the equality of all as *human beings* is quite hard to communicate; too much emotion is invested on the other side. That much overused apophegthm – 'The artist is not a special kind of man. Every man is a special kind of artist' – contains a useful truth about people's potentialities. To use it to brush aside the achievements of Tolstoy and Shakespeare and Beethoven and many thousand others is a folly which should be nailed if only in the name of common sense, as properly defined, even if that means being branded elitist and, at the extremes, both judgemental and moralistic. At this point one remembers Saul Bellow's weary but fair phrase; that if a Tolstoy of the Zulus could be found, he would be happy to read his work. That is now, unsurprisingly, dismissed as 'notorious' in some intellectual circles.

The battle for clearer argument and for language to match it, for better cultural understanding and for a sense of the importance of standards, is one of the more important any of us can undertake – but these issues are not on the whole well recognised in our universities. It should be seen as an important application of the proper witness of universities to the world around them; equally important as, say, the disinterested application of scientific findings to industrial needs; at bottom, more important. That, it is by now abundantly clear, is one of the main themes of this paper; the need to bear witness.

Is this kind of engagement in the end worthwhile? I have mentioned some inevitable losses for those who do engage, and might add the sense of displacement which can come from frequent shuttling between the two sides. But it has to be undertaken nowadays in particular when many universities, faced with an increasingly inimical world, wrap themselves even tighter into their more and more refined specialisms. Incidentally, Kosol's book, *Illiterate America*, points in its second half at American academics' failings here much more fiercely than I have done towards ourselves.

It is important for those who do go outside their university walls not in turn to become portentous or holier than thou. Some others (not all) could do these things but choose not to, often for good scholarly reasons. Those who do, do not always succeed in bringing to bear more than a fraction of the influence they had hoped to exert. In the course of things they are likely to have discovered limitations and weaknesses in themselves, in their own mental and emotional equipment, which they had not suspected. They may gradually have come to compromise more than they expected, since each step on that road looks at the time like a sensible accommodation. They will discover, also and of course, that people with none of the academic labels they possess often have at least as much insight and objectivity as they themselves have, before general issues. There are gains and losses for those who go into the marketplace and the corridors of power. I hope some continue to do so. But in general only if asked; or sternly pushed ...

University of Massachusetts, 1985/2000

LITERACY IS NOT ENOUGH: CRITICAL LITERACY AND CREATIVE READING

This essay was prompted by a year-and-a-half's experience of a new Labour Government and the growing feeling that, although it claimed that its attitudes towards education were radically different from those of its predecessors, that Government already seemed in too many ways to be treading much the same paths.

In particular, it seemed time for a better definition of literacy than was circulating: hence the argument for critical literacy.

It also seemed time to promote cultivated literacy, *that higher intellectual and imaginative level which lifts off from functional literacy, of no matter how competent a kind.*

It is now two years since the pugnacious book in which this essay appeared was published. Apart from a limited and inadequate review by the head of Ofsted, I have seen no mention of it in official or governmental circles.

I don't imagine we expected a greatly different response. But hope always survives. Perhaps some of the relevant civil servants looked into those pages.

UNDER THE PRESENT government two areas of educational activity are rightly receiving special attention: literacy and reading. Obviously the two are twinned: literacy is fundamental, the essential gateway, the starter tool; without it we cannot read at all. Yet even with it, after we have been passed as officially literate, we may be able to read in only the barest sense. We may understand the dictionary meanings of an approved number of words; we may be able to interpret what those words say when they are strung together in sentences and paragraphs, but only so long as the words are not very polysyllabic or abstract or heavy with imaginative meaning – such as the words in a well-presented guide to simple cookery, say, or to driving a car, or to putting together a very plain piece of do-it-yourself equipment.

All such gains are helpful and justify the present drive for literacy, whether that is labelled 'basic' or 'initial' or 'vocational'. They take us so far, are the minimum needed in modern society and not very demanding. Which makes it all the more necessary, as this government is insisting, that at the age of eleven many more than the existing two out of three pupils should have reached Level 4 at Key Stage 2 of the National Curriculum.

But, and it is an enormous 'but', a definition of literacy which ends at Level 4 is inadequate for effective adult life in developed, open, commercial societies such as ours. It would be inadequate for closed authoritarian societies too.

It is obvious that the ruling bodies in all kinds of society must seek to create a sense that their kind of society is self-justified and self-sufficient. They chiefly do that by persuasion and predominantly by persuasion through image and language. But the kinds of persuasion differ. In authoritarian societies the persuasion is collective and socially insistent; we are incessantly required to accept that this is the best form of all forms of society and so urged to join the great body of citizens in going the way this particular world is going, by acts of public belonging.

In open 'democratic' societies, too, we are invited all the time to approve of and join a sort of collectivity, but now of what are presented as congeries of free, self-valuing peer groups, chiefly united in buying much the same sort of thing, or doing much the same sort of thing or being amused by similar things. We are not so much asked to join the collective as a self-justifying political end in itself, but to appear to decide to become a part, each by an individual act of choice (or of what is made to look like one), of our peer groups and their group tastes. These differences between each form of society are important and decide the different tones of voice with which we are approached.

We are approached, then, in a society such as ours, by a multitude of voices, few explicitly directional, almost all peer-group-plus-individual aimed, would-be persuasive and occasionally simply informative. By this immensely elaborate, continuing, successive process do mass, highly developed, non-authoritarian societies exist and keep on existing. In that process the primary engines are the complex and endlessly developing techniques for mass communication. There is no point in doing more than mention here their manifest value in all sorts of ways. Air travel, rail travel, road travel, the transmission of essential knowledge of all kinds from medicine to weather patterns and beyond – without modern mass-communication technology, all such operations would seize up and we would be the poorer for it.

It may be said that the argument so far has been almost entirely that modern societies must go beyond initial literacy, must add to that base all the information and knowledge essential to coping adequately with many aspects of life today. That is true, but still does not go far enough. These are also the societies of competitive-commodity promoting, and that puts a different slant on the processes just described. Plainly subordinate voices are subordinate not to the bullying but to the cooing and wooing, the deceptive and corner-cutting, the selectively suggestive, so that more goods should be sold, yesterday's goods discarded in favour of today's; and so, too, must be yesterday's habits, prejudices, notions, assumptions, convictions.

This encourages and creates, in particular, new forms of two types of work: public relations and advertising. For reasons which will soon be clear, I refrain from calling them 'professions'. They have both, especially since the last war, seen major growth. But the massed ranks of public-relations operators and advertising experts are concentrated very much more on persuasion to buy what it is in someone else's financial and influence-gaining interest to encourage us to buy, rather than in objectively pointing us towards information and knowledge which would be useful for personal and social life. It is in many people's profitable interest that most of us should remain semi-literate. But, then, so are many of the persuaders themselves, and among them some of the more effective.

A slight diversion here, to justify withholding the title 'professional' from the majority of such people. To belong to a profession means having ethical principles towards your field of work and its practices. All professions, properly so called, have their own forms of the Hippocratic oath, spoken or unspoken. Medicine is obviously a profession; so are teaching and public service broadcasting and the law, and a fair range of other activities old and new for which severe training is necessary, and with that the absorbing of the principles of the work in relation to those outside, to whom it is offered; all these change the occupation from a job of work to a profession.

Most of these new styles of operator – men or women – are not professionals, since they manipulate emotions and hence language for profits or other ulterior ends. It is a sad sign of their own insecurity or just plain cheek that they cling to the word 'professional' to describe themselves. Since their ethics are never pure, always contingent on the need to deliver what those who pay them want (which is itself always and entirely contingent), their self-designed tickets of entry to the professions can never be honoured at the entrance gates. They are parasitic on and compliant to activities which are always interested, never disinterested.

This takes us to the need for a level of literary which is, obviously, not only beyond Level 4 – we have seen that that is elementary – but beyond also a degree of literacy which has absorbed information and knowledge adequate only for the more complex practical managing of important aspects of daily life. It points to the need, the inescapable need, for a degree or a kind of literacy which is alert to the manifold deceptions – carried mainly in language – by which persuasion operates in the open society. The need is, above all, for *critical literacy*, a literacy which is critically aware, not easily taken in, able to 'read' tricks of tone, selectivities, false *ad hominem* cries and all the rest.

In the face of these assaults by television, radio, the press, mailshots and hoardings and all the rest, Level 4 literacy is a vehicle with no more than solid wooden wheels – which is the level at which almost 40 per cent of us are stuck. All that phoney language and distorted emotionalising so as to take money from the pockets of all those inadequately educated people. A shameful travesty of a so-called democracy, a distortion of what might have been, if working-class people had been given a more straightforward chance to take advantage of their new greater freedom – people most of whom now have time and money to spare after earning their livings, but are lured to misspend it by other people, many of whom are verbally cleverer, or in other ways tricksier, than they are.

At this point some defenders, especially among the advertisers themselves, say: 'But most people are not taken in.' Some are not, certainly, but many are. The figures prove this, as does the willingness of the advertisers to continue throwing money into their 'useless' efforts. Why are so many well-educated people, at all levels and in all sorts of occupations, ready not to say a word against this distorted application of the billions spent on education for, by now, more than a hundred years? Not to recognise this substantial failure, to brush it aside on behalf of others who are its casualties, is a form of unconscious marking-down, and a justification for inaction.

From all this we should adopt the slogan: 'Literacy is not enough'. The level of literacy we accept for most of the population, of literacy unrelated to the way language is misused in this kind of society, ensures that literacy becomes simply a way of further subordinating great numbers of people. We make them just literate enough for profits to be made; truncatedly literate, two-dimensionally literate. One hears little of these considerations from the Department of Education and Employment.

The second slogan has therefore to be: 'Critical literacy for all'. Critical literacy means combining, with training in literacy, teaching about the difficulties, challenges and benefits of living in an open society which aims to be a democracy. It means blowing the gaff on all the rampant small and large corruptions, on the humbugging, smart-alec persuaders; it means learning how to read the small print on insurance policies and guarantees on major purchases; it means telling the doorstep-cowboys of all kinds to clear off and throwing junk mail into the wastepaper basket, unopened; it means mocking television advertisements (all too easy) – especially those which go for our soft underbellies. It means using a fine, logical truth-toothcomb on all political manifestos – and on a hundred other such things with which poorly educated people are showered, even more than are the effectively literate. Democracy is the least objectionable form of society, yes, but it has to be thought through if it is to be even marginally maintained in each generation. This movement is not being well-managed today in any of the 'advanced' democracies. One encouraging thought is that there still exist remnants of the sceptical 'Come off it – pull the other one' spirit within the long working-class tradition.

Again: the simple definition of literacy promoted today is inadequate. At its best it is like a fairly simple bag of plumber's tools, when we need a set of fine surgical instruments. Profit-driven societies are marked by the disposition of the profit-seekers to push to the limits the rules their society sets. They need a majority just literate enough to be hooked by every form of modern, industrialised fishing-trawler persuasion.

If people are made critically aware beyond that point, then the profit-promoters will have to adjust, which they will do instantly, becoming ever so slightly less deceptive, less egregious manipulators of linguistic sleight-of-voice, until one day, but not in our lifetime, they are indeed 'legal, decent, honest and truthful' in senses even a government-appointed regulatory commission cannot object to. We are a very long way from that point and, since in some respects we are all lazy and prone to flattery, may never quite reach it. It could be an invigorating ride, though. And at that point the operators may even be entitled to apply for recognition as members of a 'profession'.

The next step must be from critical literacy to a condition even more difficult. Words which don't sound pompous are difficult to find here, but perhaps cultivated literacy will serve. It means arriving at the ability to read other than functionally, which is after all only a simple matter. It means being more than critical in our reactions to what we see, hear and read, but being open, intellectually and imaginatively responsive. Creative reading, it might also be called.

Critical literacy is valuable – indeed, as I have said, essential, especially in a democracy – but still is not enough. It is in its nature reactive, responsive to a certain state of affairs, and hence defensive, even narky. It says: 'If we wish this kind of society to release its potential, such and such steps will have to be taken, ranks will have to be drawn up against as many as possible of the parasitical and piratical forces which batten on society's openness, which make it grow crooked, not straight.'

On the positive side, such a society must give all its members the opportunity to open their minds to the best kinds of creativity, to the best works of the intellect and imagination. Through this a society may begin to mature. A society which does not recognise this imperative will be populated by well-fed morons, not by cultivated humans. Of course, if anyone settles for being a plump moron, one cannot forbid them; but they should have the opportunity to realise what they are missing.

Most well-educated people, asked to name the highest of the arts, will choose music; and I would not wish to demur. Nor would I care to introduce pecking orders. I would only insist that literature is a very great art and in some unique ways. It has a different language from that of music; indeed, to speak of 'the language of music' is to borrow a metaphor and one drawn from the main instrument of literature, words. Which seems like an irony, but is not; it is, rather, a tribute to the importance of language as the root and rooted form of explicit, of would-be explicit, communication.

The key lies in the word 'explicit'. Words are the most direct, avowed, available, everyday form of communication. That is where two other words employed above – 'root form' – come in; words are rooted in the day-to-day. I remember quite well my own introduction to the pleasures of words. The home was bookless, but an unmarried aunt living with her mother, as I too was, had a unaware but acute feeling for language. She picked up images like a cheerful squirrel. I do not think she invented them; that would have been asking too much, but she knew good ones when she heard them. She would say of a woman with a particularly aggressive stare: 'Ooh! Her eyes stuck out like chapel 'at pegs.' That came straight from the nonconforming culture we lived in. Max Wall, the madly surrealistic music-hall comedian, used to break away from the piano, transfix his audience and ask it to consider what a beautiful word – its vowels long drawn out – 'coal-hole' was. A French hotel brochure arrives and promises a breakfast buffet which is *copieux*; splendidly long vowels, the suggestion of wide-open generosity, a cornucopia. 'Unctuous', which was no doubt also taken over from the French, has a similar lush beauty. Our linguistic inhibitions make us more nervy than the French about using such words.

An external examiner demurred at a sentence in one of my final-degree examination papers. I had quoted Wycherley on a woman who had 'a jut with her bum that would stir an anchorite'. I thought it a brilliant, brief, erotic image. For me, as for people like me, that early affair with language was both physical – sensuous, on the pulses – and an introduction to possible exactness of thought and a response to wit, fancy, gifted vision in action.

Teachers of English who argue for neglecting literature before 1900 in favour of 'more relevant' writings, and there are some, are so plainly wrong-headed that they would do well to transfer to instructing in the intricacies of computers. With what better help than that from great writers of all generations could we, through their insights-with-honesty, all caught in the love of language, more happily and strenuously confront life? It is astonishing to realise, from casual conversations, how many people – and these often among the 'well-educated' – have now decided that reading will be made obsolete by modern technology; and that anyone who questions this really has fallen by the macadamised roadside.

In the nineteenth century the joke was: 'Don't teach my boy poetry. He's going to be a grocer.' Today's version is: 'My boy doesn't bother reading books. He's going to be a computer programmer.'

It has been willingly admitted earlier, and is in any event obvious, that modern communications technology has many manifest rewards. But to think it will remove the case for reading is to misunderstand the nature of technology and, even more, the nature of reading. These new implements, to underline a distinction made earlier, do make it easier to build on fundamental literacy (the cornerstone) by opening the way to the acquisition of information and, if we want to go on to that level of effort, of knowledge. So much is plainly to the good. But reading gives or offers something different; reading of worth, that is – not the passive absorption of repetitive rubbish, of which there are increasing amounts nowadays, all around.

Here we have to defend the uses and meanings of several unfashionable words. To talk about the value of reading in and for itself is to talk of fine poetry, great drama, remarkable novels. It is to speak of works which show a respectful, gifted and, as may seem needed, wanton regard for language; a wish to make some sort of sense of experience, even if that is in the end a matter of nonsense; or it may suggest some sort of shape in life, even if that is no more than a mad shape; it is in most but not all instances fed by the wish to pass on all this to anyone who will make the effort to listen. A difficult apprenticeship for the reader (worse for the writer) but worthwhile, a possible source of genuine, not meretricious, comfort and delight. There are times in which communal pleasures, things done within our peer groups or other collectives, seem self-evidently right. But to learn to read properly is to say: 'Stop the world; I want to get off'; for the time being and intermittently. Reading is initially and inherently a solitary occupation. It leads from our eyes into our minds in all their aspects; we absorb it in silence – though we can, afterwards, talk about it to whoever we will. Or we could listen to someone reading aloud in a group; but each member of that group has to try to absorb if *as if* alone. It is not and cannot in the first place be a group activity. In this it is very close to the absorption of music, even when performed in very large halls.

Reading is therefore a contract, an exchange between two people, the writer and the reader. The reader is not being given something without contributing something: his or her own responsiveness to language, to tone, to temper, to argument, to atmosphere, to the stresses of the author's efforts to say what he really has to say. In return, the author's pleasure in that difficult success, if it is arrived at, is shared also. That is the basis of what I am calling creative reading. Its reward is that we are 'taken out of ourselves', 'rapt', into another world of the mind. We bring much to gain much. All this may come from honest literature. Dishonest literature, of which there is far more, is formulaic, routine in language and response, verbal marshmallow. It strokes our existing prejudices and lazinesses; it does not challenge.

What are called the classics or the canon are rarely selected by 'elitists' just to show their superiority. They survive because some people in each generation find, for example, enjoyment of a unique kind in them, and profit from important insights into the business of being human, what we do right to call lasting or even universal qualities. They survive because each generation can hear in them things which speak to their particular sense of themselves and their time. 'Universality' can be all these things and achieves much of its effect, as Dr Johnson reminded us, through pleasure. Such assertions are not popular today; they imply some effort, some isolation, selection.

Those with better than usual intelligence, if that also includes the beginnings of a sensitive response to language, will at the start read anything they can lay their hands on; and their best help from outside will be their parents' readiness to read to them. No television 'adaptation' or 'book of the film of the book' can take the place of the book itself. Television is by its nature selective to a degree that and in ways that are not true of the book; it may produce some interesting and even honourable failures, but failures they will inevitably be.

This is a basic truth, but one which many people are unwilling to face. It is a great pity that mistaken assumptions – such as that the television version can adequately recreate the book – encourage very many people to stop in their tracks at that point in the road, comfortably assured that they have 'met' Jane Austen. They really 'don't know what they're missing'.

A qualification. It may be that a greatly talented director taking off from a great book may make a great film, in its own right. It might then stand beside the book, as a different form of art. It will not be a substitute for the book; or vice versa. Even this generous olive branch will be rejected by some television producers; they firmly believe that they can recreate the book in all its dimensions and fullness, the authorial voice and all. All new creative professions gain some of their thrust from the defensive/assertive hedges with which they surround themselves.

But for whom are writers writing these days? For their own kind, for other writers; for professional critics and reviewers, and for that wider circle who are often slightly contemptuously – it not being a 'very English' phrase – called 'the intelligentsia'; those who read the broadsheets, listen to Radio 3, take journals of opinion. Yet, in a population of over fifty million, they make up quite a small minority, in some respects an important minority but one not sufficiently large to provide the amount of reflective yeast a pluralistic society needs.

My own general impression is that most writers are not greatly aware of the nature of their audiences beyond those who compose the minority above; if so, that seems a pity. Many thousands of graduates and thousands who are not graduates still compose the 'common readers' today. We cannot accurately count these 'intelligent laymen and woman', and many in the graduate minority above are sure that the intelligent lay reader has by now almost disappeared. There is evidence to the contrary from the sales of some books, from the numbers who attend the multitude of literary festivals across the country (though some of them, being bestseller-obsessed, do not live up to the more serious interest in literature of many in their audiences); from the audiences for certain radio and television programmes, from the great numbers who go to classes in adult education (and, for me and no doubt others, from the quite large correspondence I receive on this subject) that there is still an audience out there much larger than that of the relative minority of intellectuals mentioned above; they should be more widely recognised. This statement will not be accepted by many, least of all by some entrenched academics.

They tend to be convinced that the old audience outside, further out than they usually look but perhaps after all at one time a 'saving remnant', have all but disappeared, have either merged with the happy and unquestioning meritocrats or sunk in the comfortable sloth of 'couch potatoes'? University extra-mural education has, for them, had its day – unless it is vocational or entirely undemanding, a purely leisure-time pursuit.

The positive case is, again, not proveable. Almost through all its parts, this is an age of nervous intellectual insecurity. Public voices fear they have lost credibility, especially if they compose sentences which begin:

'We should ...' Accredited intellectuals tend more and more to address only those in their own known circles; the broadsheets give more and more space to what seems the fashionable intellectual froth of the moment, less and less time to slower and more considered work.

Though the old certainties about the existence of an identifiable group of 'serious lay readers' have been badly shaken, and evidence to the contrary such as is gathered together a couple of paragraphs back will not be convincing to many, nevertheless some of us remain unwilling to give up hope. Probably those readers are less identifiable by class today than they were sixty years ago and not embarrassed by that; nor should they be. On the contrary, that may be one sign of a more mature society, one in which a writer does not feel that certain tones of voice are needed for audiences from different social classes. More today will have had some form of higher education; many may have learned to be suspicious of the wooing voices aimed at the great bulk of the possible reading public. They may not all, though, have learned to suspect the more sophisticated persuasions aimed precisely at them – voices which aim themselves now at the broadsheets, the journals of opinion and Channel 4. Yet, though hardly any author today would be willing to announce that he 'rejoices to concur with the common reader', some authors can after looking and listening all round decide that such an audience still exists and is as much as ever worth trying to reach.

The above lines may have given the impression that almost all writers have a hoped-for audience at the back of their minds. A glance at what many major writers have said about the business of writing shows that most neither have nor seek a recognisable audience (and many hate the actual work). They write because they have to, because of an impulse that cannot be denied. From writers such as these one has the sense that readers, if they are thought of, are regarded as onlookers, listeners-in, eavesdroppers; and, often, critics too seem to be allocated to that category. Auden's American publisher offered him a copy of a book I had written about him. It was, I believe, the earliest book-length study. Auden had recoiled and said something to the effect that it might put him off his stroke if he saw his work analysed. Later, when he stayed with us, he was happy to talk about what he believed he was aiming at in more than one poem, was indeed impelled by.

Nevertheless, most authors wish their books to be read and many are disappointed if they do not sell well; but they do not necessarily wish to meet their readers or read their critics. The more or less recent burgeoning of those literary festivals may be changing this, to judge from the queues waiting for books to be signed by their authors, who scribble away apparently contented. Yet the biggest queues are for the most fashionable authors; that is not a surprise. It is difficult to imagine Flaubert sitting there cheerfully, or Graham Greene. I do not easily imagine Chekhov sitting there either, but am always impressed by the sense of ease with the people for whom he is writing which comes over even in translation. He does not woo but is always courteous towards those he assumes are, somewhere, his readers.

I said something much earlier and sketchily about what we may gain from reading 'good books'. In the making of any considerable claim in this respect, there is always the danger of afflatus, of claiming too much, even of offering great literature as an all-embracing panacea. It is remarkable how many great writers have in fact made large claims for their art, larger than most outsiders would have dared to make. Some are acceptable and rightly spirited: Lawrence's praise of the novel as life's 'one bright book', for instance; and Malraux's dryly ironic remark that the novel is one of the happier consequences of the fall of man. Some earlier authors, notably Carlyle, were confidently pontifical.

Still, Carlyle in that mode is not to be laughed at. One would more easily laugh at the Marxist, cultural materialist critic's assertion that books simply cannot detach themselves from the material pressures of production, from Carlyle's own 'cash nexus'. It is above all the claim of 'inherent' qualities, detached from time and space, material process and financial pressures which haunts such people, and hence does the claim that some books are more worthwhile than others. How could they be, being so contingent? Relativism again. Some then take refuge in a not very creditable let-out: 'Well, it may not be impressive in the terms of high art, but it is good of its kind.' With that, all doors are open. Perhaps 'effective' would be a better term than 'good'; that would offer the widest of all doors, and rightly reduce some books to the status of household cleaners as advertised on television.

It follows that critics such as the materialist quoted above reject the idea of exemplary moments in literature (an aspect of Arnold's touchstones). Such moments stick like burrs in the minds of others, so that they begin to wonder whether the materialists and some others lack a dimension in response, are not sensitive to, the way words can unlock emotional recesses; put brutally – can they 'read' in the fullest sense in which we find ourselves using that word? Do they respond, in a way different from their responses to words used entirely functionally (as in the guide to the use of their computer), to all those scenes, confrontations, revelations which recreate, body out, explore through language the nature of our relations, our responsibilities towards others, the inescapable burden of our free will, our fears and pity and joy; all drawn in 'material particularity ... the heft of things ... the solidity'?

Writers and readers are of course submerged in society, but the act of creating and reading literature may detach us, provisionally, from its demands. Bloom's 'solitary soul' is within but greater than its social connections. The best writing, whether tragic or comic, is at bottom about discrepancies, discordances and their possible or finally impossible resolution: between the world outside as we would wish it and as we encounter it; between what others here now or before us have made of it and what we are making of it; between the world of relationships we inhabit and the world inside ourselves – our 'solitary souls', again. In these scenes gifted writers may, if we allow them, help us to see, to learn from and enjoy the learning, better than we can manage to do unaided. We are then, of course, a long way from claiming that there is or can be a direct link between the act of reading and our resultant conduct, for good or ill. It is curious that those who claim such links, and even today there are a few people who do that, tend to claim that literature may help to improve our conduct; the rarely claim that it might tempt us to worse. We may see sin and not be inspired to turn away from it, or we might be attracted; in either reaction, the process is not a simple and direct exchange; there are many complex involvements all the way to any definable influence.

Some authors feel uneasy behind any such discussion; they just, they say, write and disclaim any influence. Emerson was bolder: 'There must be a man behind the book'; so was Elisabeth Barrett Browning: 'Books succeed/and lives fail'. Those apply to both writer and reader. And yet the nag continues, and it would be easy but shallow simply to dismiss it. There is nothing silly – it is, rather, touching and earnest – in the hope that a book which tries honestly to face experience must have a link with, may even reinforce our own efforts at better living. That does seem ingenuous, the book as morality-injector. Yet the wish has a limpet-like staying power. And is often projected onto the author. Surely someone who sees so far into personality must be affected for the better? 'We needs must love the highest when we see it'; surely something will rub off? Not necessarily. Great writers can be little men. Yet we can look back on our own reading and ask what our minds would have seemed like if we had not come into contact with that range of playwrights, poets, novelists who opened so many vistas of human conduct in all its aspects to us; and we are grateful for that nourishment without necessarily making claims for its effects on us.

Perhaps it is at best an implicit possible judgement to which we are free to pay or not to pay attention. Literature is, yes, and this is blindingly obvious, about life, about the world around us and the people walking in it; it is therefore always ethically involved, though not in a poker-motto sense. When it is handled well, it is enjoyable in a way little else is; enjoyable first of all for itself and perhaps also because it gives us the satisfaction of feeling that we have been helped to see further, to understand more, have been in very talented company. We are not *necessarily* the better for that; but it is just possible that we might be, slightly and perhaps temporarily, moved towards the better. And we have to recognise that others, who have not had our privileged access to literature, may or may not be inspired to take lessons directly from raw life itself; they have missed something, but that is not necessarily vitally disabling. That is why, though readers are important in their own right, by the degree to which their minds are open, responsive and disinterested before the work, it is in the end more important that they are open and responsive before life itself.

Against all this, the current inclination to set communications technology against the book, to the book's disadvantage, is revealed as confused and boneless; likely to be claimed by people who have never *really read* (the italics are mine and deliberate) a book of any consequence; not in a pious fashion but in all sorts of different ways – sometimes skipping, putting down what we are not ready for or which at the time bores us, being ready to be interrupted. On all this, a great many writers have written well, often irrelevantly because at bottom they belonged to the same congregation and could be cheerfully dismissive if need be. They know, all the time and in the end, that, in Auden's astonishing words, books are 'rooted in imaginative awe'. Knowing that, they do not need to be portentous; they can, as they feel like it, play.

The British Library, 1998

PART FIVE

FIGURES FROM A DISTANT PAST

*F*or many years I meant to write something for our children; a story, perhaps. I never 'got round to it', and regret that very much. Finally, in late retirement, I decided to write a memoir for our grandchildren; here it is. As I wrote, all seemed distant to me; it must seem very distant indeed to our grandchildren.

I was led then to try to write portraits of some people from that distant past. Here, in four further essays, are attempts to describe six of those early relatives, all now dead.

They are written with love, but such a job is inescapably difficult and complete success – however that may be defined – almost impossible, as others who have also known these people will point out. Above all, one must try to avoid all kinds of patronage, the condescensions of hindsight by the living.

I add only that I have tried to arrive somewhere near the spirit of that wonderful passage from Lady Chatterley's Lover quoted earlier: 'One may hear the most private affairs of other people, but only in a spirit of respect for the struggling, battered thing which any human soul is, and in a spirit of fine, discriminative sympathy. . . . It is the way our sympathy flows and recoils that really determines our lives.'

MEMOIR FOR OUR GRANDCHILDREN

I AM NOW IN my eighty-third year. I was born on 24 September 1918, just before the end of the first of this century's two terrible wars. That seems a long time ago even to me and must seem ages ago to you.

We lived on Potternewton Lane. Potternewton was a forgotten-seeming little district of houses mixed in styles and ages but most of them small, and of people mixed in much the same way as the houses; most seemed to have been washed up there. We were about two miles north of the centre of Leeds, the biggest city in Yorkshire with half a million people. I have always thought of Potternewton as a friendly, almost villagey name for a district. It seems to have been fallen out of favour as a name now, being caught up in a bigger area called Chapel Allerton; also a pleasant enough name.

Between Potternewton and the city centre was Sheepscar (not an attractive but certainly a very Yorkshireish name), a huddled and shabby district of small shops and small crafts, especially in the clothing trade. In the late nineteenth century Sheepscar came to be full of splendid and crowded courts, and for all I know some of those lingered into the 1920s. It was there that Jewish refugees from the persecutions of Central Europe had settled. Leeds called them because it was becoming a world centre for made-up clothing. It kept that pre-eminence until, I think, the 1930s; and held till about then, I expect, its reputation for having the largest Jewish proportion of all big British cities.

The men among the refugees were usually tailors, their wives and daughters 'tailoresses', seamstresses. I have seen a photographic book of that area in the early days; a miserable place full of grey, sad-looking people.

They worked hard and most native English both admired and resented that. They believed – and they were right; it was not a myth – that the more enterprising among the Jewish immigrants marked the stages on their way to success by the dates they moved north with, perhaps, a stop in Harehills and so to Roundhay or Moortown. I had, incidentally, a remote 'aunt' who lived in Harehills and taught elocution; that alone marked Harehills as posher than Sheepscar or Potternewton, for those on the way up. The rising families from Sheepscar skipped Potternewton; it had hardly any houses which said: 'Congratulations. You have arrived or are on the way!'

The trams from Leeds centre, heading up Chapeltown Road, or Roundhay Road slightly to the west, for those wealthier and higher and fresher districts three or four miles out, rattled past our lane end. To a little boy our house seemed a long way down from the main road. We took Simon, Nicola and Paul (our sons and daughter) to see it thirty years later, and I realised it was only a couple of hundred yards off the tram route.

I could no longer show them the house – no, the cottage. In our time there had been a huddle of stone buildings at a corner where the lane met, on the right hand, a street curving up to rejoin Chapeltown Road and the tram route.

I seem to see an L-shaped low wall and behind it a slightly sunken bit of unkempt earth and grass; behind that, facing over the grass to the road junction, was a clutter of two-storied stone buildings. They had probably been put up in the early or mid-nineteenth century. I only remember in detail the one which was side-on to Potternewton Lane itself. It was a cottage-cum-tiny-bakery, occupied by a woman who seemed immensely old and had two or three grey whiskers growing out of a mole on her left lower chin. Whether she was a widow or unmarried I neither knew nor was led to wonder.

She always seemed sweet-natured and calm. Coming back from school one day, I smiled at her over the wall. 'Hello, Sunny Jim,' she said. I seem to remember that Sunny Jim was a figure in an advert, for porridge oats. Why do I recall that tiny incident out of so many which must have occurred by then, by the time I was six or seven? I think it must have been because, by implying that I was regarded as a cheerful little boy, she made me for the first time see myself from outside, as other people saw me, as an individual about whom (as about everybody) general 'remarks' were made. Nor had it occurred to me to think of myself as 'sunny', happy; I was just 'me', I suppose. And unthinkingly happy.

On the other hand, Simon at about three or four years old asked his mother: 'Shall I be happy all the days?', and made her heart turn over with love and foreboding — and may have suggested an early reflective spirit in him. That again reminds me of taking Paul to see *Hansel and Gretel*, in Rochester, New York, when he was about four. When the witch was herself thrown into the oven she had heated for cooking the children, we wondered whether he would be a little frightened by the scene. Instead, he asked loudly: 'How long does it take to cook a witch?' Lateral thinking, perhaps.

The old lady — it would have seemed impolite on our part to call her an 'old woman' — made a little money from selling her currant teacakes at weekends. The smell in the yard was then all warm, yeasty, curranty and sugary. Sometimes, because she knew we were very hard-up, she gave our mother one or two teacakes she hadn't managed to sell that week. Even now, the smell and taste, the cushiony butteryness of a toasted teacake, not only seem marvellous but instantly bring back, with warmth, life in Potternewton Lane, even if I am having tea in a posh hotel. So does the smell of 'oven-cakes', basically round and flattish loaves baked on the oven bottom from leftover dough, as the loaves above are almost finished, and preferably eaten warm.

The old lady's place with its warm oven was the natural haunt of cockroaches. All the other houses in the huddle had them too; they were a part of life never finally to be got rid of. They had a semi-underground route from the back of the bakery to our cottage. We were in the adjoining little sunken area: a yard with on one side an earth closet — lavatory, but not a water closet — which men 'from the council' emptied every so often. Perishing cold in winter, that was; bits of other people's torn old newspaper hanging on string just to the left; no chain to pull, of course. A scrubbed, plain-white wood rectangular seat went right across the narrow width of the place, with a hole in its middle; very comforting, and pleasant to sit on in summer, reading the bits of paper.

So: the rear of the little bakery/cottage on one side, the closet facing it; our own place between them and facing the lane, across the flagstones.

All in stone. A little living room with a narrow coal fireplace and black iron range which incorporated a tiny oven on one side; a minute cold-water scullery at the back; upstairs two bedrooms, one small, the other very small. That was all. No hot water unless it was heated on the fire, gas lighting (a pure, white, gentle light from delicate fabric 'mantels'). No electricity nor, since we are counting: no television, of course, no radio, no telephone, no newspapers, no gramophone, no books and no junk mail.

The heart and centre of the home was the fireplace. We lived with the constant presence of draughts as with that of cockroaches. The importance of the fireplace was visually highlighted rather in the way of a chapel altar is; not by a fine cloth, though, but by a clip rug. It was spread on the floor at about the length across the fireplace itself; warm and cosy especially to bare feet, being made out of eight to ten-inch by one-inch strips of cut-up old clothing in many colours, all pricked and knotted onto hessian. The different colours were put into their own separate heaps, for choosing from. Some people showed unsuspected and unrecognised talent in making elaborate patterns. That was a regular winter-fireside occupation for housewives, accompanied by family and neighbourhood gossip. Not in our house, though; our rug had to be someone else's gift, probably a cast-off; but it fulfilled its purpose. We clustered on and round it; just us, usually without others.

We had to cluster because our mother had been widowed when she was not much over forty. From the two or three sepia photographs which remain, Thomas Longfellow Hoggart had been 'a fine figure of a man', of a good height and build, with a thick bristly moustache as went with his rank of army sergeant.

As the oldest of ten children, he had 'Longfellow' as his second Christian name. That was a family tradition based, Grandma said, on our relationship with 'Poet Longfellow'. He had come, she claimed, from her village, Boston Spa, a few miles out of Leeds; and emigrated to America. Hence 'Hiawatha'. Those few facts of his life are correct; I do not know whether the clam to relationship was. But first sons were given that name. Except for Brother Tom's son Andrew, who was born some years after Simon. If I had known Tom did not want the name, I would have suggested it for our Simon.

What little we knew of our father I must scratch together and, even as I do, will wonder why neither my brother Tom nor sister Molly nor I asked so few questions. His remaining brothers and sisters said little about him, so that it seemed as though he may have detached himself from his family quite early in his young manhood. On the marriage certificate his profession was given as 'housepainter', but that may have been intermittent. Early on, he had enlisted – a common choice for unmarried working-class men, at a time when there was little or no unemployment benefit if you fell out of work. He served in the Boer War, a century ago by now, and was presumably in his early twenties then.

Most working-class families had myths, usually about how except for chance or the rigidity of authority they might have done better in life. Ours included the belief that Grandfather Hoggart, another mousta-chioed and quite dignified-looking man had, when a foreman in a steelworks, invented a crane which automatically tightened its grip on sheet metal as it lifted the sheets higher and higher. 'If everyone had their due,' was the choral line, 'we would have been rich'; but the firm copy-righted it and paid him nothing.

Similarly, our father was reputed to have contracted Maltese fever (brucellosis, a disease sometimes caught from drinking infected milk) during his war service. 'If everyone had their due ...', he would have been given a substantial pension. What he did between those two wars we do not know; perhaps housepainting. Some time early in the First World War he met our mother, one of your great-grandmothers, at Strensall Camp near York. He seems by that time to have become a sergeant in the army pay corps, perhaps because he was by then rather old for front-line service or because of the brucellosis; and presumably because he could handle figures.

They, the Hoggarts, said Adeline Long was working in the army canteen but they always insisted that she was not the 'ordinary' sort of army-canteen waitress. She belonged to a shopkeeping and therefore lower-middle-class or even mid-middle-class family, of Liverpool. It was in those days exceptional for an unmarried young woman to leave home and seek work elsewhere. Usually that meant there had been trouble, but no one ever gave a hint of that. Perhaps she had an unusual degree of self-reliance. The Hoggarts, who were slightly in awe of her while also admiring, said she was 'well spoken', very graceful (a cracked, 'studio' photograph bears that out), keeping herself to herself, 'proper'.

Tom used to say he had a vague memory of our father, holding or playing with him; neither Molly nor I remember him at all. We do not know what he did in the short period between the war's end and his death. We do not know whether it was he who found the Potternewton house; or never knew it. Our history began in the early twenties, in that cottage with a mother looking after the three of us, clustering; turned in upon ourselves.

We were aware of a very few neighbours, who came into the house now and then. But all in all we were separated, distinctive, poorer even than those around us. There were rumours that one or two people who knew or knew of us, the children, thought we ought to have somehow been placed elsewhere – with foster parents or adopted or in an orphanage – but that our mother fiercely resisted any such suggestion.

She seems to have had no help from her family or to have sought it; she was said to be too proud to beg or reveal her poverty to those relatives who had not enquired or to those she decided had no cause to know or might patronise her. She concentrated entirely on looking after her 'kids' (funny that that word, also applied to goats – 'kids' – sounds so tender when used of humans). We were properly nourished on next to nothing; cocoa, bread and dripping, porridge, stew with little meat but lots of vegetables; those were the basics. With condensed milk at a couple of 'old' pence (one new penny) a tin as an all-round sweetener.

We were cheerful; it did not occur to us that we had anything to be other than cheerful about. I remember, for instance, the three of us walking up to and across the main road to the cemetery. There was what we called 'the potted meat' slab, a flat gravestone of brown mottled marble on which sliding was easy.

I have no memory of our mother laughing but rather an impression of someone quietly spoken and always a bit 'down', as though the consumption ('pulmonary tuberculosis' on the death certificate) which eventually took her off was taking hold over a long time. But since we were, like almost all children who are not undernourished, resilient, we did not really notice that or make sense of it; we bounced around in our own ways, in or near the home.

The main dividing line from the neighbours was in the lack of money. Even in the twenties, one pound or a bit more from the Leeds Board of Guardians to feed and clothe four left little room for manoeuvre. Most of that was given in the form of grocery coupons, exchangeable, in our case, at the Maypole Grocery Stores, a branch of a cheap chain, half a mile down the road. To have given all in cash was, rightly, felt likely to have led some people to waste it on booze or fags.

Proud or not, our mother must have been willing to accept, even seek, permitted extra grants for exceptional needs, such as new clothing. It was one of the working-class traditions of the day that children had to have new clothes at Whitsuntide. Our aunts used to recall how she would then for a few pence take the tram across the city south to Grandma's in Hunslet, to 'show us off' in our new 'Whit best', with quiet and firm pride. Particularly the aunts remembered one year when Tom and I appeared in new little 'sailor suits', with bosun's whistles in the top left-hand pocket. She must have had a grant for that kind of thing, even though they would have cost only a pound or two.

What a shadowy figure I am drawing, but so it has to be. More or less forgotten or simply ignored by her own blood relatives, loved a little nervously by the Hoggarts who could do nothing or almost nothing to help, she just went on going on. Naturally, she loved us all but, like almost all mothers, she had a special tenderness, care, protective passion, for her only daughter.

From so few, one incident now emerges in the memory. We came in one day from a small trip whose purpose we did not know. We sat at tea and she drew a pair of simple, steel-rimmed – no doubt free – spectacles from her handbag and put them on Molly. Before our uncomprehending gaze her eyes filled with tears. She had no one to say such things to but, I realised years later, she was grieving that her daughter's lovely greyish-blue eyes were now to be shadowed.

It was entirely in character that when we saw her, in bed at St James's Hospital just before she died, she said – I think they were the last words we heard from her: 'Look after your sister.' It was also entirely within traditional attitudes that she did not say: 'Look after Molly.' 'Sister' expressed better the called-upon familial link and responsibility. Girls were more vulnerable in many ways, until they found a husband. Boys had more choice and freedom. We did, we have, tried to look after 'our sister'. As to her boys, I sometimes think of her pride if she had lived to see one become a headmaster, the other a professor.

Where did those genes come from? It would be easy to say: from the Liverpool shopkeepers. But the Hoggarts were not fools. Their horizons at that time stretched to no more than getting away from manual labour, to 'a white-collar job', and some arrived there. Of our generation, even

Tom had to fight hard to 'better himself' and did so quietly but persistently. I was all along the way given unsolicited lifts from people who went well beyond the call of duty to help me. In general, for those born into the late-nineteenth- and early-twentieth-century working-class, no matter how great their natural ability, there were few organised educational ladders.

For our mother through all that time there must have been constant deprivations, for herself but less for us (or less impression of deprivation), constant 'scrimping' and calculating; all is so much easier when you have a 'bit of play', of elbow room, in the weekly budget. We did not always understand why we never had that great working-class treat, fish and chips, or biscuits unless someone brought a few at Christmas. We badgered her from time to time. I remember tears coming into her eyes again at one such moment, about one thin slice of boiled ham which must have cost no more than tuppence (one new penny); a small personal treat to which she had succumbed. She did not hesitate to give us a little each, but it must have been an effort. She also managed to give us a Saturday ha'penny (one-fifth of a penny today), and that bought a handful of synthetically flavoured sweets.

School at five was 'all right'. The district had an old-fashioned, washed-up-on-the-shore, simplicity; not solidly working class, not in any way middle class, part old residents seeing their time out, part people who had somehow landed there – it was the sort of mixture that can encourage a kind of tolerant, refugees-together, air. The school up on the main road a quarter of a mile away had that air too; it remains in the memory as, compared with Hunslet, a gentle place.

Walking back home one day, just turning the corner to home, I looked over the few remaining fields opposite and saw a cow give birth. I guess that field lasted no more than ten years after we had left. The owner would make a fair deal of money; the developer put up closed-packed, private, probably fairly gimcrack, houses at only a few hundred pounds each; another lung had been closed.

In the last couple of decades Chapeltown, as it seems to be known now, has become one of the most disturbed parts of Leeds. It houses a great many immigrants, many unemployed and some deeply disaffected. It is a haunt of prostitutes and drug dealers; its members often part of the 'underclass' – those who have fallen through the fabric of society, such as it is. Our mother and her neighbours would have been astonished and shocked. That word, 'underclass', could not have been applied to us; we were working class and we were poor, but we were 'respectable'; we had a code.

Back to our childhood there. When we were daring, we went left up to the main road to watch the trams go by. At night we only saw them when our mother was bringing us back from, say, a winter visit to Hunslet. That was best of all. None of their successors has had the Venetian splendour of a fully lighted tram car sailing by in the rain on a December evening, clashing and clattering and throwing off electric sparks as it crossed the points. The people's gondolas. Not something to regret, their passing; but a splendid memory.

In the early twenties that road had few but a gradually increasing number of motor cars; our lane still saw them only occasionally. The most evidence article of 'street furniture' as these things are called by some professional observers these days, were horse-drawn carts; especially of the rag-and-bone men (that must have been a smelly trade, and it rubbed off on its practitioners). They gave only a few pence for an armful of old clothes or, to children for an especially large bundle, a tiny goldfish in a jam jar.

The clothes were taken ten miles or so west up towards the Pennine foothills to Dewsbury, which, since the late nineteenth century, had been te home of English 'shoddy' making. Their machines tore the cloth to shreds, sort of 'mashed' it into a material which could again be woven. It came out as a dull, hard, soon shiny, bluish-grey material which was cheap but not cheerful; hard-wearing though, shine or not. My own first long-trousered suit, at the age of about sixteen and brought with a charity cheque for one pound and ten shillings (1.50), was made of shoddy and I hated it. Some of the same machines were at work until at least the sixties, though now tended by the cheap labour of Pakistani immigrants. Then it sank to a remnant as artificial fibres took over. In Dewsbury they say that the finest soft West of England cloth still contains a few per cent of shoddy, to 'give it body'.

The only other place in Western Europe to make shoddy (and on similar machines) was Wuppertal in the German Ruhr. The army blankets of both nations were of shoddy. Odd to think of the soldiers of both countries sleeping and dying on blankets made from the recycled waste of both their Industrial Revolutions. Not an early form of environmental awareness; just a tiny by-product of capitalism, of the urge to make money from almost anything; small-time parasitism.

Horses and occasionally donkeys would leave their droppings at frequent intervals. They were quickly shovelled up by the first person who got to them; windowboxes, with rank nasturtiums the favourite flowers, thrived on a shovelful.

Immediately over the main road was a walled institution, a government hospital for the war-disabled. Men came and went all the time, hobbling on wooden legs, manipulating metal arms; the leftovers of the War. I have only in one other place felt with such immediacy the pitiful, everyday, lasting legacy of war; that was when I first visited Paris a dozen years later and noticed the specially reserved seats on the Métro for the mutilated, and was shocked at the evidence of France's greater losses. Otherwise that evidence was in itself not new; we had lived near it from early childhood.

In 1926 we first saw a little of industrial unrest, in the General Strike. There was a tram depot about a quarter of a mile up the main road. Now and again we watched the trams being manhandled on the turntable inside there. Just before we left Potternewton for good, someone said the tram men were 'out'. We went up and saw them gathered outside the big doors, talking quietly; no placards, no aggression, no strike-breaking; not there, at least.

If she had been politically interested, I imagine our mother would have voted Conservative; not deferentially Conservative but Conservative because she believed in standing on your own two feet, being responsible for yourself, not assuming rights whose costs were paid by someone else; and knowing from local experience that not everyone lived by those lights.

We were in that nest until Tom was ten, Molly just six and I eight. I am surprised by how little I can remember of events and things (and have only a slight idea of what unconscious principle makes me retain those I do remember). I have a vague idea of our furniture: a plain, probably deal, table, an old armchair, a few upright chairs, a recessed stone window ledge with sketchy curtains. A general sense of the simple and, I suppose, impoverished atmosphere is what I best remember, as focused by particular incidents, such as those of the slice of boiled ham and the metal glasses for Molly. Incidents which took us by surprise and began our education in the feelings, especially of frustration, love, pity and grief.

Few other memories. One or two photos with 'Mam' in ankle-length black dresses and, for special outings, a big hat with a couple of feathers.

She must sometimes have raged within at what a hard hand fate had dealt her. Many miles from her original home, alone with three children, almost as poor as it was possible to be. Our aunts used to say that her favourite Liverpool relative was her brother Dick (after whom I was probably named). He had a shop and it was darkly hinted that before her marriage she had lent him all she could spare to start that business and had not been paid back. 'If everyone had their due ...'. He never, so far as we knew, came to see her, or wrote, or sent money. I hope I am wrong in that; and have one later, better memory of him.

It is just possible that one or two of the Longs have by now seen the name 'Hoggart' in the newspapers or heard it on the radio and felt a faint echo at the back of their minds. If so, not one of them has felt moved to follow that echo. It is difficult to feel warm towards the Longs of Liverpool.

Tom and I did have one contact, to their credit, two or three years after we left Potternewton. We were asked to spend a week with, I think, Uncle Dick. I recall a sizeable terrace house with stained glass in the front door and what seemed a long hall. We were treated not unkindly, but as if there was a clear plastic screen between us and them; perhaps they were unwittingly hoping we would not claim squatters' rights.

Clearer is a teatime visit during that trip to a cousin who had married quite well, to an officer on one of the banana boats plying between Liverpool and the Canary Islands. The house was 'comfortable'; there were two well-dressed children; a sense of satisfaction with life. And caution. They were not unkind to us, but neither were they very warm. We were sort-of-objects who were being watched and judged, but towards whom they felt some slight and temporary duty. For tea, there was a large plaice and chips for the father; the four children had chips and bread. Not the kind of division we had much seen in Potternewton or Hunslet. That might have been the practice if money was very tight and dad in heavy work; even then most would have been likely to push a little of the fish to the children. It rang meanly in that Liverpool house. We saw and heard no more of the Longs.

When the cottage was cleared on our mother's death, were there any letters, and if so where did they go? I know of none. Only a couple of letters in her hand and perhaps one or two from her husband to her might have transformed our understanding. How did they write to each other? Was he reasonably literate? I simply assume, but do not know, that she was. There was nothing; except that much later a Hoggart relative gave me our father's small pocket Bible, a relic of his war service. It is inscribed: 'God bless you To Tom Hoggart from his loving wife Addie. 17/9/15. May God watch over you and keep you safe.' There were virtually no other remains. It probably didn't take much more than a couple of hours entirely to empty that cottage.

The unseeingness of children is astonishing. Our mother must have been going downhill increasingly during the half-decade or so she was alone with us. I seem to remember her coughing frequently, but that could be a retrospective illusion. We had no sense of her going steadily to the point at which she reached 'death's door'. Did she herself realise this? Consumption was a frequent ailment and almost as frequent a killer. At some moment she must have realised that the end could not be far off.

Tom, who is dead now, told me he used occasionally to be sent to a nearby shop for five Woodbines, the cheapest cigarettes. They cost only tuppence (one new penny) even in the late thirties; perhaps less even than that in the early twenties. Strictly speaking, she could not afford them and they would do her chest no good. But who would be sufficiently self-righteous as to begrudge her that bit of pleasure?

So there we are: she remains a shadow, a wraith; in memory slightly severe, as she had to be; not greatly demonstrative but gentle; low-key; washed up in one of the more obscure minor reaches of a big and alien city; never doubting where her path and duty lay; claiming very few 'rights', unless she felt one was real, and justified, legitimate, or was desperate, but accepting many duties; bringing up three children, healthy and happy in spite of all their impoverishment, for the few years left to her after her husband's death.

The death came on 15 February 1927. I had found her lying unconscious on the clip-rug, on coming in from school. At least that has always been one of my apparently clearer memories. Molly thinks it was she who found her and may be right; memory plays tricks with us all. Or she may have picked the memory up from me and unknowingly adopted it. 'Addie' was taken into the nearby, huge, St James's Hospital and soon died there.

She was forty-seven. The city authorities buried her two days later in what the death certificate, which I obtained many years later, records as the graveyard of St Matthew's Church. That now deserted graveyard, not physically connected to the new church which is a mile away, contains no 'Hoggart'. She was, I had at last to realise, probably laid in an unmarked paupers' grave; with others at the entirely untended and unmarked area up against the back wall.

The main Hoggart relatives looked after things that day, little though there was to look after. There were, I think, two people from Liverpool. Tom remembered standing at the grave, with Molly and me held on either hand.

We all went back over the mucky river Aire to Hunslet that afternoon. The question, which was soon spoken, was: 'What's to be done with the kids?' One of the Hoggart aunts told me much later that the Liverpool two contributed: 'Orphanages are very good nowadays.' Grandma Hoggart dismissed that at once; it was entirely against the ways of working-class life. We were 'family' and we stayed family. How could they have rested with the thought of those children taken to an *institution*? We would remain in the family, though we would have to be dispersed.

The answer seemed to have been reached quickly. Tom, I suppose because he was the oldest, would go thirty miles away, to Sheffield. Alice, the second of Grandma's children, lived there with husband and eleven children.

That left Molly and me. I think it would have been best for Molly to have stayed at Grandma's, since she was, not surprisingly, the most unsure of herself. I had a speech impediment and was also thought to be a funny little lad, so perhaps that tipped the scales. I stayed with Grandma and Molly went to a widowed great-aunt in the next back-to-back street. She was, again, a working-class woman with many of the limitations which can go with lack of education; though not, I think, unkind.

Molly proved to be 'bright' but the great-aunt could not see further for her than a job in the mills such as her unmarried daughter, living at home, had. I was near and could provide some support.

So, in mid-February of 1927, that set of decisions ended the first phase of our lives and opened the second. The Longs had departed, as to another planet; Tom had gone; Molly was in the next street. I began life with Grandma, an unmarried daughter and an unmarried son. We were soon joined by one of the Sheffield daughters in her late teens; even in the unemployment-ridden thirties there were jobs for seamstresses in the large Leeds clothing factories. Ivy, a quite good-looking, good-natured and phlegmatic girl, stayed with us until she married Alf, an equally good-natured and phlegmatic Leeds barber; in the meantime she went home to Sheffield as often as money allowed, taking Alf as soon as their relationship became settled. It may have been a crowded Sheffield home, but she made for it like a homing pigeon. It gripped them all and the Hunslet house was not, on the whole, a happy place. After marriage, Ivy and Alf spent a few years in Leeds, but as soon as a job in Sheffield appeared, back there they went and stayed for the rest of their lives. They had no children but were a good aunt and uncle to their many nephews and nieces.

At just short of nine years old, I started at the new school, Jack Lane Elementary. Jack Lane was about a quarter of a mile from and roughly parallel with Hunslet Road, which ran south from the city centre. Our street ran between and connected the two. Once out of the centre and over the black, rat-ridden River Aire, the great heavy industries began; interspersed with them and running at right angles off each side of that main artery were street after street of cheap brick back-to-back houses. Most had been privately built anything up to fifty or more years before. The Hammonds in their history of those times aptly called them 'the barracks of industry'. Most houses were let by petty entrepreneur land-lords for less than ten shillings (fifty pence) a week. I notice that council houses in Farnham now cost over fifty pounds a week, apparently more than one hundred times as much. Even allowing for the difference in the value of money, those Hunslet houses seem cheap. Or were they? Perhaps not. Manual workers today earn seventy to a hundred times, in notional not real terms, than their grandfathers earned in the thirties. And their council houses are far superior to the back-to-backs.

Being huddled together, the streets had a busy life of their own: rent and insurance collectors; sellers of 'clothing checks' for 'Whit', weddings and funerals, since most people could not save enough for those times or for Christmas, or for holidays (though few rose to those); debt-collectors, hire-purchase agents, rag-and-bone men, ice-cream vans, Friday fish carts.

32 Newport Street was very slightly superior. It was an end house in a row of six or eight, which backed on to the wall of St Joseph's Roman Catholic School, though separated for all except us from that by a strip

of garden about four yards deep. Not much gardening there, but some pigeons and rabbits. At the side of our house was a double gate leading to an L-shaped concreted yard where, I was told, Grandad – by then dead – used to keep a handcart. At each end of the row, up against the school wall were two earth closets (converted to water in my day), one to each pair of houses, and a midden. No toilet paper; that would have been a waste of money. Just the *News of the World* torn up and on a string. Good for reading there on a warm day.

At some stage an attic had been carved out of our house and, no doubt later, a free-standing bath had been put up there, with a wooden 'clothes horse' covered in coloured wallpaper to ensure privacy. So there was a double distinction; space and a bath. Uncle Bert and I slept in the attic, the others were disposed in the two first-floor bedrooms, one sizeable, the other quite small. When daughters of families in the row were about to be married, they used our bath the night before the wedding. Otherwise, one had an all-over wash in the scullery.

Jack Lane School was rough in a rough district. Virtually all the boys (the girls were in a separated part of the building) assumed they would go into heavy industry just down the road. At, say, the Hunslet Engine Works which made engines for all over the world. I saw them in Argentina in the mid-nineties; and saw at the works, in the early nineties, uniquely powerful electric engines designed to carry the earth up from the Channel Tunnel workings.

Those boys did not feel they were an underclass, as many in today's Hunslet feel, now that most who can afford it, even if they still work in Hunslet, have decamped, often to mortgaged homes, in their own third- or fourth-hand cars. Those in work, a majority until the slump of the thirties, could manage reasonably well. They were likely to call themselves 'working class and proud of it'. They often had a craft which demanded skill as well as sweat; it was work only a strong man could do and they were proud of that. At the midday break they squatted against the wall of the works, looking at the traffic, smoking, eating their corned-beef-and-pickle sandwiches and talking about Hunslet Rugby Club. They were self-assured, sort of aristocrats.

That compact area could provide almost a whole way of life of the sort they knew and were satisfied with: corner shops, plenty of pubs, working men's clubs, 'Panel' doctors (free, or charging very low fees), regular and cheap trams into town; interweaving gossip for the wives, street play for the children, local elementary schools. Those who could afford an annual week's holiday went to Blackpool or Morecambe; others might get a change of air by going to stay with relatives in the country or even in another big town.

They felt, in both admirable and less admirable ways, not so much like a 'community' (that much abused word comes from another mental world) as a more or less closed group. They disliked 'Them', the authorities and the better-off people up Roundhay way. Themselves, they belonged to 'Us' and could if pushed be aggressive about that. Within their groups they could, especially the women, practise neighbourliness. Some of the men became drunkards, or violent brutes, or adulterers; and many became soft and lost in old age; Othello's occupation gone.

Their sons usually admired them and wanted to 'take after them'; tough work, wenching before marriage, weekend boozing, watching ruby and all. That was the desired whole way of life. For almost all, any hints of the intellectual life, the imaginative life, even the political life were, it almost goes without saying, closed worlds which they had no wish to enter. They were secure in their all-embracing culture, confident.

So Jack Lane was a rough school, though not excessively so. I had three disadvantages which would be likely to attract bullies: I was small; I 'spoke better' than they did. Potternewton's speech differed from Hunslet's. Worst of all, I had a speech impediment which made me unable to articulate 'l' and 'r' and so sounded a bit Bertie Woosterish. There had to be some ritualistic roughing-up of the newcomer, 'Hoggie'. That was led by a thin, rat-faced boy, aggressive and wounded and so one kind of playground gang-leader. His favourite form of attack had the Leeds stamp. Leeds working-class people, and for all I know, the middle class too, were, as I have implied, deeply ambiguous to the Jews in their midst. They sort-of-respected them while resenting their hard work, enterprise, and mutual help buttressed by a strong sense of family. They suspected that Jewish sexual habits were more sophisticated than their own. They were convinced that Jews were 'sharp' (their synonym for rapacious), all out for money.

The rat-faced boy came over to me and squared up for a fight by first of all calling me 'sheeny', the routine insulting word for a Jew. I do not remember whether we fought; I do remember standing up to him and saying I was no more a Jew than he was. That was the first time I found in myself an absolute refusal to give way. He was apparently thrown off course by the stubbornness, the accent and the articulateness, and, with his group, moved away a little. Nowadays, I suppose he might have drawn a knife. That was my first lesson in a truth which provided my best weapon throughout the time at that school; a facility with words could sometimes disconcert bullies as much as a straight left.

Back to number 32. The centre of the household was Grandma. She must have been well over seventy when they took me in and on. Not that I could have been called a difficult boy; but I soon showed that I was going to be a strange one to them, nosing my way blindly to worlds they did not know. But there was love there, on both sides, and that made up for a lot. I never heard Grandma raise her voice, but I often saw her sad, and with good reason.

Soon after I arrived the elder of her two unmarried daughters, Clara, who had for some years worked in a women's outfitters fifteen miles away in Huddersfield, came back home and found work in one of the clothing factories. She was soon made a 'passer', an approver of the work of a line of seamstresses. She must have been a tough nut at that job. She had made a women friend in Huddersfield and they remained partners for life, exchanging weekends at each other's homes. They were well suited to each other.

So now, with Ivy, there were six of us and seven on some week-ends. The two not so far described were Aunt Lil, a nervous, gentle woman who all her life suffered from erysipelas, an inflammation of the skin; and Uncle Herbert, who was a salesman in a furniture shop in the centre of Leeds, and had a good tenor voice, much in demand for chapel oratorios. The stage was set for endless recurring battles. Aunt Clara was a congenital and violent jacket-straightener; Aunt Lil didn't want to 'row' with anyone but took a lot of the flak; Ivy walked through it all, inviolate, her head full of Alf and Sheffield; I sat at the living-room table trying to get on with my homework; Herbert regularly drank after work and came in late to an overcooked supper and a barrage of denunciation; Grandma sat near the fire, rubbing her hands one over the other in distress.

As I soon half realised, Grandma loved me but was anxious not to be soft with me; so did Aunt Lil, in her bemused and soft-hearted way; and Clara in her tortured way. Clara hated much in her life and knew she could have done better (she did, years later, in partnership with her friend Elsie, running a woman's clothes shop); she could not until then afford to live away from home and anyway had a strong bump of daughterly duty, especially since she did not trust any of the others. Her life was largely angry and unhappy.

Aunt Lil was entirely less demanding and more intuitive in her kindnesses. She arranged for me to meet her at her workplace in Holbeck once a year when Holbeck Feast (the third largest fair in Britain, it was said) was on, so as to have an hour there before going home together. Aunt Clara would probably have liked to do that, but her sense of propriety forbade it. The seamstresses might have seen her. Aunt Lil was saved also by a surrealist sense of humour. She picked up and pocketed mad images like a gifted squirrel. So I loved her uncomplicatedly; hers was an undemanding affection, whereas with Aunt Clara one had to navigate, negotiate through angry seas to reach her narrow, obstacle-strewn, loving landfalls; and even then you might be repulsed.

Late in the thirties Lil was wooed by a widowed coalminer with six children. Clara erupted at this, believing the union below our status, so fine were the gradings between parts of the working class. I think Grandma felt, as I did, that all in all that was a better fate for Lil than staying at home.

I don't want to give the impression that Hunslet was simply a rough and unpleasant place. In many ways it was friendly, mutually protective and self-respecting. There were tough parts two or three streets from us; mainly families of Irish labourers who had, we believed, been tempted over originally as 'navvies' ('navigators', who dug the canals and later laid the railway lines). They were Catholics and that was why we had St Joseph's Catholic Elementary School just over Grandma's back wall. Years later, I met a man who had been a pupil there; by then translated into a professor of sociology. Another from the same streets was the actor Peter O'Toole. We didn't mix with 'the Catholic lot' but maintained a kind of guarded respect and keeping of distance.

When I went to grammar school, the first inhabitant of those streets to do so, most were quite impressed. Early on, some of the lads liked to knock off my silly grammar-school cap (chocolate brown with crossed banana stripes – a marked badge of distinction). I do not remember being upset; I simply put my cap in my trouser pocket when I got near our streets on the way home. Many years later, when the Jack Lane Elementary School had moved and the buildings became the home of a local-authority athletic centre, I was in the office of the

Director of Education for Leeds. He showed me the honours board from the school, with my name as that of the first who reached grammar school.

Having homework to do each evening, I had to leave the groups playing in the streets, but never minded that. I had become interested in other things. Yet was there little social life, even at weekends? There was the Parkfield Picture Palace along Jack Lane, for Saturday, matinées at threepence or sixpence. Molly often came over. The Primitive Methodist Chapel, near the corner where Newport Street met Jack Lane, was the most important social centre. Sunday school was run by a deeply believing spinster, blind from birth. We respected and loved her because of her own loving spirit. Making a film about Hunslet in the mid-1980s, we found her. She was by then over ninety, still managing on her own. I knocked, walked in and said hello to her. Before I had spoken my name she said: 'It's Bert. I'd know your voice anywhere.'

One or two well-intentioned bodies made it part of their practice to help poor children. Leeds Rotary Club had a camp for poor boys (I do not remember if girls were included) in Silverdale, near the Lake District. I expect the members felt all the better when they voted the money for the camp each year. They were not very attentive to the way the camp was run. It was in the hands of a large man, his wife and helpers. In principle, some thought had gone into what we might need. Each of us was handed a pair of stout boots on arrival but size was decided by a quick glance. If anyone came back to say their boots didn't fit, they were casually told to swap around till they found some which did. That was typical of a sort of offhand near-cruelty which pervaded the place, a small-minded heartlessness, typified also by the fact that the staff ate very well, much better than we did. I have had only two other experiences of Rotary Clubs, each marked – though on these occasions in the members themselves – by a kind of self-assured insensitivity. Oddly, on each of those subsequent occasions, the Rotarians had invited me to be their guest of honour – giving them a free talk after one of their regular lunches; and being treated, during lunch, to the self-important, insensitive ponderousness of a Hull city doctor, and the racism of a London city businessman.

A happier act of charity appeared after, I think, about two years at Cockburn High (grammar) School. I contracted pneumonia and, once over the worst, was sent by the local authority for one or two weeks at a

convalescent home in Bridlington. The rubric was that walks in a croco-
dile through the fresh sea air and nutritious food (I had that at home but
most didn't) would do us all good. I remember hardly anything of the
other boys except for one typical oaf who, unnoticed by the staff (he had
the usual low cunning), bullied boys younger than himself. Much more
important was a very gentle nurse who was kind to all of us beyond
anything I had experienced at, say, Silverdale. I came away unwittingly
but strongly moved by that early experience of unself-regarding, natural
charity from outsiders. It is plain that experiences such as the behaviour
of the Liverpool relatives at our mother's funeral, of those who ran the
camp at Silverdale and one or two others are particularly known to
orphans from time to time unless they are very lucky. It is the sense of
being at one remove from the most close of all ties, that to a mother and
father, of being in the second line, the one who has to be thought about
as an act of will; or not thought about except casually. You register it in
tones of voice, in particular words and gestures; you do, *they* probably do
not.

To have something of your own, something to love and be continually loved by, then becomes an unconscious search. There was love in the
Newport Street house, certainly; from Grandma, from Aunt Lil and in her
complex way from Aunt Clara. But even that was not quite what one was
after. And it was set against the constant fights. Uncle Bert was drinking;
Aunt Clara was back home from Huddersfield to work in Leeds. The
spark and the tinder met.

That kind of love came in the shape of a little, timid, brown mongrel.
Strange that I have only recently recalled her. I do not remember where
she appeared from. It was a great kindness that they let me have her; there
wasn't really room for her. Perhaps they realised without putting it into
words that I needed such an object of total and reciprocal affection. She, of
course, became my shadow. Inevitably, since she had never been to a vet,
she became pregnant. They cleared a little cupboard at floor level next to
the fireplace and there she gave birth to three or four. I remember giving
her, as she lay there, milk on a saucer while she intermittently licked my
hand. I remember no more. Was she lost, run over, stolen; or did she just
die? The way memory works surprises me more and more.

The unprompted kindness of the young nurse at Bridlington was the
first in a line of five or six such people, apart from family, who I now
belatedly see have run through my life, who went out of their way to be

kind, to give me a leg-up. They knew I wasn't in very advantageous circumstances; I was small and had that lisp which invited mockery from some other boys; they thought I was also 'bright', 'very promising' and conscientious. They could have noticed all that, registered sympathy, and passed on. They stopped and helped.

I have just realised that, in a small way, the manager of the Sunshine Grocers' branch near us was one of the first in that line – when he asked me to tea at his little semi, partly out of unaffected and not publicly prompted kindness, partly to indicate to what I might aspire. By contrast, the Rotary Club had meant well, but their charity had a distanced, impersonal quality to it. Unexamined charity can do more harm than good.

Mr Harrison, the headmaster at Jack Lane, was near retirement when I arrived. Moustachioed, dressed in a dark, striped two-piece suit, he looked like a bank cashier. How he had landed in that rough school I do not know, but I never doubted his authority or his commitment. He seems to have thought after a few months that I must just be the one who would at last – and be the first – to pass the eleven-plus exam from his school and go on to grammar school.

The first hint we had of this silent laying-on of hands appeared when I took pneumonia and, as was often the case in those days, nearly died. They put me on a bed in the living-room and called the Panel doctor. Afterwards I learned that one evening before going across the city to home Mr Harrison had called to ask how I was. Astonished, they asked him in; indeed, it was a remarkable gesture. At this point it would be routine for me to ask rhetorically whether the headmaster of a slum elementary school (not that it would be called that today) would do that nowadays. The answer would have to be 'I hope so', not automatically to assume the contrary. Grandma and the others seem to have realised either from something the headmaster said, or from the mere fact of his making the visit, that he thought particularly well of me as a pupil.

He paid me at least one more special attention, but unrevealed until long afterwards; he was a true professional of his day. He put me in for the eleven-plus exams. At ten and a half on a bitterly cold winter day, I walked over what was antiquatedly called 'Hunslet Moor' (it was by then a few acres of black clinker) to sit papers in arithmetic and English. I failed the first, having been taught by an incompetent. Four years later I took a distinction in maths in the matriculation exam. That was of no use in 1930. I was not awarded a scholarship.

Unknown to me, Mr Harrison moved firmly again. He went down to the education offices in the city centre, carrying an essay of mine, to insist on my ability. Whether an officer there read the essay, looked up and said: 'Yes, indeed, this lad should have a scholarship'; or whether they looked at Mr Harrison and said to themselves: 'Poor old chap. He's near retirement and never had a success at eleven-plus. Let's give him one' – of that I will never know the truth; and do not remember where I heard about the visit down town.

But both of us were very happy. Mr Harrison retired with something of the honour he sought; I was full of trepidation but knew that that was where I ought to go, wherever it might lead. I did not dislike Hunslet or the people in it, but knew I must leave. Sometimes even now I wonder, perhaps in a plane or car on a solitary journey, what would have been the shape of my life if I had stayed at Jack Lane until I was fourteen and then gone into the working world. I suppose I would have broken somehow, as have very many before and after.

So Mr Harrison was the first main giver, outside the family, of a lift on the way. In a different manner so was the doctor, the young and at that time little known Dr Cook. The best-known doctor in the area lived opposite the school, in one of Hunslet's very few large houses. Of stone, with an attached coach house, it had almost certainly been built in the mid- to late nineteenth century for one of the few professionals who lived in the area. He was old, very distinguished-looking and rather forbidding in manner; a great city personality. Other than that, since he was not our doctor, I remember only two things about him: that his wine and spirits were regularly delivered by van; and that in assembly one morning Mr Harrison told us that the doctor opposite had been awarded the Freedom of the City and that he, Mr Harrison, had gone over to offer him the whole school's congratulations.

Dr Cook was of another generation and breed. A soft-spoken and gentle Irishman, he had with his sister, Dr Jessie, put up his plate right down on the noisy Hunslet Road. They must have known they would attract almost entirely working-class people, many of them poor, and likely to run up debts. Hunslet soon discovered that they were 'a lovely couple', which meant dedicated and in every aspect unthreatening.

I learned many years later, and without surprise, that the Cooks had continued their life of devotion, in Britain and far afield. They intervened or tried to intervene crucially in Molly's and my life. When I had pneumonia, the brother called in each day until the one on which he told Grandma: 'The crisis will be tonight.' She knew, as did virtually everyone in those days, that you either passed through the crisis to recovery or died. Dr Cook appeared, after his surgery and visits, late that evening and sat with me until the small hours, when I began to breathe steadily. He then said: 'He's over it. He will be all right now'; and left.

Dr Jessie's attempt at intervention was unsuccessful. She had formed an affection for Molly and thought her clever, mild-natured and rather lost. She told the half-aunt that she would like to adopt Molly and bring her up as her own daughter. The offer was refused, with some heat. No doubt a mixture of reasons and emotions led to that refusal; I do still regret it very much.

So I began a new day-time life at Cockburn; and, as is common with 'only children' and especially with those who live within an older-than-usual family, the school became the centre and pivot of my life, the opening to a world our bookless home had never envisaged, a succession of realisations that the world is bigger, wider, more varied, more free and challenging, than I had up to that time conceived. 'An eye-opener', in a sadly revealing Hunslet phrase.

As I cleared te back-to-back streets each morning, passed over the bridge at Hunslet station and the works yard whose wall had a plaque commemorating the dead from cholera in the middle of the previous century, over Hunslet Moor and up a few better-set-up streets of houses to the school, so I left behind, in spirit, one life; and braced, opened, myself expectantly for the emerging one. That district of about 30,000 people had the one 1902 Act grammar school and took in one or perhaps two classes of thirty each year. One or two entered as fee-payers, at a minute sum; most were selected racehorses sent by the city which, of course, owned the school. There must have been some clever children who fell just outside the free limit chosen by the city and whose places were taken by the fee-payers who could not enter on merit but whose parents ran small shops, were foremen or had loving grandparents with a bit of money to spare.

The teachers were specialists, some gifted, some crammers, virtually all graduates. Some inspired you, others force-fed you. Grammar-school jobs were hard to get in those days, so one met a few of an entirely new breed, Southerners. The French mistress, a model of her kind, told us she was from 'Virginia Water'. I imagined a lovely lake with Lutyensesque houses, around whose shore strolled people with soft accents such as I had never met before. In general, the staff saw us as promising material picked out of the working class and destined, perhaps, to go on to slightly higher things; probably at the limit to a teacher-training college and teaching below the grammar-school level. They were restricted expectations but not undignified or self-seeking; there was a sense of service hidden within them.

At Cockburn there appeared two more of the Encouragers. One was, predictably I now see, Mr Kerry, the English teacher. I say 'predictably' because I was already becoming preoccupied with words, whether in poetry or prose. They were to become, pre-eminently, my way out. Teachers of English, unless they go against the light, are the great openers of the imagination. Self-evidently.

Mr Kerry, I would guess, especially from his accent, was from the respectable Yorkshire working or lower-middle class. He was not an inspired teacher, but he was sound and respectful towards his material, whether that was books or pupils. He organised each year a week's camp, in bell tents, in a field owned by Flowers the brewers at Stratford on Avon, so that three or four plays could be seen. It did not occur to me that I might go. But one day he called me over and said I could go for nothing. He had arranged a 'whip-round' in the staff room; and told me that this was to be kept 'sub rosa' (a magical phrase). Believing, like a good Yorkshireman, that you didn't – shouldn't – get 'owt for nowt', he added that the condition was that I write a report on the week for publication in the *Cockburnian*. I reread it some years ago and almost, but not quite, blushed at how as a thirteen- or fourteen-year-old my attraction to language had led me into a range of fancy-but-ponderous cliché images. Samuel Butler of *The Way of All Flesh* was the first to start pulling me out of that mode.

At about that time Mr Kerry pointed north out of the classroom window and told me that, if I 'played my cards right', I might one day live up there, in Roundhay. The limits held. He was, of course, delighted when I did well enough in the Higher Certificate exam at eighteen to gain a Senior City scholarship to Leeds University. That city of half a million gave thirty such scholarships a year; there was no question of going to any university other than Leeds. That was in 1936, when your grandma and I both went to read English there, she from the other side of the Pennines.

By chance, in 1939–40 your grandma, as part of her postgraduate training course for teaching, was assigned to Cockburn for her school practice. Mr Kerry soon asked her if she knew Hoggart. She said she did. By that time we had been going out together for three years, but she felt no need to expand on that to Mr Kerry. One evening we went to see a play at the Leeds Grand Theatre, in 'the gods' (the gallery) of course. The next morning Mr Kerry accosted her as though she had been wilfully keeping a momentous secret from him. He'd been at the play with a school party and seen her 'with Hoggart!'.

Among other omissions about which I feel shame, I regret that I never wrote to Mr Kerry – say, when I became a professor – or sent him a copy of one of my books. I thought of him frequently, with respect and gratitude. Perhaps I did write and have forgotten. That has happened more than once with other people. So I can only hope it did with Mr Kerry.

The other special helper was not so close or continuous. At some point in my time at Cockburn a new headmaster appeared. He had taught at Dulwich College. I do not know what led him to seek the headship of a Northern grammar school in a working-class area. He was, as we realised later, slightly other-worldly. He left the school not long after I did; to become an Anglican monk, it was said. It was also said that one year he forgot to send in the school's completed papers for the Higher School Certificate exam. That may have been an invention, a backhanded tribute to his remote abstractedness.

I have only one sharp memory of an encounter but it proved to be – seminal, I suppose one would say. Mr Kerry, I imagine it was, fell ill one week, when I was in the sixth form. The headmaster, gowned, swept in on the small group and told us to write an essay on some author we admired, and left. I wrote on Hardy, one of whose novels was a set text; that had led me further. The essays were handed to the head's secretary.

A day or two later I passed his office as he was coming out. 'Ah, Hoggart,' he said, 'Your essay begins "Thomas Hardy was a truly cultured man ...". What does "cultured" mean there? Am I "cultured", I wonder ...' and so on. That was an important double illumination. I had until then never seen a mind at work handling an intellectual abstraction and, more, trying to relate it to his own life; and, though I realised this only much later, I was just beginning to see – indeed, I was groping towards this insight in going out on to the semantic deeps with that one word, 'culture' – something of its ambiguous meanings and its relationships to intellectual and eventually social status and their cultural forms. I remember no more of Mr Norden but remain grateful to him and still impressed by his skill as a teacher, a mind-opener.

So: home each night to the living-room table to do homework. A limitation? No warm and quiet room to work in? In some ways it was constricting, and when the exams began to loom I went to the study room in the new Hunslet Public Library. But one side of me liked to be in the middle of the family and its talk. I imagine it was no more or less of a distraction than is the pop music in a warm bedroom which is said to accompany much homework today. So I was intrigued, and pleased, not long ago to see our granddaughter Amy doing her homework on the end of the table in the eating area off the kitchen/breakfast room, while family talk went on all around her. She preferred that, I was told; and understood.

There were other, extra-mural, openings in those years. Such as the occasional autodidact, one of the very few in the streets who had his own shelf of books, and who liked to talk about his most recent intellectual discovery. One of them introduced me to Pelmanism – associational memory control and recall, I suppose it might be called; or an early form of lateral thinking. It still comes in useful occasionally.

Above all was the opening by a local Labour MP, Arthur Greenwood, of the new Hunslet Public Library. Right in the middle of the district. Looked back at from the end of the century, it stands out as a remarkable indicator of trust in the power of books and the potentialities of people living in the most unpromising circumstances.

A few of us, grammar-school pupils and autodidacts especially but also lonely old widowers, immediately made it a part of our lives. Above all, for me, it introduced poetry. Through Swinburne, which I picked out by chance and was immediately – one can hardly say 'entranced' or 'enchanted' these days, so 'caught up by' must do. Thus it was, from the first line: 'When the hounds of Spring are on Winter's traces ...'. It was an introduction to the taproot of literature: the love of words.

The introduction to music came more casually. Someone gave me an old wind-up gramophone. I bought for sixpence from a market stall a record of the violin-haunted entr'acte from Verdi's *La Traviata*. Conducting to that up in the attic lasted for months.

Meanwhile at home, life went on in its increasingly unhappy way. The terrible angers, the only-just-avoided shame as Herbert went downhill – and brooding miserably over it all, sitting in her chair near the fire-place, Grandma; rubbing her hands one over the other as if to smooth it all out. Herbert, the youngest of her ten, with the good tenor voice and good brain, had been the love of her early middle age and onwards.

Of course, I did not know at the time the role I began to play in this backstreet Greek tragedy. Herbert she still loved, until she died. But also she began to put hope and love in me and my progress. I was another 'bright' member of the family who might go on to great things, so long as she did not 'squander' his talent.

So, with all the love, she could be stern about any falling-off she thought she detected; I mustn't go Herbert's way. She was sparing with praise, but occasionally I heard her saying to a relative or neighbour: 'Bert seems to be doing well at school.' And she told everything of this sort to Miss Jubb, the regular visitor from the city's Board of Guardians.

One well-remembered week I particularly cherish. There was no chance of a holiday at the seaside. But it was arranged, when I was about twelve, that she and I would go fifteen miles away to Harrogate where one of her sons, married but childless, had a job in a 'select' men's outfit-ters. Uncle Harry. A sad man, as it proved; when the war came, he was sacked without mercy by his employers of many years; presumably they, having sold the business, settled back into their comfortable villas and thought no more of Hoggart. 'He got paid each week, didn't he?'

Harry's wife was a rather silent person. She took in dressmaking and that occupied the whole of the 'front room' of their small 'semi'. The back living room had a tiny fire and we were usually cold, the more so since a fat little terrier stretched itself out in front of the fire all the time. The food was somewhat sparse. One day Grandma decided that we would go for a walk; that must have been one of the few walks she had taken for other than dutiful purposes since she had started to have her ten children. Though there was a purpose on this occasion: to buy me an apple. I talked most of the time.

Uncle Harry was a soft and soft-hearted man, a perfect victim for the sort of treatment his employers subjected him to, in the times before he could have had much protection from a trade union. Perhaps he would have objected to any such help. I imagine he was deeply conservative with both a lower-case and a capital first letter. He was shown an army airmail letter from me in Italy telling my aunts among much else that I had been promoted to captain. Whatever else he said then I do not know;

they told me he'd volunteered that if I really wanted to 'get on', I would need to have a better 'hand' (handwriting). But a well-meant and kindly man.

Back to Cockburn High School and the four years to matric (School Certificate). In spite of the tensions at home – much eased also by affection – school was a happy time; as in a different way grammar school was for your grandma over the same years. Her home was loving and protective, but being an only child is often a lonely business. Manchester High School for Girls made up for that, abundantly.

My particular friend at Cockburn was a boy of immense self-assurance, Stanley Binner. His mother had I think been deserted by her husband, leaving her with two or perhaps three children. She had to work for their living. In those days the State did not offer anything like adequate help. The only available work was 'charring', being a 'charwoman' – cleaning other people's homes or various kinds of institutions, such as schools. Mrs Binner became a cleaner at Cockburn. Many of the boys there would have been ashamed by that and afraid it might become known. Not Binner. He made no attempt to conceal the situation. He was a sturdy youth and it was silently known throughout the school that if any boys sneered at the revelation Binner would knock their blocks off. He did not do well enough at eighteen to win a university place, so began work as some sort of technical trainee at the Yorkshire Copper Works just down the road. He should have been nicknamed 'Binner the Beaver', for within a year he had sorted out a scholarship to allow him to read one of the sciences at Leeds. The first time I ran into him there he told me with his usual assurance that, taking over his mother's maiden name, he had registered as 'Stanley Peel-Binner' since he thought double-barrelled names impressive. We lost touch after graduation, but I think he went on to a good technical career. He was staunchly protective towards his mother and, I think, sister. Though of much the same age, he was more mature than I was; not a bookish boy but one who confronted life unabashedly and cheerfully. He was one kind of Happy Warrior, though rather a rough-edged one.

I did well enough in matric at sixteen for the headmaster to write at the bottom of my report for the year: 'Should think of professional life'. Grandma could hardly grasp the meaning of that. She realised it meant I had done well, but this was the limit of her comprehension. Here Miss Jubb came in.

Miss Jubb, on behalf of the Board of Guardians, had to visit children in their care regularly so as to check they were being well looked after. I think she called in about once a month. She seemed to have established a bond of confidence and mutual respect with Grandma, who had probably never before had a continuous relationship with such a middle-class professional lady. Very upright and proper; and very observant and sympathetic.

Grandma showed her the school report and asked what it meant. Miss Jubb had one of her strokes of brilliance. 'It means that he is clever enough to become a doctor or a parson,' she said, citing exactly the two professions Grandma would have had experience of. It would hardly have been useful to say: 'or a solicitor'; Grandma would have met none of those in a life untouched by house purchase or wills or legal disputes.

She was obviously torn by this news. On the one hand it offered a prospect which startled and impressed her. On the other hand, the seven shillings and sixpence (37½p) a week which the Leeds authorities paid her for my upkeep was becoming increasingly inadequate for a growing young man; and a successful grammar-school career might at sixteen lead straightaway to a decent collar-and-tie job – to that of railway booking-office clerk, say.

Miss Jubb left but came back some time later to say that, if Grandma agreed to let me stay at school, the Guardians would henceforth pay her fifteen shillings (75p) a week. Almost incredible as it may seem now, such a sum was just about adequate then; so long as it was supplemented by clothing checks and the like.

I went into the sixth form for the two years to the Higher School Certificate examination; a group of six or seven for the humanities and much the same for sciences. We were expected to work hard and with not much supervision; it was a happy time. We had been so much selected at each level that, for a working-class grammar school, our subsequent record and that of the years before and after was a credit to the teaching: several professors, diplomats, solicitors and businessmen eventually emerged. The little racehorses.

I mentioned earlier that I had from birth a speech impediment by which 'r's and 'l's came out as 'w's and that, naturally, I was mocked or teased about it. A crucial moment came in the sixth form, since sixth-formers took it in turn to read the lesson at morning assembly. That promised to be a dreadful occasion. Again, the kindness of the place went into action. They found a biblical passage which contained few 'l's and 'r's and coached me in delivering it. The hurdle was surmounted quite well.

Perhaps it was that occasion which made me try to be rid of the handicap before going – as I hoped – to university. Much earlier, I mentioned the half-aunt who lived in a modestly well-to-do district, Harehills, and taught 'elocution'. 'Elocution', a word I haven't heard for decades. One of my dictionaries calls it 'the art of effective speaking'. That edges near to what I think of as rhetoric. Elocution in my half-aunt's understanding was the practice of *proper* speech; and that meant a modified form of what used to be called 'Marshal and Snelgrove's tortured vowels', thought to be superior. I don't think my half-aunt would have recognised or accepted that description. She offered a better model. She gave lessons in particular to young ladies whose parents wanted them to talk as if they were 'reciting'; which indeed some were led to do, especially at church and chapel functions – poetry, parts of 'Hiawatha', for example.

She was a pious churchgoer with a husband of similar persuasion. He was the spit-and-image of Dickens' Joe Gargery in *Great Expectations*. He even looked as I imagine Joe Gargery; large, slow-moving, soft-spoken when he did speak, manifestly an honest man. He was a self-employed craftsman in ironwork. 'Never a cross word between us in fifty-odd years,' his wife used to say and one believed her. But I think he might have been rather boring; she had the liveliness for both of them and he obviously and silently adored her.

She had a large pot cast of the human head in her professional office, the front room, and with its help quickly discovered the source of my minor disability. She listened to me speaking passages with many 'l's and 'r's, and immediately showed me with the pot head's help what I was not doing. For 'l's I did not put my tongue up to the front of the roof of my mouth; and for the 'r's I did not do the same at the back of the mouth. We selected the passage from *Macbeth* which ends: 'Like syllable of dolour'. The one which tested the 'r's I have forgotten (but am sure it will surface some day). I repeated those passages morning and night, on the way to school and in other odd moments, and in a few weeks was cured – though in moments of stress I can still revert, as your grandma usually notices. I went up to university virtually cured.

That tells you how, even though as we've seen, uncovenanted kindnesses existed, children from working-class homes were given little incidental medical help in those days. For almost seventeen years I had that impediment and of course desperately wished I hadn't. No one referred me to a speech expert, who could have removed it in a few weeks.

Which recalls the dental treatment. The Leeds schools did have a free dental service. What the authorities had not sufficiently examined was the actual practice of some of the dentists in the pay of the service. Children from Hunslet schools were treated by a casual, cruel, young man who saved time by not offering a painkiller even for fillings which required much drilling. As in the instance of the Silverdale holiday camp, reality fell a large, unexamined distance short of the apparently highly satisfactory paper provision.

At eighteen the Higher School Certificate exams were taken and most of us in that small sixth form did well. One girl was kept behind for an extra year to prepare for the Oxford entrance exams; her father was a teacher at Cockburn. I heard of no one else to whom that opportunity was offered. Most went to training colleges for teachers, for a two-year qualifying course.

I do not now remember exactly how much the Senior City scholarship was worth. I think it was perhaps a hundred pounds with fees also paid; it may have been less. Out of that you had to pay for everything else: board, lodging, clothes, books, incidentals of all kinds. It was reasonably manageable if you lived at home and if your parents did not ask much for continuing to keep you; many did not, even among the poorer. Otherwise, it needed very tight management. Once, some time later, I worked out that I had a shilling (5p) a week left for fun-and-games after everything else had been paid for. But I did manage to find grants from charities, and work in the summer vacations. I do not remember how much I passed to Grandma each week; she died towards the end of the first term of that first year (1936–7).

I was bereft; she had been the main magnet of my affection. Aunt Lil had by then gone to Kippax, ten or so miles away, to her coalminer husband and stepchildren; Ivy had returned to Sheffield with Alf; Uncle Herbert had married and was up on the Middleton Council Estate; only the tinder-dry Aunt Clara was left and she was making plans with her friend Elsie to find a shop in which they would set up as ladies' outfitters. They found a corner place quite soon, up in Armley not far from the gaol, and managed quite well until the war came. Then they flourished;

the wartime allowance of coupons for stock meant that until some time after the war ended they were safe from predators, buyings-out, being undercut, sold short. By the time their market became competitive again, in the late-forties, and because they were shrewd and sharp, they had made enough to buy a 'nice semi' on a private development in Morecambe, a nirvana for Leeds retired lower-middle-class people.

That move to the shop did not happen until some months after Grandma died. Those months were tense. Aunt Clara's difficulty in living at ease with anyone else – except perhaps with Elsie, and that had periods of warfare prompted by one or the other – was at its most exacerbated, especially as they moved through all the worries of setting up in business. It soon became clear that I should try to move out, preferably to a university 'hostel' as Leeds called its student residences. The main and obvious one was Devonshire Hall, not much more than a mile from the university; but that cost more than my grant would bear. I got down to London somehow and went to the British Legion; after all, our father had been a regular soldier. They gave me a grant sufficient to allow me to enter Devonshire Hall (and later gave more than one clothing grant). By then we were halfway through the second term and it became clear that Aunt Clara would be quite pleased to see me out since plans for the move to the shop were going ahead.

Another act of kindness. The head of hall was always an academic, at that time the portly professor of education, Frank Smith. I am fairly sure that Bonamy Dobrée, the professor of English, had explained to him that I needed to move if I was to get the best out of my studies. Frank Smith saw me round about the middle of the second term, told me had no room until Easter but he would do what he could until then. He put me in the sick bay and, luckily, there was no call on it until that term ended. Bonamy Dobrée also persuaded the Leeds Director of Education to give me grants (in 1937 and 1939) to go youth-hostelling abroad.

At the freshers' 'social' in the first days of the first term I looked in but did not dance; I couldn't, and anyway was too shy to ask for a dance. I was just eighteen and had never walked out with a girl. I saw a very attractive, a 'very nice-looking', girl at the far end of the room in, if memory is correct, a brown silk dress. I noticed but did nothing.

She proved to be another of the first-year students of English, so we saw each other at lectures most weekdays; but nothing happened for weeks, months, until the second term. She started to walk out with a junior member of staff in the Department of Agriculture, who came from near Stalybridge, her own home town. He seems to have been a decent as well as very intelligent man and rose to become a professor in those days when the breed was rare, and established an international professional reputation. He was taken to meet Mary's parents that Christmas vacation.

It took me until the February of 1937 to ask Mary, your grandma, out. We had over the weeks become used to talking in the bay of the Brotherton Library allotted to English students and it gradually became clear to us that we were becoming particular friends. But boys had to make the first moves; which I did in that February, on the outer steps of the Library, by hesitatingly asking if she would like to go to a matinée at the Paramount Cinema in the Headrow to see *Green Pastures*. I think we each paid for ourselves, not out of ideology but mainly because it was clear I could not afford more than my own ticket. Mary's father, your own father's or mother's only grandad, paid the costs of her hall of residence and gave her ten shillings a week for other expenses. That was not extravagant but certainly adequate.

I do not now remember exactly what was the next outing or when we began to walk together, most nights after the library closed, to Mary's hall which was two or three miles further from the university than Devonshire but on the same tram route. There was a very good fish-and-chip shop early on the route and on 'flush' nights we stopped and shared a modest package. By the end of the Easter or soon into the summer term, Mary told the other man, Gordon, that she had a steady relationship with me.

Farnham, autumn 1999

BROTHER TOM

THE GREAT PARISH church of Grantham was packed for my brother Tom's funeral service. There were former pupils from his years as the first headteacher of Corby Glen Secondary Modern School; colleagues and clients from his work for the Samaritans, members of the Stroke Club which he had founded, and people from other voluntary activities of which given his normal reticence, we knew nothing. It was an astonishing tribute to a quiet man who avoided the limelight but sought out opportunities for good works.

There is a common disposition to try to find in our early backgrounds what followed many years later: 'given his childhood, we might have expected just that'; or 'given his childhood, he must have been all his life reacting against it'. If such easy observations have any value, then the second would be more likely than the first to be true of Tom. But not very true or revealing.

When our widowed mother died, we were divided among those relatives who were willing. I can only guess what criteria decided who went where. There was an aunt in Sheffield, married to a former railway drayman; they had eleven children. Most people would have thought that enough but they thought otherwise; one more wouldn't make much difference.

I always, or for many years, thought of Tom as less happily placed than I was. How could they shoehorn another into that crowded house? Still crowded, although at least two of the siblings had already married. Say, eleven plus one. The house was in a long brick terrace, Petre Street,

leading into the city centre via somewhere – was it a railway bridge? –
called The Wicker. There may have been more than three bedrooms and
perhaps an attic. A tunnel between each two houses led to a yard where,
I think, the lavatory was. The main living room was at the back, thus
ensuring little sunlight; the front door faced on the street into the best
room, which I hardly remember ever being occupied; no doubt it was
opened for celebrations, Christmas, weddings, funerals. Many of the
unexpansive aspects of early-twentieth-century working-class culture
were embodied in that house and its setting (though 'setting' is surely too
pleasantly countryside-evocative a word here).

The father of the house was thought by the Hoggarts of Leeds to 'rule
with a rod of iron' and to be assured in the rectitude of his way of going
on. He *had* to be firm and ordered, with that size of household. Thus, one
of Tom's allotted tasks was to clean all the family's shoes on each Sunday
morning, I think it was. I found Uncle Jack fascinating but remote,
though some of his grandchildren remember him with warmth; but that
is not surprising – most old men mellow.

They arranged for Tom to see Molly and me from time to time, so
that was a kindness. Tom came to Leeds and I occasionally went, without
Molly, to Sheffield. As is the way, I remember vividly one practice. Aunt
Alice, by then a large figure, spent the evenings in her big chair near the
living-room fire. Each evening Uncle Jack would bring her a glass of
stout, with an: "Ere y'are, muther', said unctuously; a sort of ritual.

Tom never did more than make a passing humorous remark about
some of Uncle Jack's countryman's attitudes. He seemed to get on well
with the nine offspring of the house, and particularly with the youngest,
Leslie; and later with the handsome cheerful girl who became Leslie's
wife. Leslie graduated into becoming an illusionist at working men's
clubs, holiday camps and the like; his star turn was cutting his wife, who
was in a wooden box, in two.

Tom rarely spoke about that home and never with rancour; sometimes with wry humour at its size. He was a good example of those
who 'swallow their own smoke', keep their own counsel. Quiet, elusive,
self-contained but not self-concerned, not shy but not pushing himself
forward, one row back and usually slightly amused; apparently not
expecting much, phlegmatic, not concerned to project his personality.
He seemed in some ways to think little of himself; for instance, at one
point he told me that he shaved with ordinary soap and ignored all

special shaving creams and the like. Something of all these things.

He could, his second wife used to say with amusement, have flashes of irritation at, for instance, the laziness or incompetence of a local council. 'Don't expect too much in most things' was one of his ground rules; laid out cheerfully. When he became head of that modern school in rural Lincolnshire, he found himself sometimes addressed by often misguided advice from the local lord; from his secretary, that is: 'His Grace has observed that ... [there followed some fancied breech of deference by some of the schoolchildren. One was an account by a pupil, in the school magazine, of being slightly peppered on one of the Earl's shoots at which he had been employed as a beater]'. His Grace was not amused. Tom enjoyed those and remained unruffled; he also became professionally friendly with a lady on his board of governors who seemed to him intelligent and unbuttoned – the Earl's unmarried daughter.

In appearance he reminded me after about the age of thirty of George Orwell. He was about five foot nine inches tall, always slim or even thin; his face was lean too and as he aged became, thinly but deeply, as vertically lined as Orwell's did; sometimes the similarities were striking.

He was from an early age attractive to a good number of both men and women. There was little intellectual or artistic nourishment in Pitsmoor (the working-class district of Sheffield where they lived). His quiet but friendly manner, lack of push but suggestion of a half-hidden wellspring of unmalicious humour drew people to him. I do not think he was positively a believer, but he went regularly to the local church and became a welcome member of a mixed group of about his age; it became his unofficial youth club and necessary for him. He had a very tuneful light tenor voice which the church valued. Underneath, there was the suggestion of a sense of firm conviction but one which came out only when it had to. His best friend of those days, Ray Coates, and Esme from the same group, whom Ray married, stayed close right through to his first wife's death and to Tom's funeral about twenty years later.

I have often tried, but with little firm success, to isolate the source of Tom's attractiveness. Something to do with the mixture of strong but hidden purpose and the capacity to find something ironic or funny in so much of life; in pomposity, self-importance, bungling incompetence. That's as near as I can now get, though I may have another try later. Except perhaps to stress again here the gentleness, the permanent suggestion of gentleness. Which is why, I suppose, that he got on well with women; perhaps not with all women – who does? – but with those who liked thoughtful and kindly looking men. My wife Mary liked him from the start and was particularly happy, when I was in the Army and she teaching near Sheffield, to be asked to go with him to concerts in the city. The same kind of good nature attracted children too; when he was in the car with us on a visit to some local landmark, or walking from the beach to our 'digs' in Filey on a holiday we shared, he was usually asked to sing. He usually began with 'Shoo fly, don't bother me ...'

I imagine the Petre Street people, the Manterfields, recognised that he was 'clever'. That ability led to a turning point, when he passed the eleven-plus examination and so was offered a place at the city's central grammar school. Only much later did I learn that two of the Manterfield boys, older than Tom, had also won places but that they had not been taken up. So it was not to be taken for granted that Tom's scholarship would be accepted; not out of ill will but because it was something quite out of the ordinary. I was told at the time that Uncle Jack finally thought Tom should take up the place because he now realised that a grammar-school education might lead to a 'white-collar job'; two or three years must have changed his outlook. That those two older boys stayed where they were illustrates yet again the awful waste of talent among working-class children at that time; a gate closed before them as it did for thousands of others.

The scholarship carried the right to travel without charge on the trams to and from school. Tom did his homework each evening and morning on the tram. Eventually he passed the matriculation exams at sixteen. There seemed to be no suggestion that he might stay on and finally become – say – a teacher.

He joined one of the large steelworks on the Sheffield perimeter, as a 'stell-stock clerk'. That was presumably one kind of 'white-collar' job. There, he seemed to get on well, be highly thought of and likely to be quickly promoted. He had a girlfriend, met, I seem to remember, at church. She was a well-built, handsome girl with much brown wavy hair; she seemed fond of Tom and he, in his slightly just-off-the-ground but attentive way, of her.

Then trouble set in. It was the middle-to-late thirties, when we all, unless we insisted on pushing our heads into the sand, recognised that in a few years war was highly likely. Tom became involved with various political movements, usually anti-war, within Sheffield, and finally joined the Peace Pledge Union; that decision showed in a quite unqualified way his strength of purpose, usually hidden by what could have looked like that friendly easy-goingness.

Understandably, the Manterfield family must have been largely uncomprehending, as though the boy to which they had given shelter had turned into not quite a cuckoo but certainly into a bird of incomprehensible colouring. I do not remember hearing that they rejected him. There can be in people in such places and circumstances a kind of phlegm, when faced with situations they do not fully understand, which yet stops them from mounting a big moral horse, as some in a more articulate, more self- or class-conscious family might.

On the other hand, and predictably, the steelworks, when war arrived, sacked him peremptorily. It would be going into full-scale war production and could have no place for a conchie, even if they did not harbour suspicions that he might turn into a saboteur; the principle was enough.

It was enough for his girlfriend's brothers too; they immediately persuaded her – with what unwillingness and unhappiness I do not know – to end the relationship. There then began for Tom what proved to be a year or two of casual work – if casual is the right word; he could only find jobs in places which were hard-up for labour and didn't ask many questions, least of all about applicants' political or moral positions; chiefly because their jobs were arduous and ill paid. He survived; and stored up Chaplinesque stories of the comic horrors and misdemeanours of such places. There was one prepared-food factory which was rife with sudden pregnancies, just as soon cut short once the employee had got rid of the side of bacon she had hidden up her skirt as she was leaving in the evening; there were strange sexual exchanges also concerning transactions with food. Best of all was the cheap-and-nasty biscuit factory which in the interests of profit ran the conveyor belts coming out of the ovens faster than they should have done, so that the workers gasped and sweated to keep up. Worst, said Tom, were the cream crackers; 'they were murder', since they went through the ovens on the belt fastest. One day Tom and his mate on the other side of the belt slipped or in some other way misfired. The trays of cream crackers rolled on and were thrown on the floor, in pile after pile, as the two of them collapsed laughing and crunching among them. They weren't sacked; labour in that place was too hard to come by.

Meanwhile, I had gone into the Army and was being made ready to go overseas. Tom was called to a tribunal for conscientious objectors in Manchester and asked me to support him. If an ungifted would-be-dramatist had written that script, he could hardly have been more to the point; no, he would have been accused of obvious banality. A clutch of self-important, elderly local bigwigs who clearly had no sense of what led a manifestly decent young man to take up that stand, which might well lead to considerable unpleasantness and probably to prison. Tom was not a rigid conscientious objector; he told them he would not kill but was willing to serve in a front-line medical unit. They did not take the point – that in that role he would have seen more and more directly of battle and blood than almost all except the absolutely front-line infantry-men. I was in uniform and, true to type, they contrasted my sense of national duty with Tom's cowardly refusal. His application was rejected. It was sickening. We left making comical remarks about it all, but aware that one day soon a policeman (or military policeman) would call to carry Tom off.

No one called. Manchester had an air raid and, we learned, the papers of that board were destroyed. Tom waited and, after at least a year, his call-up papers came: for the medical corps. He landed with the Normandy invasion, saw a lot of fierce combat, was promoted rapidly to sergeant and offered a commission; which he refused. He saw much more front-line battle than I, in the artillery, saw. But those experiences were only revealed under direct questioning, and not much then. He really did wish to draw a curtain over all that and carry on. It was the typical rhythm of his life, whether any part had been dramatically unhappy or happy.

As to happy parts, one stills stays with Mary and me. It was the early summer of 1940. Tom was waiting to be called up after what proved to be that semi-abortive tribunal; I had finished an MA and was due to be called up in a few weeks. We went walking in the Lake District, from youth hostel to youth hostel. The only other visitors seemed people such as ourselves; taking a break from the saw. It was a lovely, companionable trip with a lot of laughter which touched our easily touched funny bones; such as Tom pretending to be a porpoise in a small lake. He also had the delicacy to take some short after-supper walks, assuming that we would value odd moments on our own. That was of course a typical touch. But there was always a touch of sadness in it. In that Sheffield house, with no one he could really talk to about his main intellectual interests, and by then without his girlfriend, he had learned never to put himself into positions in which he might have seemed and felt an extra; it was a sad sign of an inward loneliness; and sometimes, as then, excessive.

Underneath, he seems always to have wanted to be a teacher. The cut-off had come at sixteen, when he left grammar school for work. Having joined the army late, he finished his service after I did, in the Far East; but eventually came back in 1947. He immediately applied for a place on the Emergency Teachers' Training scheme. It seems hardly credible now, but that scheme turned out qualified teachers in one year. That some such as Tom were trained by that means indicates at least some success for the experiment. But it was a compressed experience. If you slipped out of an English-literature lecture for a quick pee, Tom told us, you would be greeted with the cry, on coming back: 'Sorry, we've *done* Wordsworth while you were out.'

Most of the young women at Sheffield Training College for Teachers were at the usual age, about eighteen. Tom started to walk out with Joyce, from a family in Tamworth. It seemed a happy and promising relationship and so it was through to marriage and for some years afterwards. They shared some holidays with us, paid us visits during the usual breaks and eventually started a family, a boy and a girl; and acquired a Jack Russell terrier. Tom got a job in Nottingham, where his merits were soon recognised. He took a course in education at the university there and carried off at least one and perhaps two good qualifications. He was very attentive to his widowed mother-in-law; she went more than once on holiday with them to the same small hotel in the Vendee – she had not been abroad before, but loved it. Eventually, he gained the headship of the new secondary modern School at Corby Glen and they bought a house in Bourne, not too far away.

All seemed to be going well. I do not now remember whether we had indications otherwise before they left Nottingham. Tom said almost nothing but later hints began to emerge that Joyce was not well. I remember going over to Bourne at Joyce's invitation to speak to the local Workers' Educational Association, of which she was secretary, so it would seem that up to that stage she was managing well, was indeed organising some things. She was also teaching. So we really did not and do not even now know for how long she and Tom had to cope with that intermittent but severe illness; it may have been for years. We do know that for as long as ever possible Tom kept it unspoken. He never complained; he simply did not mention it; again, he swallowed his own smoke, while giving constant loving care.

From that time onwards Tom had much more to cope with: a wife who was not always well, and the running of a large new school. They had some holidays with the Coateses, their long-time friends from the early Sheffield days; and it may be that they were more in touch with the details and progress of things than we were.

We went to live in Paris in early 1970, for more than five years. In that period I had a telephone call in my office from Tom to say Joyce had died. I left and was in Bourne for early evening. Esme Coates was already there, helping with anything at all. Her husband, also a headmaster, came over as soon as he could. That friendship, which lasted more than sixty years, must have been one of the stoutest reinforcements in Tom's life from his early days in Sheffield up to his death.

After Esme had gone to bed that first night, Tom and I broached a bottle of cognac I had brought over; I think we finished it. Tom was more outspoken than I had ever remembered. There was no hint of maudlin sentiment, let alone of self-justification, or of: 'If only I had ...'. Better and most touching of all was his recollection of how particularly enjoyable had been their early married days. It was as though he was at the moment of deepest despair holding on to that as the most shining of memories before those curtains had begun over the years to fall.

Mary came over for the funeral. Afterwards, Andrew the son went back to school; Eleanor the daughter and Tom came to Paris and stayed until they felt ready or simply had to leave for other commitments. All very low-key, as sad as possible, but also in some ways recuperative. Which is, one might say, a sort of relief; but the word doesn't suit, sounds ill-fitting; but it is hard to find one which does express that dense inter-play of powerful emotions to which Tom above all, and of course the two children, must have been subject.

Before I write about Tom's decade and a half, after his remarriage, I feel the need – as I hinted earlier – to try to assess more closely and directly what he meant to me and, perhaps, guess what I may have meant to him.

I can recall only one unfriendly moment between us and that was very early, when he was about twelve and I about ten. Tom was over in Hunslet for a short stay; we played in the backyard. For some reason he began to tease me in a way I found unpleasant. I was provoked enough to throw a piece of wood at him; it missed. That was all. It did not affect the basic relationship.

Our sister Molly and I always 'looked up to him'; he was the reliable big brother from the day of our mother's funeral when he led us away. We never doubted that his instincts were good and for our good. Over the years one or two incidents occurred which made me realise that our casts of mind did work differently; sometimes I preferred my way, sometimes his; sometimes I was not sure.

In my early book *The Uses of Literacy* I had made a reference to the uncle in Grandma's household who drank. I had thought little of the decision to say that. It was a well-known fact; it had plainly and publicly caused his downfall at work. I said little more than that. If I had thought that he would be put out by the reference, I would probably have omitted it. Surely, I had assumed, he must recognise that about himself? Later, I heard that the uncle took offence at the reference and I was surprised. I told Tom, who at once said that we all have endless reserves of self-deception. Of course Uncle Bert was hurt. Tom was drawing from another well. He could perhaps have added that for many people there is 'all the difference in the world' between recognising, and knowing that those around you recognise, a perhaps embarrassing fact about yourself and seeing it in print. I now think Tom was right.

On another occasion Tom was tougher than I. I told the story of a trade union official who had supported one of his members, a temporary junior lecturer who was, immorally in my eyes, in confrontation with Goldsmiths' College. He was relying on an accident of drafting by the registrar, who was ill, so as to claim an open-ended appointment. We paid up, much to my anger. 'Naturally, the union official stood by his member,' said Tom. 'That's his job; and the mistake was the college's.' I replied, no doubt sounding portentous, that there was or should be a difference between a legal right and a moral; but Tom stood firm. That's what trade unions were for; they had no moral role and it was a mistake to try to father one on them.

Tom had, naturally I would say, been best man at my wedding. I assumed I would be his. He invited us, of course, but did not ask me to be best man. That was his friend Ray Coates. I do not think I was most hurt for myself, but my bump of familial piety was bruised. I then realised that that bump was stronger than his. He recognised a bond which was, in some respects, stronger than the familial. Ray had been his friend from the early and quite lonely days; he honoured that. I never mentioned this to him and I do see the strength of his case.

He action there showed a lack of sentiment for traditional actions which I sometimes found surprising. As I noted in the preceding essay, it was a tradition in the Hoggart family that the eldest boy was given the middle name 'Longfellow' in honour of the belief that the poet of that name was an ancestor. Tom did not do so, not wishing to burden his son with so unusual a middle name.

Tom was an acute reader of my typescripts and always frank and therefore helpful. If a book was then well received, he did not, so far as my memory suggests, congratulate me. I do not think that was in any way due to jealousy, neglect or casualness. He would not have expected or wanted praise if he had been the author; and he never by the slightest word or gesture tried to speak against or reduce anything I had written; except if he thought I had been thoughtless, and even then he was never hurtful.

Sometimes I wondered whether he felt as close to me, as aware of me as his brother, as I was of him. Perhaps, I occasionally thought, those early years, those in some ways rather lonely years, had caulked up a few of his more overt expressions of emotion. But when I remember his always-present sense of humour, his kindness to anyone in need, his fund of gentleness which was so easily drawn out.

One day, at Goldsmiths', a lecturer on the staff introduced me to a friend of hers who knew Tom from his work in Lincolnshire. She was a rather brusque woman who obviously made a virtue of plain-speaking. 'I know you are more well-known,' she said straightaway, 'but I know your brother and he is the greater man.' Gratuitious, uncalled-for, a bit rude (how did she know enough to make the comparison?). But one side of me was pleased, since I felt, had always felt, it to be a fair distinction; and was glad to hear it recognised.

It is time to come back to the main chronological line, to the last twenty years of Tom's life. After Joyce died, he spent about a decade before retiring. He filled them, crowded them, with useful works. He joined the Samaritans and eventually became the coordinator for his county; he later invented a club for those who had suffered strokes and needed help in recovering strength and confidence. We saw as much as we could of him, but of course he spoke little of these and other activities, all on behalf of the unhappy and in need. At the Christmas some months after Joyce's death he came to us in Paris with Eleanor. It was a surprisingly relaxed and even happy visit. I can still see him standing in the embrasure of one of our large windows on the Boulevard Haussman, laughing at some funny remark, probably by Simon. On Christmas Day we went for a walk all around the Bastille, when Mary suddenly remembered that, having confused kilograms with pounds, she had failed to put the turkey in the oven in time for the evening meal. Tom and Mary immediately took a taxi back to the apartment. A tiny and rather silly incident to remember after so many years – about twenty-five – but it seemed to capture at the time the more light-hearted mood which had begun to surface.

Tom's luck turned. He had met at the Samaritans the widow of a clergyman who had several years before, and after a long illness, died of Parkinson's disease. She had nursed him throughout. They had a son and daughter. Tom and Ida married and he moved into her rented eighteenth-century house in the middle of Grantham. She is a devout churchgoer, spent years as an accountant's senior clerk and had become the unpaid accountant to the parish church.

'Towards the end he sailed into an extraordinary mildness'. Tom would have given his dismissive anti-romantic smile at Auden's line on Melville appearing here; but it fits. They had about a decade and a half of happy years. She made a comfortable, relaxed, unruffled and tolerant home at which all four of the children were always welcome, and got on very well with each other. Ida went to church each Sunday at Grantham and when with us at Farnham. Tom was by then an undeclared unbeliever but walked down from our house to meet Ida after the service. They liked sitting out in the garden while Tom recalled odd funny events for the benefit of Ida and the two of us.

Ida recalls an incident which for her typified much in Tom. They soon began to go for walks in the remoter Lincolnshire countryside; Ida was a very knowledgeable bird-watcher; she did not know until it was quietly and as if incidentally revealed on one of those early walks that Tom had an extremely detailed acquaintance with wild flowers and plants.

Then, cancer was diagnosed in Tom. The Grantham Hospital was not, of course, a leader in cancer treatment; so they sent him to Nottingham for examination. Weeks passed with no diagnosis from Nottingham being reported by Grantham. Tom's obstinate streak where his own health was concerned would not allow him to enquire. Finally, Ida prevailed on him to do so. The report had arrived at Grantham weeks before but had been misplaced. I do not know whether the lost weeks allowed his cancer to take a firmer hold. Perhaps not; but it certainly galloped at the end.

In Grantham Hospital Ida had the miserable recollection that her first husband had died there, also after several weeks of final illness and daily visiting. We went up, naturally. He was in a room of his own. One day he ordered champagne and delivered a short, rather wryly amused sort-of-sermon to his children; including a gentle ticking-off as well as expressions of love. Andrew though it was all a bit like *This Is Your Life*, but Tom told him this was his last speech and he was going to deliver it the way he wanted. He died a day or so later.

I was asked to make a short speech at the funeral service but was choked and made a mess of it; few seemed to think it mattered; the greater sense was of a tribute being made by all who had come, to a good man who had emerged against many odds.

Ida packed and went to live near her sisters in their native Oldham. She still cares for and keeps close to that one family she made out of two, is as warm to them as the best of parents. Tom would have smiled on that.

In addition to Auden's passage on Melville, Tom's life as a whole recalls for me George Eliot's recognition of the worth of people like him, who 'increased the growing good of the world ... by unhistoric acts; ... that things are not so ill with you and me as they might have been, is half owing to the number who lived faithfully a hidden life, and rest in unvis-ited tombs'.

I am sure I have missed out many things which would have made a fuller and more accurate picture. On these occasions odd memories spring out like gouts of water, suddenly from between rocks. How they are selected I do not know; I know *I* do not decide; they decide themselves or are decided by forces I am hardly aware of. But that is a common expe-rience. Are there ambiguities? I ask this only because I have come to think that in almost all – or indeed in all – our relationships, no matter how loving or admiring, there are always some ambiguities; that those are among the terms of our humanity. I cannot at this time see them here and have to hope that most, if any there are, have been flushed out or at least faced. 'Some hope, but worth trying,' I can hear Tom say, dryly.

BILL AND LIL

BILL VARLEY CAME into my Aunt Lil's life at a pub one night. She must have been in her late thirties; unmarried of course and living at home with her widowed mother and a mixed foursome of us.

Lil was one of the hundreds, perhaps thousands, of seamstresses who sat at their machines in huge halls, turning out the ready-made clothing for which Leeds was said at that time to be pre-eminent in the world. The commercial king of all that was Montague Burton, who had a chain of shops for men right across Britain, lived in the poshest outskirts, and in the thirties worked hard and spent freely for peace, including endowing a chair in international relations. I imagine he had come over, probably with his family, in the later half of the nineteenth century, when pogroms in Eastern Europe drove many Jews to the mecca of Leeds.

Montague Burton was one of the most successful of those. It must have been no more than a few years later that he realised the size and force of the German menace and, later still, knew that if Germany were to win the war he would have been despatched quite early to the death camps.

I heard him, a most distinguished – and patriarchal-looking elderly Jew, introduce in Leeds Town Hall Sir Norman Angell, also a tireless worker for peace, whose efforts had been rewarded with the Nobel Prize in 1933. This must have been about 1936, as I entered Leeds University.

Aunt Lil would have known hardly anything of all this. She knew, since she worked at Burton's that there was somewhere in the stratosphere a Burton boss. She also shared the general feeling that 'Burton's aren't bad to work for', had an edge of paternalism towards their workers. That would have been about all.

So, like Auntie Ann on the other side of the Pennines, she walked each working day from Hunslet to the neighbouring working-class district Holbeck and back again each evening with a few local friends. That, for working-class women, was overwhelmingly the standard pattern. At home she joined Grandma, her elder sister Clara, her younger brother Herbert, Ivy, a fugitive from the Sheffield Means Test Man (he would have docked her family's allowance if she had stayed at home and worked) and me.

Grandma was in her seventies and hardly left the house. It was not a happy house, and the recurrent spark to its formidable 'rows' was Bert's drinking and Clara's fury at that and any other form of disreputable behaviour. Lil had to have an outlet.

Unmarried seamstresses of 'a certain age' tended to drink in small clusters – on their own they might have been taken for prostitutes; they knew precisely the pubs at which they felt safe, and the safe, preferred drinks. Port-and-lemon was habitually talked about but among Aunt Lil's group stout – especially Mackeson's – seemed more favoured for non-celebratory drinking. They sallied out only at weekends, not counting Friday; they were never 'the worse for wear' (nor could they afford to be; and they were leery of men who too easily offered them drinks). Yet, when Babycham appeared they quickly decided to leave that to the younger lasses.

Theirs was distinctly not a habit of the 'respectable' working-class and as a family we were certainly respectable; and Aunt Clara was our overwhelming moral mentor. She had a restricted vocabulary but one whose elements she could deploy in multiple ways to meet all her purposes. She knew as surely as Moses knew the commandments that Aunt Lil had gone a full step down from her family's status by drinking in pubs at all: 'It's disgusting. Boozing in those places at your age.' Ivy and her boyfriend Alf remained inviolate, were soon saving up for marriage; apparently their greatest excess was a cuddle in the angle of our two backyard walls. I do not believe that any of the used condoms (in matchboxes – delicate touch) which used to float over our yard wall were theirs.

Even Aunt Clara could see that there was a cultural difference between Uncle Herbert's and Aunt Lil's drinking. His was that of the man with a job which he knew to be below his capabilities; he loved talk and was quite gifted at the easy story-telling of the saloon bar; he gravitated to men of a similar disposition, who propped up favoured town-centre pubs in the early evenings and then made for home, often to a tongue-lashing from wives, parents or siblings. They were, most of them, thought to be 'on the slippery slope', 'going downhill'.

For Lil and her friends the weekend outings were a relief, in her case from a home which too often had the sense of approaching storms hanging over it. I imagine they also found congenial the attentions of some men, also of a certain age, who approached them 'with respect'; they weren't for 'picking up'. That seems to have been how Bill Varley appeared on the Hoggart scene.

He was kept well in the background for quite a time; Lil was nervous had cautious – she loved her mother and was rather uncertain about how she would take to her daughter being courted by a widowed coalminer with six children, four still at home. Lil was also afraid of Aunt Clara, who might well be expected to erupt, on the grounds that no one who had made friends with Aunt Lil in a pub could be up to much, that this one was a miner and so indelibly of a lower social order, ignorant, common and merely looking for a compliant housekeeper and bed companion (if she ever thought of that aspect); a 'real come-down'.

That he existed and that the relationship was serious gradually seeped through, like a whiff from beneath the floorboards. Aunt Lil was habitually timid but, as people of that disposition can be when something captures them emotionally, ready in this instance to stand up to Clara. Grandma said very little, least of all to me – still at school and to be kept ignorant of major family problems. But Grandma, I imagine, realised that there was little joy and no future for Lil at home; and that she might manage better with a home of her own, however odd that miner's council house seemed as a home for one of ours. Aunt Clara sniffed with a dreadful majesty but had to yield.

My memory of the actual wedding is uncertain, but I seem to remember Lil in a two-piece with a frilly white blouse and a flower in the buttonhole; looking hesitant but not unhappy; rather wobbly in new shoes, peering from behind her thick glasses and from time to time stroking her face. She had erysipelas, inflammation of the face which produced itching and seemed never to leave her; it was thought to afflict 'people of a nervous disposition'. Nor do I remember her ever having medical treatment for it; it seemed an immovable act of fate; and doctors had to be paid, even if little.

So they married and moved to Kippax. Kippax had once been a small hamlet seven or so miles east of Leeds, just past Garforth; and a mile or two north from Castleford, which was essentially a coalminers' town (and the birthplace of Henry Moore). The local council expanded Kippax by building a sizeable housing estate on its fringes, especially for the miners. They walked to the pit each day, meeting at the pithead the miners coming from Castleford itself and round about there. For the Kippax families to visit Leeds and its wonderful cornucopia of a covered market was a bit of an expedition on Saturdays; Castleford was a shorter bus ride and its street market good enough for most weekly purchases.

The council houses were of the usual thirties pattern and, for the time, not at all bad. A 'kitchen-living-room', a 'front' or 'sitting' and so slightly posher room, three bedrooms and a bath with lavatory upstairs; a small front garden and a longer back garden backing on to that of a house in the row behind. Most gardens were unkempt unless occupied by retired miners; working miners were too tired with shovelling underground to set about the gardens. They were the homes of washing lines and some kicking-about of balls.

I remember someone saying to me that Bill was a bit rough but a rough diamond. That was a romantic cliché. I don't think he was rough in the way some miners were violent at home. I do not remember any suggestion that he struck Aunt Lil, though that was fairly frequent on that estate. But he was rough in the way most miners were: very little educated and so hardly literate, tough rather than rough if any of his children strayed; able to keep his end up with his mining group; and probably in some ways shrewder than the average, as his post-mining career showed.

When Lil married him, one son was in the British Indian Police, the next was married, a miner and living in Kippax; then two boys, one somewhere between his late teens and early twenties and a miner, one in his much earlier teens and a victim of what I imagine was petit mal, and two girls just a little younger than he was.

Some time after Lil arrived, the married son and some of his family were killed. An entirely predictable death. He had bought an old car and was driving a group to Leeds. At a crossroads near Garforth they had a pile-up. The car would not be likely to have been serviced properly, possibly for years; that would have been true of many of the old bangers which had begun in the last few years to appear outside the council houses. It is doubtful if the lesson was taken widely.

So, for Bill: four children at home, the place to be kept clean, food provided for all, clothing for all but the working young man, and order maintained. Managing on his own, Bill had been and remained after marriage like an on the whole fair but firm sergeant major; he had to be. The older youth liked his beer and had the usual undisciplined eye for girls. He particularly enjoyed telling me of his racy adventures there. Was he inventing them so as to see how I responded? Perhaps. But I suspect most were true.

Did Bill know of such things? Probably; the kind of thing, if not the precise incidents. They were part of the ways of many young miners and not necessarily thought heinous; as was 'mucking up' the American cloth of the living-room settee, an incident described below. Bill was a strict household manager, the rules of indoor and outdoor management finely graded and distinguished from each other.

I do not remember Bill ever taking notes of aid his routines; he seemed to keep the weekly pattern in his head. He went down to Castleford Market on Saturday evening as the stalls were about to close and selling off what they had left. So every Sunday's midday dinner seemed to be the same: a cube of Argentinian beef for which Bill had paid about a shilling (five pence); it fed all plus any visitors. Then, mashed potatoes, carrots and cabbage; and, naturally, Yorkshire pudding. It was 'very tasty' indeed; he knew how to make gravy too. Well, with Bisto.

That routine was indicative of his whole 'going-on'. It was complemented by a big weekly wash and cleaning of the house. For a working miner it was an admirable way of coping with widowerhood. When all was done, he took himself each weekend evening to the Kippax working-men's club. That, rather than the pubs, was the main free-time focus for almost all but the abstemious miners. One custom (they had as many as a London gentlemen's club) was to 'take the wife'; wives gossiped together but usually without breaking the links with their husbands.

I am anxious to reach Aunt Lil and her married life, but something else about Bill occurs to me which I wouldn't like to forget. He was very direct in his speech and had an eye for the significant detail; qualities which many better-educated people do not necessarily have, being a gift, a sense of the 'telling'.

Early on in the marriage he volunteered: 'Eh, Bert, yer Aunt Lil were a virgin when we got married!' He was obviously startled; perhaps a thirty-odd-year-old spinster in Kippax would have been expected to have had at least some sexual experience. I was startled too, at the idea that my Aunt Lil had been assumed not to be a virgin; that wasn't part of the Hoggart closed culture of the thoroughly *respectable* Northern working class. Aunt Clara would have been outraged at the very idea. I was also rather flattered that he thought me old enough and fit enough for such confidences (though I suppose he may have told his mates also).

Once, when Mary and I were over there for a weekend, as a break from university – we kept close to Aunt Lil, though I do not exactly remember how they fitted us all into the bedrooms – he looked out into the back garden where Mary was sitting in a low chair reading some required text. He came in and said with unabashed admiration: 'Eh, Bert, that lass o' thine's got some rare limbs on 'er.' I was flattered, too.

On the other hand, he was furious one Saturday evening. They had been down at the club. The older boy was courting a local girl, but they had left the house before Bill got back. He looked at the brown American-cloth sofa and saw it had been somehow damaged; he assumed by what used to be called 'necking' and is now called 'snogging'. He must have known what happened with couples who were going steady but, like Lady Macbeth, he wasn't having it in his house; or on his American-cloth sofa. Aunt Lil told me that story, with a mixture of disapproval and amusement.

I imagine that Joe, who at that time had a very great deal to learn from his Dad as a mature human being, took more care after that. Later, he was called up into the pre-war 'militia'. Just before he left, he and some mates robbed a hen-coop; casual theft was a part-time occupation. 'Bloody idiot. He deserves what he'll get,' said Bill. Joe was very surprised that the police were able to trace him and pull him in for questioning. They let him go with a caution; he was more use training to be a soldier for the coming conflict than in jail. Later, he came out of Dunkirk with his infantry regiment.

It might be unkind but would not be entirely inaccurate to call Joe, at least at that time, 'a bit slow on the uptake'. He also had the rather cocky assurance often found in people such as that; he seemed to be without doubts as to the rightness of his very limited world; all the rest seemed beyond him.

He married and after the war moved to a heavy job at the Yorkshire Copper Works in South Leeds. They found their council house nearby. His wife proved to be a much more powerful character than he. She ran that household efficiently; placed simple nourishing food before Joe every evening within a few minutes of his coming back from work (I remember a steaming large plate of liver, mash and vegetables); she did not tolerate nonsense. They had one child, a quiet and studious boy, whom his father totally failed to understand and whom he seemed chiefly to look upon as a much cherished appendage of his wife. I don't think he was unkind to the boy; he would have had a clip over the ear for that from his wife if he'd tried. But to see anyone engrossed in a book was something he simply did not comprehend. When last we heard, the boy was hoping to be a librarian.

After Bill Varley had died – to jump over a few years – Aunt Lil was found a small maisonette just across from Joe and his wife in a more-or-less enclosed council-housing-estate circle; Joe died first. His widow kept a close, slightly managerial eye on Lil, who was by then in her eighties. From visits at that time I remember especially two remarks by the widow, one indicative of her very limited knowledge of the public world, the other honest and thoughtful about experience. We told her that our son Simon had found his first job; on the *Guardian*. 'Well, yer've got to start somewhere, 'aven't yer,' she said encouragingly. On another occasion, sitting with Aunt Lil in her tiny living room, the talk – surprisingly – turned to the Pill and the freedom it gave to girls in their relationships, including the new tendency to live in a partnership without necessarily thinking of an inevitable marriage. 'I think that's all right,' she said, 'If Ah'd lived with Joe for a few months, Ah doubt Ah'd have gone on to marry 'im.' That was an open-minded wisdom not always found among women of, say, the middle class faced with the same social change; or, for that matter, in the very consciously 'respectable' working class.

Back to Bill and Lil and Kippax. She had taken on a tough and complex job. She was not used to doing large weekly washes, producing at least one solid hot meal a day, keeping a household of six in decent order and being a bed companion. She sort of wandered through it all, in her own way effective, habitually 'nervy', but helped by her natural, soft, good-heartedness. I guess Bill spotted that and knew she was not a woman who would ever turn nasty. She hadn't, as the local saying was, 'a mean bone in her body'. Never malicious, even though Clara's treatment of her sometimes gave grounds for that, she liked a quiet laugh with me about some of Clara's excesses, and she also had to a high degree, like Auntie Ann in Stalybridge and to some extent even Bill, that eye for the telling incident and for language which captures it. At those moments she too gave a little giggle – 'Yer've got to laugh, 'aven't yer' – they were a relief, since at the moments when she was actually being ticked off she sometimes looked fed up. Later no doubt, Bill's robust and even raucous judgements on Clara helped her a lot.

Of all the support Lil brought to that household I imagine the most important was that she helped the two girls through puberty; for that Bill would have been ill-equipped. Lil would not have been able to articulate her role then, but it existed; she apparently had a fair idea of how to cope. I may be mistaken here, but heard of no panic about the girls' behaviour at that time. Neither showed any urge to come out of their culture, but both showed energy in finding a solid place within it. When I last heard, one was, with her husband, managing a tough pub near Leeds Market. The other, also with her husband, managed a working men's club in that other South Leeds working-class area, Holbeck.

Incidentally, I came to know that that field of working-class enterprise was riddled with, at the least, small corruptions. I was told later that club management committees assumed and ignored roughly up to 10 per cent of fiddling by the manager; above that, they moved in sharply. When the daughter of the Holbeck Club manager turned eighteen they bought her a while coupé. It would have been difficult to do that on a manager's basic salary. That family moved to western Canada and I lost touch.

Perhaps they had learned some of the tricks of the trade from Bill, who, on leaving mining a few years early, had become manager of the Hunslet Carr Club. He didn't straightforwardly water down the beer but he increased its volume with a brown chemical itself dissolved in much water – and was convinced that the people who sold him that tincture were charging him too much for it, 'the greedy buggers'; and that the members preferred the beer in that form.

Back again to the Kippax years. How can one sum them up; but, in particular, were Aunt Clara's fears and predictions borne out? I think not, all in all. Lil may have had to endure things about which I didn't know.

But she did not seem to grow dismissive or routinely critical of Bill. She knew he was rough but she would have said, I think, that he treated her properly; and I think she knew he was faithful. She felt that she had some status; the children grew to recognise that her instincts were good and that she cared for them and for what might become of them. In any event, she had to a degree which Aunt Clara would not have recognised a capacity to roll with the blows. Her sense of her new role was best exemplified in her enjoyment of the company in the club at weekends; that was very much better than the 'hen' groups in the Leeds pubs after a week's work. She enjoyed a role she could never have had if she had stayed at home; and when he finally died after that second career, she found that Bill had 'left her all right'.

That is to go fast-forward. Before it happened, the Kippax years had ended and Bill was launched on his new career. He took over the working men's club in Hunslet Carr as salaried manager, with accommodation on the premises. The front opened on to a fairly busy road going nowhere in particular but feeding the Carr and connecting it with its neighbouring districts. I never saw that door opened. Everyone used the back door, which faced a short, cobbled, dead-end street of back-to-back houses.

Bill seemed happy there and Lil too. Nor did she seem to mind the petty criminality endemic to many such places. The war was not long over and food was still rationed. In the cupboard of her one downstairs living room Lil soon had a store of tinned food (ham, chicken especially) which, she hinted, had been acquired from restaurant-car stewards on the Leeds to London expresses. If she had been offered anything stolen from someone she knew nearby, she would have rejected it and been upset. Large anonymous organisations such as British Rail – that it was nationalised made it no less anonymous – were legitimate targets; in a small way. They were assumed to be wealthy, not to be likely to miss small pilfering: and not friends of the ill-paid working class.

I used to cycle down south from the university over the river to the club each week to hand over my washing and take back last week's lot, washed and ironed. Grandma had died at the end of 1936. Aunt Clara and her friend, having set up shop together, were busy making it prosper, so Aunt Lil offered to do my washing. I enjoyed those visits. I had to have a mug of tea and 'something to put me on'. Bill would come up from the cellars where he'd been fixing the beer and tell me some outrageous anecdote for which he knew I had a sweet tooth.

I cannot remember why I was there one Saturday and looked in on one of their evening shows. Those years, just before television invaded, saw the boom in working men's club entertainments. A great range of 'artistes' went from club to club each weekend: singers male and female, single, joint or in groups, illusionists, stand-up comedians, musicians. One club up near the Pennines was so successful that they booked Louis Armstrong. Others paid the best very well but were merciless to those who did not please. Mine was an average Saturday night from which I recall chiefly Aunt Lil sitting in her favoured corner surrounded by her cronies, elderly ladies, mainly widows, each cuddling a glass and smiling myopically: 'Eh, it's yer nephew, in't it Lil? Int'e doing well!'

In the autumn of 1946 we, with Simon a few months old, went up to Redcar on the north-east coast so that I could start my first job, extra-mural lecturing for the University of Hull; in half of a rented house. That was a bitter winter, rations were adequate but dull, coal was short, Mary was feeding the baby and struggling to make the chill place a home, I was going all round the area by train and bus to evening classes.

Suddenly Bill announced that he would like to come and stay for a few days, during Redcar Races. With money in hand, probably for the first time in his life, he had become one in the long line of working-class adherents to the sport of kings. He had always had a slight touch of the dandy, with a tilt to his trilby whose slightly rakish air was only cancelled out by his evident flat feet. With them he had a rolling walk, something I have noticed in ex-miners, as though they have only just got off their knees from a confined space.

He was a well-behaved guest and appreciated that he was being fed as well as we could manage. Nor was he 'under our feet' much of the time. If he wasn't at the races, he was down at the Redcar Club to which he had reciprocal member's rights. He went out after lunch and after what could, I suppose, be called high tea, after which I left for my class each weeknight, and he for the club again. He had soon made acquaintances and picked up from them the sort of anecdotes he loved and loved to relate. He did not roll up late though we were by then usually ready for bed. We had warning of his return from the recognisable wobble of his feet on the pavement and sometimes from the sound of talk as one of his new pals saw him to our door.

He usually had a good story about an aspect of Redcar to which we had no access; nightly, we recognised our innocence. One night he told of a chap in the club who had been boasting of the money he made by some devious practice. Bill was intrigued but not so much as to neglect a certain kind of typical conversational delicacy. "E offered to tell me how much 'e'd earned by it this year. Nay, I said, I wouldn't ask you to tell me that. So Ah said: "Tell me what yer paid in income tax: that'll do." So 'e did. [pause]. He wor doing alright, ah can tell yer.' Complex rules of engagement.

That is the last close encounter with Bill which I remember. In 1949 we moved to Hull. Bill died and was given a fitting funeral by family and the club; he had become a sort of minor patriarchal figure to both groups. Lil missed him but took the change quietly, almost phlegmatically, to an observer. She spoke little about him but what she said usually gave a sense of mild satisfaction about the man who had taken her away from the low spirits of Newport Street, and given her a fuller life than she would have had there. She did not hesitate to recall some of his odder ways.

She had to leave the club accommodation, of course. But she discovered that, of the half-dozen back-to-back houses facing the club in the cul-de-sac, Bill had bought two. They would cost only a very few hundred pounds each but they were valuable bricks and mortar; and a house for Lil.

Which she made into a typical Lil home. We moved from Hull to Leicester to Birmingham, but always came up at holiday times to Mary's parents (and then to her widowed mother), and en route, going or coming, to Aunt Lil's and to Aunt Clara's, by then in Morecambe.

Lil's gift for making you welcome never deserted her. Within minutes of the three children tumbling up the steps straight into her living room she had gone to a cupboard and brought out 'snowballs' for each. Surprisingly, I noticed on a market stall not long ago that they still exist – round balls, in size between a golf and a cricket ball, chocolate covered with shredded coconut all over them and, inside, gooey, sweet, imitation cream which stuck to the teeth. Nowadays, they look as if made in a backstreet by a small firm on which the public-health inspectors are keeping an eye.

The children loved those little treats, as I had done. Inspired little gestures, gifts, were integral to Lil's personality. After the 'snowballs' and before getting ready to be off, one or the other of the five of us needed to go to the lavatory; or lavatories, since there was a communal pair, in a brick embattlement at the end of the street, up against the cul-de-sac's enclosing wall. That was not an uninteresting experience. You first took a key hanging behind the front door and tied to a small block of wood so that you didn't lose it if you dropped it into the lavatory bowl. With that and some squares of torn-up newspaper, also from near the house door, you were equipped.

When you got back, Aunt Lil had laid out some sandwiches, biscuits, tea and 'pop'. She was by nature hospitable in the old, characteristic working-class way, especially to children; who responded with affection. Her step-grandchildren knew this from the time they were walking, and spoke of her with the kind of humorous affection reserved for the very old who to them have ever-so-slightly dotty manners but are on your side.

She retained her capacity to surprise. One day, when we were calling at the little back-to-back, she revealed with a mixture of shyness and relish at something comic, that she had a courtier. An old widower, very shy, had become attentive at the club and had graduated to calling on her. She had always had a gift for collecting lame ducks and obviously he was the latest. He was very lonely.

She had been keeping it quiet, but now he had asked her to go to Bridlington with him for a week. A perfect conjunction; Bridlington was more working class, less bustling and with fewer pretensions than Scarborough. One side of her would like to have gone; another side of her knew she couldn't. Not that there was any question of 'hanky-panky'; just a matter of giving him company. And he was well behaved. Then she produced a sentence which seemed to have come out of a Northern cartoon: 'He's a very clean old man, ye know'. She knew that Clara would have blown up if she had heard. 'Very unwise. Bringing the family low once again.' Lil didn't go, of course; but the old man continued to call on her and she was always kind to him. We saw him – to say 'met' would be an exaggeration – once. He sat silently in an upright chair near the door. He was certainly a clean-looking old man, in a tidy dark suit with his hat on his knees. He had a nervous smile, like a weak sun through the mist. He nodded once or twice and Aunt Lil took care that he was, by all kinds of quiet implications, made a member of the party. I am sure that he felt that and liked it. It would be the nearest he got by then to recreating the companionship of his dead wife; and he recognised Lil's good heart.

So Lil was quite comfortably settled, had various visitors and her niche at the club where she still met her pals. Then a shadow came over her life which led her to turn to me for advice; presumably as one of the 'really educated' members of the family. Bill's eldest offspring, the one in the British police in India, came home, probably as a result of Indian independence; with his Eurasian wife. Aunt Lil let them have the second of the two houses that Bill had bought in that street, two doors away from her. The husband died soon. His wife proved to be a termagant. She asserted to Lil that as the widow of Bill's eldest son, she had a right to his estate. Whether she was importing Indian law to England I do not know. I know she was persistent and deeply unpleasant. She caused Lil enormous worry. Would she be right? I did my best to reassure Lil, whose rights were clear; and advised the other widow that she had no case. It was a nasty instance of where simple and uncomplicated ignorance of the law in a well-meaning woman met a distinctly harridan-like character who tried to have her way over someone she recognised as not likely to put up a matching fight. In the end it all blew over.

In the sixties we lived in Birmingham, in a very large old house and garden near the university. It became clear that the aunts would like to visit us. That was almost as complicated as moving a military platoon. The two of them stayed for a few days, much impressed by our style of life and of course warmly looked after. The peak came with a state visit to *The Sound of Music*, which they loved, especially Clara. But it was like seeing the old relationships in a large goldfish bowl. If a friend called and was introduced, Clara assumed her shop assistant's regal manner. She had to boss. One morning she saw that Nicola's bedroom door was open and looked in on a typical young girl's tip. She did not hesitate to pronounce vehemently that we should not allow such untidiness; if we did, we could be sure that Nicola would grow up to be 'a tart'.

Lil took most of the domineering quietly but by now clearly resented it; she reduced her resentment by laughing about it with us. She was the younger sister and Clara had said, when Lil must have been already a long-married woman, that she still had to act for their mother in making sure Lil was all right and did right: 'She'll never learn any better,' said Lil.

When she became less able to look after an old house with an outside lavatory, Lil was put into the council maisonette opposite Joe and his wife. Her Eurasian pursuer had lost and, on Lil's death, no doubt her stepchildren divided what was left of her inheritance.

She was reasonably content in the little modern place. But inevitably she weakened; and was finally taken to St James's Hospital on the other side of Leeds, where the poor have gone for decades to die. I talked to her soon after and discovered that the local doctor was 'a blackie'; she had the local, habitual, narrow, ethnic prejudices but not strongly. It could be that white doctors tried to steer away from poor working-class districts – and Hunslet was by that time sinking as heavy industry declined and those 'with anything about them' decamped. I asked if her doctor had looked after her well. 'Oh, 'e gives me a prescription for Valium every time I see 'im, that's all,' she said. She had lived for some years on Valium.

I went regularly to see her at St James's. She was kindly looked after but died after a few days there. On my last visit she did not recognise me; I simply held her hand, hoping that something was getting through to her. It seemed extraordinarily peaceful.

I do not know what that sensation meant. I do think I know that in some important respects Lil was a good human being. I do not mean to disparage Aunt Clara; she was haunted by her own dreadful ghosts, but she also had saving graces, moments when she broke out of her awful, judging, unhappy prison and expressed love underneath.

Lil was of a different kind: simpler, less forceful, perhaps not as 'sharp' as Clara but in a deeper sense in the end wiser. At bottom, she just assumed that we should be kind to one another; she taught us implicitly, by example, that in face of the horror all around us day by day we should offer continuous understanding and sympathy. That attitude can be a small but shining light which we might always, and often against the odds, cherish.

I think Bill Varley had made a good choice.

AUNTIE ANN

I MET AUNTIE ANN for the first time soon after starting to go to Stalybridge, to 'my girlfriend's' home. Then regularly, except for war service abroad; after marriage, with the children and through to her death.

Auntie Ann was small, probably no more than five feet tall. She was into early middle age when we first met. 'Dumpy' looking by then, of course, and as though she had been dumpy all her life. In those days it was usual for women of about forty and after to be much aware of 'me corsets'; and 'me false teeth'.

One can sometimes see in a woman of, say, thirty-five and still good-looking, how she might look at sixty-five. It is harder to look the other way; often moving but not always sad to see, in the face of a sixty-five-year-old, what must have been so attractive at thirty-five.

One could find something like that in Auntie Ann. Not imagine an earlier face of conventional beauty but rather a young woman's good-natured face, open before life, gentle; a face to attract a quiet, honourable young man. A friend of my wife Mary's at Leeds University had and has such a face.

Unusually, there seemed to be at the back of Auntie Ann's face, in her eyes and lips (perhaps since she was a girl, one felt), a slightly comical look as though she was expecting any minute to find something which would amuse her.

She would go to elementary school and just as inevitably expect to leave at thirteen. The Fisher Act of 1918 lifted that to fourteen but Ann left well before then. She went straight into 'The Mill' – a generic term for any one of the cluster of mills in Stalybridge and the other townships around it.

She would take all that for granted, as a fact of life. It was anything but a fact of life; a fact of the Industrial Revolution, rather. Immediately to the east of Stalybridge and its sister towns was the great bare-backed range of the Pennines. Over them was Yorkshire, its biggest city Leeds; another landscape, another country, another culture, took over, with its own form of the revolution; based mainly on wool rather than cotton. That other side felt more foreign than does many a move across American state borders.

For that first visit I hitched a lift on one of the 'wool-waggons' which constantly crossed the hills; through little industrial townships on both sides, well before the arrival of M62, the clotted Pennine motorway of today.

To the west lay Manchester, the maw for the products of cotton mills for miles around, such as those of Stalybridge. The mills crept eastward from the Manchester metropolis to the foothills of the Pennines and the dividing ridge.

It was a classic illustration, a microcosm, of the mid-Imperialist phase of British industry. The material to feed those machines came from the southern states of the USA and the wide empire. They were fed into that particular ravenous mouth of European frenetic activity partly by the Manchester Ship Canal, a willed profit-driven domestic penetration unlike that traumatic incursion of the Dutch up the Medway two centuries before.

Ann's half-century of work saw the end of that cycle of raw-imports-into-manufactured-goods-into-exports to the original growers and many another place. Gandhi had appeared on the scene well before she retired but his campaign, which was to have a major impact on her work, meant little to her or her mates, apart from the meagre and distorted material the popular newspapers put out.

Ann did as she was bid, tended to the machines; and at the end of the week took her small wage packet home. For how long did she hand it over to her mother? Did she feel exploited by the bosses? Not so far as one could tell. In so far as she was at all politically aware, she was a typical working-class, Church-of-England Tory. She was 'put off' by working-class Labour activists, likely to think them 'loud-mouthed'. Her life outside the home revolved round the church and its cycle of activities: especially Sunday school and theatricals. In one play, in her younger days, Ann had taken a man's part. Her parents were furious.

So all around were the great hills and the great mills, pumping out their daily contribution to England's unevenly spread prosperity. As a boy, I simply assumed that Blake had particularly in mind that scene when he wrote of 'dark, satanic mills'. Inaccurate history, that, but imaginatively correct. Auden knew and relished the view from the top westwards; a dark, green, smutty grass plain interspersed with dozens of great, uncompromisingly functional, fuming structures. He said they made one of the most astonishing perspectives in the world. True: they exhibited the rape of a striking landscape, the uninhibited encroachment of insistent industrial energy, the entrapment of tens of thousands to its service. After Ironbridge and the coalfields, that was one of the major foundation sites of the Industrial Revolution.

Among the tens of thousands of 'hands' and working there, as it proved, for several decades, was Auntie Ann. She left very early indeed each morning for a sizeable journey to work, in the beginning probably on five and a half days a week; down the slope, across the cobbles. Not in clogs but in stout, though not expensive, black shoes. Black would have been her dominant colour, or grey; certainly not the often unrestrainedly colourful girls' and women's clothing which came into being as late as the end of the last war. That was before the dominant days of the cheap chain stores for working-class women's clothing, with C & A as one of its peaks; much would then have been bought a couple of miles away in Ashton-under-Lyne's street market. Many such markets exist today and are now especially popular with Asian stall-holders selling riotously coloured fabrics. For the English shoppers they tend now to be something one 'takes in' as part of a pleasant Saturday afternoon, not a lynch-pin of the family's economies in clothes-buying. A different experience – 'shopping' as recreation.

In those years from the early teens up to an expected marriage, nature makes sure of a blooming period, in which most girls put on attractions hardly imagined some years before or in late middle age; attractions which live in the eyes, or the way the hair waves, or the bone structure (especially high cheekbones) before extra flesh comes to hide its fine main frame; or the shape of the mouth or nose; or simply in the basic expression. I guess that when Auntie Ann had her bloom it showed above all in her expression, a 'very nice' expression. No obvious sexiness at all; but probably a good, honest, and ready-to-be amused homeliness.

Did some young men recognise that and become drawn towards it? Where would she have met eligible young men of that kind? Not in pubs, for sure; she wouldn't have 'set foot' there, would have heartily disapproved of them. Not in the mill either; most of the employees would be girls and women. Such men as worked there, foremen, maintenance men, odd technicians and odd-job men, were as likely as not to be married or in early middle age and onwards. The church was the most likely place for a meeting. It was rumoured that one young man, whether met at church I do not know, tried to court her but her parents disapproved of him. So the relationship ended.

At any rate she went on; and on and on; one of the many millions on whom fortune did not smile at birth. Tending the looms, standing up, practising a skilled but entirely repetitive trade whose almost unique interruptions came when a thread broke and had to be quickly caught and mended. All amid the ceaseless rattle and clatter of scores of other machines in a great, echoing, dusty hall. Life on the conveyor belt of a chocolate factory would have been easier; or that of a machinist sitting down in another type of great hall, producing ready-made clothing. But those belonged to other areas and most young women wouldn't have thought of migrating to any of them from Stalybridge; any more than most young men thought of leaving the coal-mining areas across much of England in which they had grown up. There, it seemed manly to go down the pit and join the tight, macho groups of miners in the working men's clubs at weekends.

The house to which Ann returned each evening was still her family home for many years after she started work, and long occupied by her father and mother. Later her married sister and her husband joined them. From a relatively early time in her married life, the sister Mary was an invalid and couldn't do much about the house. Nor could her husband, who came home each evening from heavy work near Manchester and needed food and rest. In any case, working men were generally not expected to help about the house, except *in extremis*; some paragons did help of course. Three children, two boys and a girl, appeared, so that made eight.

The house was within a short terrace, named 'New Street' by its linguistically ungifted developer, plonked on top of a very steep hill or 'brow'. The houses faced up the hill, looking at nothing except odd clinker and scrub. They were somewhat larger than the usual working-class terrace dwellings, and had a cellar which acted as a go-down-and-walk-in refrigerator; and an attic. Outside lavatories, though. To get to the house from Mary's home one had to walk down and up, across the sharp valley of the polluted little River Thame which Stalybridge straddles.

Ann must have slowly and as if remorselessly slipped into being 'the unmarried daughter who stayed at home and looked after her ageing parents'. With knobs on, since she also had another five to bear in mind. The chances of marriage for herself must have receded ever further. Of course, we didn't know – I doubt if anyone knew, given the inhibitions of the time – whether Ann had ever really looked forward to marriage or whether she was, by a rather unkind because blind assumption, what used to be called 'a born spinster'. She seemed at least on the surface not to be kicking against any pricks.

So she became one of the stock figures, the typical *dramatics personae*, of the day, of those lives and times. What a burden it must have been over so many years; with so little apparent resentment, and so much resigned acceptance, at least on the surface. There was a big family party up at New Street each Christmas. Apart from much else, that party illustrated the almost self-sufficient domestic and neighbourhood culture of such places. The mince pies had to come from a particular shop; everyone knew, correctly, that hardly anyone else could make such good ones at home. Rumours about oddities in that family were as accepted as was the excellence of their mince pies. It was traditional also to get your boiled ham from so-and-so's shop; it was always 'very tasty and moist'.

Ann was busier than ever then, this time with some helpers. She seemed to enjoy it all at least as much as the others; in her characteristically unself-regarding way. Did her faith help her throughout, assuming she needed help? As I said earlier, she went very regularly to church, not to any nonconformist chapel. To one brought up as 'chapel' it still seems odd that working-class people could so often be 'C of E' ('The middle class at prayer?') as it does to think of them voting Conservative. Methodist preachers seem to have had less impact on that side of the Pennines than over east in Yorkshire. In some ways Ann might have been called 'devout', but equally in some ways the word doesn't fit. She went to church, presumably she believed in God and the afterlife; she had a strong, puritan moral sense. She did not seem to show thought-through religious faith; but, then, that did not come with the country. In this she was presumably like many around her, spinsters and others. Religion was more ethical than spiritually philosophical.

She had at least one long-standing friend, also unmarried; Mary Oates. She tended to appear at, for instance, the Christmas tea parties and had the honorific title of 'Aunt'. She and Ann did not seem ever to go on holidays together, not even in Stalybridge's annual 'Wakes Week' when the mills all closed and crowded trains took off, chiefly for Blackpool. Did she feel she could 'hardly leave me father and mother for that length of time'? Did she never feel that she needed and was due for, had earned, a rest? Did no one ever say: 'Ann does more than enough all year. She needs a break. We must try to get her a bit of time off'? Initiatives of that sort need ready money and ready persuasiveness; it is more usual just to let things ride, just to go along. But perhaps someone did try to arrange a break for her but failed.

So, presumably, Ann moved on into and through early middle age, to middle age, and elderly life to retirement. Any bloom of youth went gradually, but as inevitably as dusk falls and then gives way to dark. She became the dumpy, grey hair slowly turning white, little woman I first knew her as, and as she remained. Not complaining; not outwardly, at least. And still capable of the occasional chuckle when something caught her fancy – which indicated her native wit, half-hidden imagination; tempted out only from time to time, like a witty small creature kept hidden but *there*; a quality not greatly obvious in most of those she moved among. There would be some in the mill – there always are – calling out the latest funny notion from time to time. 'Well, yer've got to see the funny side of things, 'aven't yer.' Those moments would often include sexual innuendos when one of the men who worked there passed by. I guess Auntie Ann did not like those at all.

From the first time I saw this quality in Ann I realised she was a sister in spirit to my own Aunt Lil. Has anyone written about this quality, this gift, in people without much formal education? I expect so. It is a form of perceptiveness in people who are not handy with abstract language but at home with images and able to recognise the incident which *tells*. Of course they exist in fiction, with Sam Weller as their archetype, their grandfather. It is as though they have been granted a wellspring of quirky insight, a comic eye, of which they are themselves hardly aware and which those most often around them may hardly recognise. Others do respond and decide that so-and-so is 'a bit of a card', as though that a gift allotted to few, like flaming red hair. I do not remember anyone in the family saying something like: 'Ann has a hard life. But she can be very funny when it strikes her.' Perhaps I simply wasn't around when they said it; or perhaps they responded to it without ever articulating that response.

Eventually, the population up at New Street drained away. The two nephews and the niece married and moved off, one to Australia for good. The grandfather and grandmother had already died. Mary, the ailing sister and mother, died. Ann continued looking after her brother-in-law and the house, as though it was an irrefrangible commitment, which to her it plainly was. He was by then retired and 'not at all well', but Ann solidered on as ever, though the house had become a burden to her. Until her brother-in-law also died; then she was alone, 'rattling around' in a house far too large for her. The nearby niece and her husband were concerned and attentive. They knew something had to be done about Ann. It was decided to sell the house once a more suitable home had been found for her.

It must have been about this time that Ann began to feel low. It was as though clouds had been gathering in her mind, piling up with the years, kept at bay perhaps by the busyness of her life, the stifling of her own inclinations, the hiding of her own wishes, needs, impulses; and now, when the busyness had gone, breaking out with force. She may well have felt compassless, rudderless, directionless, rootless, even useless, lost. She went after a while into the first of two deep depressions.

Mary's parents suggested that they might come over to us in Hull with Ann for a few days; to see if the change of air and situation might cheer her up. This was in the fifties. She was certainly not her usual self; the responsiveness to something comical was muted; she spoke little, and on what were meant to be recuperative little car trips around the area was virtually unresponsive. But she was still not in any way complaining; she was just *there* now, embroiled within herself, fighting her own battles, involving and blaming no one else. It was impossible to be sure whether or not the break did her any good; at least one hoped it did no harm.

Today she would, I feel sure, have been diagnosed as suffering from clinical depression; that seems obvious. From fragments of incidents and near-admissions, that depression seemed to have had two main and interleaved elements. One was a feeling of guilt, and from that the conviction that God would duly bring her to judgement. Interleaved appeared to be the further conviction that that judgement would include punishment for having wrong thoughts. The horror for her must have been terrible. It was as though repressions in all those years had burst out and over her in a great all-enveloping flood.

She had no keys for unlocking anything like that, at any stage on the way. It all hardly bears thinking about. Was the unhappiness chiefly in revulsion from those thoughts-in-the-head which, brought into the open, might well have seemed simply mistaken, quite exaggerated? At any rate, she was burden with guilt with which nothing in her surroundings, her culture, her education had made her capable of coping. This is immensely delicate ground which can be approached only with the utmost charity, and the realisation of how little one understands it.

The second depression was more severe. Again she was brought for a short stay with us. That ended in an incident of pathetic, near-tragic, comic force. I was driving the Stalybridge party home when, just breast-ing the higher Pennines – this was before the motorway was built – I had a puncture about a mile above the nearest village. Not remotely a good amateur mechanic, I nevertheless had to set about fitting the spare wheel. With the party standing on the verge looking out of place, slightly like stateless refugees all of a sudden, I jacked up the car ready to remove the useless wheel. Incompetently, I put the spare wheel against the car's side; where, perhaps disturbed by the wind from a passing lorry, it detached itself and began to roll down the steep crest towards the township in the valley. I took off in pursuit, managed to draw abreast of the rolling wheel and kicked it over.

Everyone climbed back into the car once the wheel was fitted, me feeling surprised and slightly pleased that I had managed not entirely ineffectually. Not for long. In the back Auntie Ann was moaning gently while the others tried without success to comfort her. For her the punc-ture was an act of God, another proof that he had noted her sins and was choosing his occasions to bring them home to her once more.

The worst stages fell away and Ann became once more her usual self. A relative was a local councillor and quite soon – this was very much the way things worked – a suitable small council house came up. On the other side of town, near her niece and family.

She was also a few hundred yards behind what had been her brother

Harry's. He had been, always and in many ways, her stay. She was of course very proud indeed of him, a headmaster. To Ann this must have seemed an altogether remarkable achievement. The main thing, though, was that he was her prop more than anyone else. I can still see him, listening with his head on one side, twiddling with the gold watch-chain across his waistcoat (Sunday suit), listening attentively to her as she sought his opinion.

Harry and Doris, devoted parents and grandparents, regularly came to stay with us from 1946 (up on the north-east coast), through to Hull from 1949 to 1959. In that summer we moved to Leicester, but within a month or two Harry was found to have cancer; he died in January 1960. Ann's main prop had gone.

The council house proved to be a short-term arrangement. She was by now very old and no doubt her relatives noticed that even managing for herself in a small house was becoming too much. She needed to be looked after. Quite soon a place was found for her in an old people's home run by the council. It was as though layers of shutters were relentlessly closing.

The home was up the Mottram Road, which clears town and rises towards the hills. There the wealthy or well-to-do of Stalybridge and the neighbourhood – from mill-owners to doctors and solicitors – had built their stone houses within half an acre or more of garden and so well set back from the road. There would be six or seven or even more bedrooms, some large enough to be converted into two. Auntie Ann's place put two into each large bedroom. A pity, since many old people value their privacy as much as do those of any age; and some fear that their neighbour will have unpleasant habits or confuse personal and private belongings. That arrangement was probably a matter of cost. Doubling up doubles the capacity of the house; there is a saving of scale.

Arrangements for the seating in what was called the lounge were no happier. Each resident had an allotted easy chair and was not supposed to use any other. The focal point of the room was, of course, the television set; hence the force of the fixed arrangement. Rather as some German holidaymakers pre-empt the best deckchairs by running out with towels to put on them before breakfast, there would, but for a fixed plan, have been the Stalybridge old people's home's equivalent: of regular and selfish early appropriation. What they did when someone died I did not ask. Did all move up one? It recalls reputed behaviour on tour buses, where one couple always tries to get the left-hand front two seats with a clear forward view. Some bus companies allot the seats when the bookings are made. One excessively 'keen' Farnham woman was always at the door of the bus company before the office opened on the day bookings began; and boasted of having those two left-hand front seats on every holiday. Surely some bus companies have thought of a daily rotation? Or a raffle each evening, with no one able to win twice?'

All in all, that home did not seem a happy place. The woman in charge was given to restrictive rule-making. Probably some of her rules had at bottom been prompted by an inevitable cautiousness. Residents were not allowed to go to their bedrooms during the day. No doubt this was partly to discourage theft. What if someone wanted, *needed*, a rest after lunch? Perhaps they were supposed to take that in their chair in the lounge. Pettyfogging rules, but sometimes inspired by petty undesirable behaviour.

All contributed to a feeling of constriction rather than relaxation. it was eventually discovered that the woman in charge had been fiddling and so had to be dismissed. One wondered whether before that the councillors on the committee which oversaw the home, and who were expected to pay regular visits, ever sensed the restricted air of the place and tried to do something about it.

We called on Auntie Ann during our visits to Stalybridge and sat in the faded provincial portentousness of the entrance hall until she slowly appeared, very plainly glad to see us. She would not grumble; she had always had an intuitive sense that you did not burden others with your troubles. Yet she was evidently not all that happy in the place. But her sense of humour could still surface. On one of the last times we saw her a particularly old lady shuffled across the hall at an almost imperceptible pace.

She gave us a small shy smile. 'That's Mrs so-and-so,' said Auntie Ann in the broad Stalybridge accent, 'We can 'er Twinkletoes.' Not 'wild laughter in the throat of death' but a small relative of it. I doubt if Ann had herself made up that gentle nickname, so there may have been a wit among them. But Ann predictably picked it up.

That incident recalled a much earlier one at a meal in our house at the time of her first depression. She was urged to have a second helping of the pudding, I think it was. The sun broke briefly through, she gave a wide brief smile and said: 'Eh! No thanks! If Ah go on like this they'll be calling me "poowerky" [the Stalybridge "or" in "porky" coming out as "oower"].'

Mary went to the funeral. It seems right that we should particularly remember that late Twinkletoes remark as typical of her. She was also a sort of English cousin of Flaubert's *coeur simple*, the rustic servant, endlessly self-effacing and loyal. But not so simple after all. More, much more. Her sense of the comic was enough to ensure that.

HARRY AND DORIS

I HAVE MOST CLEARLY in memory two snapshots of my father-in-law, Harry France. In one, he is sitting in his armchair by the fire, set as a triangle at the junction of two walls in the corner of their small living room. That happened each evening after he returned from running his school. He and his wife Doris had then a modest and agreeable high tea; they had a hot dinner in the middle of the day. He pulled back, of course, when Mary and I and, later, the children were visiting; but that was his usual setting. Doris often sat at the table on the other side of the window, mending something or looking at the local paper or reading a book. The man had been out at work all day gaining the family's only income; in those days that applied whether he was a heavy labourer or a sedentary clerk It was of course assumed that most if not all work about the house fell on the wife.

Radio arrived later at 'The Mount' than for most – in the mid-thirties, as a reward for Mary's success in matriculation – and did not seem greatly to disturb Harry's reading. For us, radio came earlier than for them but television only in 1957, on our return from America. Harry and Doris bought a set in 1956, on our going to America; perhaps they thought it would help them along in our absence. Since he died in January 1960, his television experience was limited; he hardly had time, even if he had had the inclination, to become a television couch potato.

After he retired Harry took up bowls just down the road at Ashton-under-Lyne's park. That is my second characteristic picture. He didn't go there 'too much'; he didn't do anything too much; I never heard of him going to the pub; he didn't do much about the house but he faithfully paid his other dues to married life, the unbreakable dues he recognised from the start. That could have been one of his mottoes: 'he paid his dues'; never too much, never too little. He could not mend a simple fuse, nor did he wish to learn; Doris learned how to. He could not, would have found this even harder, change a tap washer. In such matters he was at the far end of men who are regarded as of no use about the house. He comforted himself, as the plumber was called in, with one from a range of favourite phrases: 'The labourer is worthy of his hire.' He was a person of fixed and proper and regular habits and epigrams to match. Another sententious saying was something to the effect that good food needs no sauce. But at some stage he had virtually lost his capacity for smell and so had little taste; he made up for that by using large amounts of salt.

In such things he was typical of much in Stalybridge life and culture. It was in no sense a boastful culture as often emerges in cities, especially if they have a football team. Stalybridge did have a football team, but I never heard anyone boast about it; nor did it seem to be much to boast about.

Stalybridge's culture was nevertheless almost all embracing to its native inhabitants. That is, or was, before the age of television, true of Lancashire towns all around. The mills on which so many of the population were dependent gave each town a different week off each year for holidays. 'It's Wigan's Wakes Week so they'll all be off to Blackpool.' Other cardinal points in the year – Christmas, New Year, Whitsuntide ('The Whit. Walks' by the churches and chapels) – all had their regular, firm and traditional practices.

Those shared ways spread into most of the interstices of everyday life: eating habits, recreations, styles of clothing, courtship and marriage. They were unquestioned. Come to think of it, they were probably much the same in townships all over the country, and in other countries, from the Middle West to the villages of Pakistan. Until I started going to Stalybridge, I hadn't at all realised how strong collective habits were in places such as that; smallish and, even if only slightly, separated from large cities. I knew something about class-defined – working-class – habits in a big city; nothing about the collective habits of single townships.

I had been brought up in a big city, Leeds. Leeds didn't have 'a culture'; it had several cultures and those largely class-decided. It had several centres too, marked out by the different ways in which each class used the city centre but, of course, overlapping. Leeds also had different cultures encouraged by the existence of a university there and what went with that intellectually – some very strong grammar schools such as those of Manchester, Stockport and some others not far away from Stalybridge, plus perhaps a nationally known newspaper, two or three nationally known theatres and a regional broadcasting centre.

By comparison, Stalybridge was a one-class town (with the inevitable one or two professionals – parsons, dentists, doctors, solicitors; but they were a very small element); it had virtually no provision for intellectual life – at that time the public library hardly counted in that sense. In the early years the librarian asked you what book you wanted, decided after a glance and perhaps a few questions whether you were suited to have it and then went for it. That system remained for children after the shelves were opened to adults; no place for inspired browsing and fortuitous discoveries if you were under sixteen. Even quite small towns had their own mayor, town hall, council, many of them extremely small-minded. Many are no great loss.

Until the closure of most of the mills blew fresh winds through Stalybridge and its kind it had been for almost a century a more or less static, enclosed, largely one-industry, habitual community. Even though Manchester was so near, it belonged to another world; chiefly for special shopping trips.

A good many working-class and lower-middle-class natives of Leeds, who had saved up enough, tended on retirement to move to, for instance, Morecambe or, slightly posher, Scarborough. Stalybridge people of that level tended to stay put – and, the men, perhaps to take up bowls.

Harry France was born into a working-class family about a dozen years before the end of the last century. He was quite small, perhaps five feet five or six inches tall; but stocky, at least by the time I first knew him. He was always 'a good son' and from an early age recognised by his proud family as unusual, a clever and hard-working lad. He was a few years too old to be able to take advantage of the 1902 Act which authorised local education authorities to set up grammar schools. Whether he ever realised what he had missed by being born a few years too soon I do not know, but doubt that he did.

Instead he took one of the few routes available to a bright working-class boy; he went to the local elementary Church of England school and then served a year or so as a 'pupil teacher'. There his headmaster had become and remained his patron. He was then awarded a place at Chester Church of England Teacher Training College. As a regular churchgoer, a former pupil and now pupil teacher at the church's school, he presumably came to realise that he might reasonably aim for a place at Chester; but it was a big jump.

Chester had been founded by Gladstone as the first teacher training college. It is now the Chester College of Higher Education. One is bound to wonder what the intellectual and imaginative levels of Chester College were at the turn of the century. Probably not very high but certainly devout and steady. If we wish, we can turn for enlightenment to a body of acts on all aspects of public education from 1902 to the present. In Harry's day, and though there had been much public attention to national education from the mid-nineteenth century onward, that attention was more functional than enlightened in terms of, let us say, its examining of the interweaving of educational opportunity and social class (though there was much attention to the needs of 'the labouring masses', it was not greatly fed by comparative analysis; some would have regarded that as subversive); or of the problem of how to do right educationally by both the 'bright' and the no-more-than-average pupils; to take only two such major questions.

Harry was clearly a very hard-working student; he also enjoyed his two years at Chester enormously. One can gain a sense of this and of its cheerful-young-men's delights in those relatively simple, pre-motor-car days from two large framed pictures, each a talented and crowded confection of caricatures of days at Chester drawn by one of Harry's friends. Our son Paul, who has a particularly strong sense of family history, now has those pictures hung in his own work room: 'Happy Memories of Chester College' and 'Reminiscences of Chester College, 1905–07' reveal Two-Men-in-a-Boat activities by young men (Chester was of course a single-sex college), contentedly smoking their pipes with feet up on the common-room chairs (a spiral of smoke from the pipe contains the form of a buxom young woman – 'when the day's work is over Lady Nicotine transforms the past into the present'). Many sport fashionable flat caps, breeches and long socks, Norfolk jackets and natty ties. They make routinely funny, dismissive but innocent remarks about all kinds of college activities from lectures to chapel, and from lecturers to chaplains. The Cadet Corps commandant orders: 'Form Fours – to two volunteers.

It could all seem, to someone of that age today, as from a much earlier time even than the last hundred years ago to which it belongs.

Harry must have loved it – to meet young men from other towns than Stalybridge and perhaps even from other parts of England; perhaps young men who came from not altogether bookless homes. If Harry had been just old enough to benefit from that 1902 Act, he would at eleven have entered a similarly selected but still local community, a group more intelligent than the average, with some in it who had found and read intellectual books while still living at home; and wanted to talk about them. Harry entered something like that world only in his very late teens or even early twenties. It must have been an eye-opener. Today, it seems likely, a boy with those abilities would have simply expected, unless he had an antagonist family, to go to grammar – or comprehensive – school and so to a university.

He came back to Stalybridge a qualified teacher, to the elementary school he had attended as a boy. His favourite subject was mathematics, especially when taught to the older boys, between eleven and thirteen. He could not be called a roving spirit. That disinclination would be strengthened by the hold of Stalybridge culture, but also, and this was itself of course an integral part of much in that culture, his filial devotion to his family; and probably also to the sense that he owed them close loyalty since for his sake, so that he could have higher education, they had sacrificed some years when he might have brought wages into the house. They were as proud of him as he was grateful and devoted to them.

He was not an intellectually questioning spirit and not closely attentive to educational changes in fashion. He continued teaching maths in the old way while the New Maths sailed past him – until ideas changed and he found himself in fashion again, as he taught what he had learned at Chester. But his best opportunities for teaching that were lost when reorganisation took away his eleven- to fourteen-year-olds.

He stayed at the same school until eventually, and I do not know against what competition, he was made head. That could have been helped by the continuing patronage of his own old headmaster; again, how closed and indeed parochial those societies were, and hence consummate practitioners of the word in the ear.

Harry was, as was only to be expected, a most devoted headmaster. Perhaps that settled him even more firmly into the life of Stalybridge. To be still near his family, to be now head of the school he went to as a boy; what more should one want? I doubt if he ever looked further. Was he ever approached to move and take over a new school? That is doubtful too. I feel fairly certain that he would, while being chuffed, have rejected such an approach.

So far, apart from the Chester interlude, Harry has sounded Stalybridge-bonded. But he loved the Pennines, just a short bus ride away, as they climbed eastwards over towards Yorkshire; all springy heather and gorse and reservoirs and curlews and peewits. Mary also remembers those excursions with great pleasure. He would probably have come to know them first with the mates of his unmarried years; he carried that affection over to marriage.

I imagine, but have no evidence, that he met Doris through church. I imagine also that their courtship was a decorous affair. They were well matched in this, each rather careful and cautious. And yet ...? Is that an inevitable supposition? In a long and not very adventurous or often bouncy marriage it is especially easy insensibly to grow more like each other, though with more influence from one party than from the other. My guess is that Harry and Doris were drawn to one another initially by their shared unmelodramatic expectations and inclinations. And habits; he could reasonably be called 'a creature of habit', for that kept the world in order, manageable. He bought fifty Craven A cigarettes each week and smoked seven a day; and presumably eight on Sunday unless he had given one away. If he opened his pack after lunch on Sunday and I was in the room, he would, with a slight hesitation which he soon overrode, hold out the pack to me. I hope I learned to refuse; in any event I, most of the time until giving up tobacco altogether, smoked a pipe. No embarrassment.

There could be some embarrassment over 'household money', that given regularly to Doris for all household expenses. I do not think Harry was mean and I expect the allowance was adequate though not lavish. Doris, to whom such carefulness came naturally, 'managed'. Except now and again, when someone came to tea. She would buy, say, boiled ham or fish to cook, allowing for the presence of visitors but sometimes slightly undercalculating. Mary remembers being embarrassed in adolescence as she watched her mother in the kitchen most carefully calculating the servings, transferring a little of this or that and finally pointing to one rather more generous than the others, for Mary to take to the table:

'That's for so-and-so [the visitor].' I wonder now whether Harry was aware of these occasional wobbles; perhaps not, and Doris was not likely to have told him. She knew such attitudes of Harry were ingrown, not mean but protective of them both; so she respected them. I wonder whether later, when Mary was 'off their hands', Doris relaxed. Certainly her grandchildren – and we – enjoyed their meals there and never hinted at a shortage in the frank way that comes easily to children. She was a very good 'home cook'; we still remember with pleasure her Lancashire hotpot.

Why did they have only one child? Perhaps they were warned after the one birth that it might be dangerous to try for another. Doris was seriously ill in her thirties, not long after Mary's birth, with pleurisy and phlebitis; the phlebitis plagued her for many years after.

That child, Mary, was born in April 1918, just over seven months before the war ended. Harry had served with the infantry, in his local Pals regiment, in the trenches of Flanders. That too was typical: to go straight to where his kind of people were joining up and in the least romantic of military arms – and in some ways the most dangerous. He was lucky; he caught 'a Blighty one', a foot injury from, I imagine, shrapnel, and was no longer useful as a front-line soldier. All his life afterwards he had to wear one boot built up to compensate. All his life he refused to talk about his time in the trenches. All his life he refused to contemplate leaving Britain for a holiday; he had simply had enough. He enjoyed reading books about exotic travels, but for himself 'abroad' was the blasted muddy fields of Northern France; that area which is dull even in peacetime. In this he was, I suspect, like many thousands of other squaddies; some of the officers were more likely to be acquainted with Deauville, Biarritz or the Riviera, the playgrounds of the pre-First World War well-to-do. The Second World War was less static, more far-flung; when cheap air travel began to arrive in the late fifties, our generation embraced it, being less traumatised about 'abroad'.

So, as the war ended, Harry and Doris, with their baby, began to put their married life into regular shape. They had several homes, rented in the first years, one a little terrace house in town, one three miles out at Heyrod. They saved, of course, and eventually were able to buy (I believe with a mortgage), a newish, neat, three-bedroomed, bay-windowed house on the slope just above Stalybridge centre and near, sideways-on-to and fifty yards from, the Manchester–Leeds main cross-Pennine road.

The house was much like the average semi-detached but one of three, after which the street continued going away from the main road as a terrace. Next door but one, at the beginning of the street, was a confectioner's shop. Relations were always good with the shopkeeper; which was a help, since right through married life there and Doris's ten-year widowhood on her own in the house, they had no telephone; and, of course, no car.

That was the only France house I knew; and came to see as a welcome and welcoming second home, especially after we left Leeds University. Mary started teaching near Sheffield, and I joined the Army. It was to that house that we gravitated whenever leave allowed.

To me, it was often rather like being in, but not part of, a Lancashire soap opera, *Coronation Street* without actual involvement with the booze and adultery and fights. They existed, of course, but we were onlookers, recipients of some affronting but juicy gossip. The oddest and mildest memory of all concerned a turkey. The houses each had a very small fenced backyard, useful for hanging out the washing and not much else. One year the amiable middle-aged childless couple next door acquired a turkey, live; presumably for the next Christmas dinner. The bird, soon quite tame, wandered for a long time in their yard like a displaced but dignified spinster. They became fond of it, couldn't bear to have it killed and gave it a name: Sally. It made a great gobbling outraged sound at intervals and delighted our children. Like the Roman geese, a useful burglar alarm? No: one Christmas a local petty thief made off with it in the night. I hope it proved very stringy indeed when it arrived on somebody's Christmas dinner table.

It would be wrong to give the impression that Harry and Doris lived a virtually enclosed life. He was for many years secretary of the Stalybridge branch of the National Union of Teachers and carried out those duties conscientiously. The union's annual conference was held during the Easter break each year and the three then went off to Blackpool or Llandudno.

There was also each summer a four-week holiday, often at the same place year after year – such as Cleveleys on the Fylde Coast, north of Blackpool. Inevitably, they had 'an arrangement', one much favoured by working-class and lower-middle-class people in those parts (it may have been common more widely then; I have the impression that it has by now more or less died out). Each family paid for their rooms and for the cooking of meals; sometimes there was a small additional charge for 'cruet', meaning the salt, pepper and sauces on the table provided by the landlady. The advantage of this system was obvious; each day you could provide your landlady with food which you knew would suit your own family. The disadvantage was slightly tricky; when several families were in the same house over the same period, the effort of juggling the preparation of different dishes for different families at the same time would call for willing accommodatings on all sides. Sometimes the provision of – simple – puddings, such as rice, sago and tapioca with jam, was left to the landlady. Some people, including the Frances, went year after year to the same landlady and formed a friendship. The pleasures of Cleveleys and its kind were unexciting but humane: fresh air, pleasant and healthy walks, small-boat trips, some seasonal entertainments. We went there as a family years after it had accommodated Harry, Doris and Mary; we rented a semi and thoroughly enjoyed ourselves. The quality of the local grocers and greengrocers – in such things as home-made bread and cakes, locally grown tomatoes and home-boiled ham – was particularly high; no doubt most have today given way to the supermarkets.

So back to Stalybridge and the settling in for autumn and winter; and all the usual occupations of those seasons. Undramatic, undaring, usual, all of them. It is tempting to call Harry timid and in some ways both of them may have been. But, once again, when the war came he answered the call directly and went straight into the worst of it. He tried to steer by his moral lights even though some of them could seem simplistic.

We bought out first house in 1951 with help from him; for £1600, in Hull. We left for Leicester eight years later. We were as innocent as Harry about house sales but shouldn't have been. Under Harry's quite firm suggesting, we decided it would be wrong to ask for more than we had paid, plus perhaps £50 for a major internal structural improvement we had made. The buyers, childless college lecturers, were more cute than we were. After agreeing to pay the £1650, they pleaded shortage of ready cash to pay the deposit of £100 and asked us to halve it; which we did. At Leicester we paid over £3000 for a house; on looking at the deeds, we discovered that the previous owners had paid much less than half of what we paid them. They had been in the house only four or five years. Our solicitor was aghast – and he was a Quaker.

Harry was stubborn in all such matters. One Christmas at Stalybridge I asked if I might use one of his member's cards to borrow a book from the local library which bore on my work. He read out from his library card the words 'Not transferable', told me he couldn't therefore lend me one of his cards, but added that he would sponsor me as an applicant for cards of my own. Since we were only there for a few days I did not take up the offer.

Another Christmas inspired similar moral firmness. Doris and Harry always invited Doris's brother Joe, his wife Florence and daughter Anne, for Christmas dinner; making a total of seven to ten of us, depending on the size at any particular time of our family. The complimentary remarks were all much of a muchness: 'Well, Doris, if we never eat worse than that, we'll not be doing too badly.' 'That was a lovely pudding, Florence' – Florence always made the pudding. On one occasion, perhaps inspired by us, a bottle of beer and a large bottle of lemonade were brought in for the making of shandy. For six or seven adults. After one helping for all those qualifying, Mary proposed to offer the small amount left to anyone interested. Harry spoke up, as if warning of rapids ahead: 'Now, Mary, don't you go haphazard with that liquor.' He was always aware that a boat, the family boat, could be easily rocked.

So ran the even temper of his way, in all things temperate and modest. Conservative with a small 'c' he certainly was; whether he was politically Conservative I do not know; I would not like to think of him as a deferential Conservative and probably he was not. Always one comes back to the way he paid his dues, to his loyalty to family in the extended sense; a dutiful husband, father, son, brother. In all these matters he was, at least to someone not daily within those historic close relationships, equable; it was as though he clung to that almost above all else.

Every Sunday the trio crossed the valley up to Harry's mother's house, to what was still thought of as the traditional family home, the base. Not surprisingly, Doris eventually began to take less pleasure in those routine visits.

On Saturday evenings Mary, when a little girl, was taken to her maternal grandmother's while her parents went off somewhere – perhaps to visit friends, or to see a film, or perhaps there was some leisure activity at church. Grandmother gave Mary sixpence to buy chocolate at the nearest shop and they settled down to card games or had an earpiece each of a home-made radio (a 'crystal' set made by an uncle). That remains a particularly happy memory.

Incidentally: thinking back about the ways of life of all that family, and of all such people, one is bound to wonder just what their religion meant to them. In what sense were they believers? Did they really expect to meet on the other side those of their loved ones who had gone before? I think so. Those gravestone assertions and newspaper rhyming couplets were surely neither merely routine nor insecure. Now, in this third-millennium world which has known so much actual destruction and intellectual undermining, it seems almost incredible that people should have believed in that way; and still do. It suggests that the process of filtering-down of major changes in ideas still comes up at some point against rock-solid traditional assumptions and for a long time has no more effect. The popular press does nothing to alter that; it starts and ends with where people are, not with where they might be or, terrible circulation-wobbling idea, *ought* to be. The increase in access to higher education of the last three decades will eventually have more effect on those who enjoy it; their parents are likely to remain unaffected for longer, unless challenged by their liberated offspring; but such challenges will be uncommon. I never asked Harry about his beliefs; he would have been surprised if I had done; as surprised as if I had asked for details of his yearly finances – only more so. There was a tacit understanding that we did not discuss such things; I would have been an earnest clot to have done otherwise. What good would it have done? And how could I have responded to justifications which would have been bound to seem, in no arrogant sense, so simplistic, and might have led to actual challenges; or, better, to an embarrassed withdrawal on both sides: 'Leave thou thy brother ...'

The unspoken definition and practice of 'neighbourliness' in such places took many subtle forms, from those of people who were 'forever dropping in', not just to borrow a bit of something but also for a bit of a natter, to those who 'kept themselves to themselves'. It will be no surprise by now to hear that Doris kept well to the second end of that line. She knew how to respect neighbourliness and to practise it, especially in those small to larger aspects when an urgent need arose. But you didn't expect as you arrived at the house to see a neighbour sitting there for a gossip. Their degree and style of openness to visitors, like so much else, followed a known and regular and limited pattern.

Of which the main weekly figure was 'Uncle Bert'. He was an honorary uncle, in deference to the existence of Mary; to whom he paid some avuncular dues over the years. Uncle Bert was unmarried, a sweetheart had died during the First World War and he had had no other. He lived with a married brother in another but not distant part to Stalybridge and led a very ordered, quiet life. Each year he took several holidays, often to establishments run by a society or societies designed for quiet and friendly people who liked nice walks; with names such as The Holiday Fellowship. That name is evocative of the pre-war era which nourished the Cyclists' Touring Club, the Ramblers' Association and the youth hostels; groups of the kind – well, the more earnest among them – of which Orwell made mocking fun.

Uncle Bert had a rather reddish (not through booze, though) and uneven face whose most prominent feature was an unusually large nose; not so much a hooked or aggressive-seeming but rather a bulbous nose, a friendly nose, which would harm no one and undoubtedly meant well. He did not speak much and prefaced all speech with a slightly nervous clearing of the throat and a shy smile. In some ways one felt sorry for him, since life had dealt him so poor a hand; but that could have been patronising; he was so obviously a well-disposed and kindly man.

Uncle Bert came once a week to play bridge with Doris and Harry. No one was invited to make a foursome. They played on the table in the back living room, at least after I came on the scene; perhaps before then they played in the sitting room at the front. After that Mary and I were given that room and read and worked on the settee. After a certain time there was movement at the back which indicated that the moment had come for Mary to go to the kitchen and prepare the hot drink – perhaps cocoa or Ovaltine – and to cut into portions the meat pie bought from the nearby shop, very tasty, and perhaps some cake and biscuits. We sat down at the table with them for that. Shortly afterwards Uncle Bert gave the 'harrumph' and throat-clearing which meant he would soon be on his way.

An only child is, unless there is dissent in the house, sheltered and fussed over; an only daughter is likely to be treated like a ewe lamb. Harry and Doris were the sort of couple who were extremely anxious not to 'spoil' their only child; that went with the puritanism. On the other hand, and of course, they were devoted to her. If she came back late from Manchester when some evening event followed school, Harry would be waiting anxiously on the station platform. If she had fallen asleep and did not appear, which could happen, he would run down all the carriages in a miserable, increasingly frantic, fuss. Later, we became used to noticing him, Hunter watch in hand, looking anxiously out of the front bay window for sight of our car, we being later than he had expected.

Of course, Mary knew she was loved; but she missed the company of siblings. She was clever and Stalybridge was somewhat limited in its provision for such children. At that point Harry and Doris took a momentous decision; they sought entry for her to Manchester Girls' High School, a Beale and Buss Foundation; they had estimated that they could and would pay the fees. She gained a place and, a year later, a half-scholarship.

Nothing could have been better for her at that point in her life. She had, at least for the heart of every day, acquired a family of congenial sisters; she was among girls often as clever and curious about life as she was and sometimes cleverer. She loved that company, and the classes and the out-of-class activities.

At one period Doris – Mary thinks it may have been during her menopause, and in addition she had been very much below good health, with the recurrent phlebitis – became depressed. Her condition may have been compounded by the repetitive nature of their lives, the fixed Sunday visits to Harry's mother, the calculation about each holiday and outing, the endless weekly planning on a fixed and not very flexible budget, the unvarying tightness of it all. It may well have been that at that time all these things came together for Doris. Mary remembers finding her crying silently over the kitchen sink. And perhaps she was not able to put the various elements together and see further into the cause of her low spirits so that she might have been able, to some extent at least, to ride above them. We do not know. We do know that Harry found it difficult to cope with such things. Words and phrases would probably come to mind, about 'moods', 'women's ailments' and 'change at her time of life'. He would perhaps have been unable to discuss it all openly with Doris or with friends; and I doubt if he went to ask their doctor for advice.

He did seem to be affected and worried by it and – Mary by now being away at university – he began to propose new outings and holidays to places such as Felixstowe, Ilfracombe and Lyme Regis; occasionally, on warm summer evenings, he suggested that Doris accomany him to the bowls in the park, where there were benches.

She pulled out of the depression and moved from middle to old age and something very near to serenity; in all this she was greatly helped by her daughter's family and children, by their very existence. She became a greatly loved grandmother. I am sure that in his own even less demonstrative way Harry was deeply attached to us. From mid-1956 to mid-1957 we were in the United States. Mary wrote to them every week but it seems hardly believable now that we couldn't have simply picked up the phone and spoken to them regularly. It must have seemed a barren time to them but nothing would have persuaded them to complain. When we came back in early September, straight to Stalybridge off the boat (in one sense it was lucky that there was no direct competition from other grandparents; though I expect we would all have behaved ourselves if there had been), the children – at eleven, nine and five – tumbled through the doorway and the joy all round was almost palpable; but still not all that demonstrative on Harry and Doris's part. Doris gave what had become her standard false expression of surprise: 'Ee! Well, I never did. Who's this here then?' Not 'fussy'; deeply felt low down but not publicly much displayed. I imagine some people – say, the French, and certainly Italians – would find that hard to decipher.

Doris loved them all, of course, but had a special feeling for Simon. This is, again, not to say that she loved him more than the others. She took great pains to 'treat them all alike' and that was a genuine impulse. But Simon – the first grandchild and in a sense the son she never had – had a certain glow about him for her. That is the sort of connection which strikes deep, no matter how much love is given to all other grand-children.

I realise now that in all I have written so far I have not mentioned their attitude towards me; perhaps I felt underneath disinclined to take that step outwards. Years later, we heard that Doris had spoken warmly to a relative about me as son-in-law. Those were extremely still and deep waters.

Mary and I had begun to walk out in the second team of our first year at university. I went over the hills to Stalybridge that summer; invited to meet the parents – the sign of seriousness. I was eighteen and 'young-looking' for my age. After I had left, Harry apparently said: 'Well! He's nobbut a lad.' Mary does not remember that, but I doubt if I invented it. I do not remember ever shaking hands in greeting with Harry or giving a kiss in greeting to Doris; though, again, memory may be faulty.

Looking back, I am surprised at the degree of freedom they gave Mary after she left home for Leeds. They must have worried a great deal and hoped she didn't 'get into bad company'. They trusted her silently.

Mary remembers only one remark, when she announced that the two of us proposed to go on a week's cycling holiday. Doris had managed to say something about 'taking care'; Mary had assured her that I was to be trusted, or something to that effect. I doubt if the conversation became more explicit than that.

In September 1959 we moved to Leicester. A few weeks later Doris told us that Harry was ill and not likely, at least for some time, to come down to visit us. I had the impression that the local doctor, a Welshman who had practised there for many years, was not entirely up to date in some elements. Prostate cancer was diagnosed. We heard of no referral to Christie's, the noted cancer hospital in Manchester. The National Health Service was not much more than ten years old then, so sophisticated referrals from small towns were no doubt less common than they are today. At any rate, Harry was put to bed in the front room and seen by the doctor at intervals; Mary went up frequently. He lingered until the 10 January 1960. The children were looked after in Leicester while we went to the funeral; and then Doris came down to stay with us for as long as she wished.

Doris's widowhood was naturally lonely in some senses; you do not move easily from a shared bed and life of about fifty years to a solitary home. In some respects, though, her widowhood had a pleasant autumnal quality, one in which aspects of her character burgeoned, came into their own.

She insisted on keeping her own house. She fed herself sensibly and well; no 'making do' with scratch meals. She was always glad to come and stay with us at Leicester or Birmingham several times each year. She soon learned to be at ease with our visitors, some of whom must have seemed strange birds to her. We took her on holidays with us each year, but not abroad; that was not on the agenda for her, though we sometimes felt she might have enjoyed a week at a quiet French hotel by the sea.

She played card games with the children to an extent that we had not; she helped Nicola to learn sewing and darning; she helped Simon clear his buttery debts at university and took care to give the same amount to the other two. It was all, inevitably, a much more varied life than she had known and she learned to enjoy it.

She learned to laugh more too. One day, sitting on the beach just outside the French window of our borrowed East Anglian bungalow, her deckchair collapsed into the soft and shifting shingle. She was left flat on the ground, her legs in the air and her Directoire knickers in full view. The children, falling about laughing, came to the rescue. She caught the mood and joined in. I had not before seen her laugh so wholeheartedly.

We never felt, and I do not think she ever felt, that she was 'a visitor', an addition. She was one of the family, who came and went often from her home/house which we too had long felt was itself part of the family living-places. She just merged.

In the summer of 1969 I had three professional approaches: one from New York, one from Brisbane and the third from Paris. Our first thought was that we did not wish to give up being close to Doris. Hers was that she must not 'stand in your way'. We all finally agreed that I might accept the Paris offer, on the understanding that Mary could fly to Manchester each weekend.

That autumn, after a late warning to us (she had tried to treat herself with Savlon ointment from the chemist, telling no one of this), she sent us – of all things – a brief postcard (those being cheaper than letters in an envelope) saying she was going to see the doctor about an eruption on a breast. Mary went up at once. Very soon Doris had a mastectomy, which seemed successful.

The economical postcard was typical of her laconic style. One day she wrote that 'cousin Joe has bought a second-hand car. I suppose it's the engine that counts'. She could also be elliptical and inconsequential. As an old lady staggered on to the road in front of our car, she called out: 'Ooh! Don't run her over, Richard. She goes to our church.'

We brought her down to Birmingham for the Christmas of 1969. But the mastectomy had not solved the problem of the cancer and she began to feel very poorly. She went to bed and our local doctor became admirably attentive. It was soon plain that she was in the last stages. She lived through Christmas, an uncomplaining patient; that was where puritanism became iron stoicism. We each went up regularly and sat at her bedside; she obviously cherished that; she had an extended, attentive and loving family all round her. She died just into the New Year. We took her up to Stalybridge to be buried not cremated. This time the children came with us.

We had kept from her the late news that I had been asked to start work in Paris only three weeks later. One always manages and we did. We flew from Birmingham at the month end, the two of us and Paul. Simon was working at his first job, on the *Manchester Guardian*. Until he had found digs nearer the office he had stayed with her – a lovely coda; Nicola was at university.

Their lifetime savings were very modest; about £7000, mainly in such forms as post office savings certificates. As to the house, we repeated our incompetence on leaving Hull; we let a local estate agent or solicitor dispose of it and asked no questions. We were altogether too busy settling into life in Paris, at UNESCO.

In financial terms theirs was a meagre harvest for a whole lifetime; but it had been modestly and honestly gathered, not driven by the hunt for profit.

In writing about people such as Harry and Doris it is easy to slip into a sort of patronage by faint praise, and that's not justified. They were, if I understand that phrase, 'God-fearing' people. They had not had much in the way of an intellectual or imagination-stretching education. They practised by instinct and local tradition, even within their own puritanism, a tolerance which disinclined them to make powerful moral judgements on others. They would never have joined a gang demonstrating in front of what was assumed to be a paedophile's house, or uttered racist sentiments, or taken a stand in favour of capital punishment. They had their own kind of liberalism. They had no cupidity and would have made poor fodder for the consumers' society. There were in so many ways *decent*.

No society will flourish without its portion of intellectuals and artists, its articulate and questioning eyes. Any society gains from its share of Harry's and Doris's. Their lives can seem dull, over-habitual. But the class and kind to which they belonged was, and is, not in any way 'flash' or out to con anyone else but a solidly stabilising element, to a degree which makes the philistine, blind distinctions of class-snobbery themselves irrelevant.

PART SIX

SUMMING UP AND SIGNING OFF

LOOKING BACK: AN INTERVIEW WITH NICHOLAS TREDELL

I do not think there is a need for me to say much about these pages except perhaps that, to the subject of the interview at least, Nicolas Tredell seems to have done a good job – in eliciting some of what might be the publicly interesting aspects of a life which still seems to have been, to its principal, in many ways disordered; but which was always at bottom a bit of a search for order. Whatever value that may have . . .

NICOLAS TREDELL: IN the first volume of your *Life and Times: A Local Habitation*, published in 1988, you say, when you're describing your time at Leeds University in the late 1930s, that 'my own emerging intellectual life had three main focuses: politics, documentary and poetry'. I wondered if we could look at each of those interests as they've interwoven with your life and work – starting with poetry, which has been a constant concern of yours, though in your multifarious activities it's not always been the concern that's been most noticed.

Richard Hoggart: I have always thought of poetry as the queen of the literary forms. I used to write a little poetry at the university and had it published in a student magazine. A friend and I wrote a joint poem which was banned by the professor on the committee of the university magazine. My friend threw everything up and went down to London to become a poet; which he became, though not very well-known. He had a particularly 'good war'. I did not have that strength of single-minded feeling but I remain fascinated by poetry and somewhere inside still wish I had stayed with it. It's linguistically and hence imaginatively the most taxing form. I went to the war and in five and a half years as a soldier could have written poetry; many did. I read poetry throughout, notably Auden, and *The Four Quartets* as they came out one by one. A year before demobilisation, still in Italy, I began to write a study of Auden. I wrote twenty thousand words or so of that, down there, with no access to relevant books except the poems themselves. When I came home I wrote more, up to about thirty or forty thousand words, and sent it to Day Lewis at Chatto. He said that if I made it into a full-length book they would publish it; which they did. I have not started seriously trying to write poetry again.

My main interests turned to writing about culture and society. Strangely, the passages people sometimes mention as being most often remembered by them – there aren't many – are usually passages which remind me that I would have liked to be a poet. I once met Betjeman and, it's almost embarrassing to recall, he said: 'You know, you're a better poet than I am.' That seems very odd but I think I just know what he was meaning; that sometimes the way I look at things and the way I try to capture them in words is rather like the way some poets work. I couldn't say more than that. Funny, I now realise even more as I talk that, as I said a moment ago, somewhere inside myself I seem still to think that I might, someday, start trying to write poetry again. I don't know.

Nicholas Tredell: Could we turn to the second of the intellectual focuses which you mention, politics. In *A Local Habitation* you say that 'The politics were socialist, as they still are'. Socialism has become very beleaguered of late, not least in England. What do you feel to be the roots of your continuing socialist convictions?

Richard Hoggart: That is at the front of my mind just now. I am writing a book about this town, Farnham – where, incidentally, we came to live almost by accident. The book has an opening chapter about why I decided to write about the town. It's Cobbett's town, it's George Sturt's (Bourne's) town (it's also the town of the man who invented that humane helpline for the soldiers, TocH, during the First World War and of the man who composed 'Rock of Ages'). I can still sense the impulses which made them look around and capture the feel of places like this; something peculiarly English, for good or ill. Then I write, in those opening pages, about how I set to the book. You start as if you are going to write one kind of book and end writing one of a kind you could not have predicted. The main thing is not to resist your impulses. If something takes hold of you, let it run away with you. It reminds me of a lovely phrase of Lawrence's which I like to quote: about how, if you try to nail a novel down – to your conscious purposes – the novel will get up and walk away with the nail. So one of the things which seems to be coming out of this new book is a clearer understanding of my socialism. Not that that is any greater matter for surprise. My socialism is a moral (I hope not moralistic) socialism, an old English style, not theoretic or ideological but humanist, liberal, ethical, qualified because we all live foggy and qualified lives. It requires much more from its adherents than is required from Tories because it's rooted in the sense that we all belong to each other; all of us. That is quite different from declaring before you go over the top that 'the chaps ... they're the salt of the earth'; that's sincerely meant, no doubt, but it's class patronage.

I remember, when I was at Goldsmiths' College, being shocked to the core by a young postgraduate geographer [this is the incident briefly referred to in the essay on Brother Tom]. We took him on as a temporary lecturer, explicitly for six months, to fill a short absence. The registrar was ill and failed to ask him to sign his agreement to this. Towards the end of the period he invoked a rule which said that, since we had not stipulated a terminal date, he had a continuing, tenured post. He knew the facts and so did his trade union, which supported him. The person whose place he had filled was now back so we had to buy out that awful young man; his equally awful union official then withdrew, as one who had completed a good, not a shameful, job. It suggests to me that one good basic socialist precept might be: 'What is legally correct is not necessarily morally correct.' I don't mean to suggest, of course, that Tories couldn't think like that; but I believe it to be at the very heart of socialist fellowship. I do not think I will ever break from that conviction. One result is that in the new book I criticise Conservatism a good deal because Farnham still shows many Conservative attitudes (though in its voting turning towards the Lib-Dems). I then find myself also criticising left-wing attitudes strongly, with more force than I had expected.

A lot of left-wing writing today is violently abusive to a degree that is not justified. Some far-left journals can be illiberal, unimaginative, intellectually shabby, given to foreshortening argument by abuse. No doubt many far-right authors are too, but I rarely read them. I simply expect more from my own kind. There is also a certain sort of sentimentality on the left. One event I cannot easily watch is the singing of the Red Flag – arms linked and swinging, as for 'Auld Lang Syne' – at the end of the Labour Party Conference. That's bogus, self-deceit of a high order; not English socialism.

Two other stances which I sometimes find particularly unpleasant when they are held – in the way they are often held' would be more accurate – by people who claim to be good socialists, are anti-racism and political correctness. They naturally merge. I am of course anti-racist; what thoughtful person in good faith isn't? My objection is to crude, self-righteous anti-racism by which you cannot say anything, you mustn't say anything even if it is a straight matter of fact, if it can be misconstrued by the absolutists as racist. That is a new kind of censorship.

I could give many instances but one will do. I mentioned it in the book called *A Sort of Clowning*. During the war, when we were with the American First Army, I had to make a long and urgent journey over the mountainous Algerian and Tunisian roads with some delicate radar spares. We drove all night. The driver, who was new to that job, skidded on a wet clay road – it was a rotten road anyway – and we went right off it, down a steep bank and overturned. It was about 4 or 5 a.m. We scrambled up to the road, both bleeding quite badly and waited for something to appear. Fairly soon an American jeep came along, fast, and we signalled to it. It put on yet more speed and swerved right round us and off. Inside were two black soldiers. My driver – they always knew these things or assumed they did – said: 'Of course they've been out on a drugs run; that's why they can't stop.' He may have been wrong about why they were out; that may have been anti-black prejudice. They were certainly out illicitly or could have stopped (unless, of course, they were totally careless of the state of two wounded men). What is a matter of fact, because we both saw it, was that they were two black soldiers. My book appeared at the height of early anti-racist activity. The word 'black' was removed somewhere along the line to production not on the grounds that I was being racist, but because I might be accused of being racist. I do not remember how I came to accept the excision and now regret it;

perhaps it was taken from the text too late for me to object. It should have been kept because it was a true part of the little nasty incident. I blame myself if I knew about it in time and let it pass. When you begin to remove things because somebody else might misconstrue you, you are supinely conniving at a form of unacknowledged censorship.

Nicolas Tredell: The third of those early focuses you mention in *A Local Habitation*, and one which has clearly been very important in your writing, is that of documentary. How did that interest develop?

Richard Hoggart: The immediate explanation is that the thirties were a very good period for documentary, from mass observation to the films of Grierson. Auden's 'Night Mail' had a great impact, and there were documentaries on coalminers, fishermen and other dramatic labourers. I wouldn't class even the best of those with the best novels; it was more like valuable raw material. So it was all in line that the first thing I published, in *Tribune*, after coming back from the war, was a documentary piece on the magistrates' bench at Stalybridge, my wife's home town.

In addition, being an orphan brought up entirely with adults aged from about twenty-odd to seventy, in a poor home, also sharpened perceptions, many of them not so easily available to someone brought up differently. When a friend took you home for tea and his parents knew what your situation was, they looked at you and registered at once that your socks were very cheap and your short trousers had cost about ten bob at Woolies; and you knew they were looking; X-ray eyes are common on both sides in those situations. You lived with such telling details. All that must also have fed my fascination with accent, intonation and style. Some people think I dwell too much on that and they may be right. Thin-skinnedness. Still, it heightened some ways of looking.

That early visit to the magistrates' court taught me a few things about making everyday observations. I had imbibed the usual notion that magistrates were self-important and often insensitive but knew as I went in that I mustn't take that for granted. They proved to be just like that, as did a bench at Goole five or six years later; aided by their clerk, they showed collective, implacable stupidity which might have come straight out of Shakespeare or Dickens. I've since seen a better bench in action at Farnham. At Stalybridge I knew I mustn't simply stroke easy prejudices, nor for that matter implicitly flatter; no obvious anger, no soft soap.

That's the beginning of the documentary style. The second piece I did, again for *Tribune*, was on the old men who haunted the public library reading rooms. Easy sentimentality was the main danger there.

I've just had a new thought about documentary, and about how *The Uses of Literacy* came to have its shape. I started by writing about the mass media of communication along the lines pioneered by Mrs Leavis, Denys Thompson and one or two others. Then I felt that wouldn't do, that I had to relate it to the lives and attitudes of the working-class people who bought such material. That produced a first half of the book. I see now that that lateish impulse came out of my documentary sense, which had started to show itself, if in only a few things, much earlier. It produced what I suppose might be called a contrasting diptych, two pictures set side by side; the material and those who read it. In part also, I had been led to that by dissatisfaction with Mrs Leavis's contrasts, in *Fiction and the Reading Public*, between popular novels and a much earlier generation of working people; that did not seem a true match. Mrs Leavis did not realise that I was, there, in some ways but implicity and politely making a criticism of her approach. I was glad to acknowledge my debts to both Leavises in a lecture at Downing College later. They had sent apologies for not being there. Later, she told a postgraduate student that Raymond Williams and I had climbed to fame and fortune on her shoulders. Mistaken on both counts; and said.

Nicolas Tredell: In *A Sort of Clowning* you mentioned that Dr Leavis was said to have remarked that *The Uses of Literacy* had some value but that you should have written a novel. *The Uses of Literacy* does evoke 'felt life' in a way that sometimes calls a novel to mind. Given your views on the superiority of the novel over documentary, did you ever in fact consider producing it as a novel?

Richard Hoggart: Trilling once remarked that there are two kinds of writer: the centrifugal and the centripetal. Tolstoy and Joyce? Taking the world as your parish or revolving on your own axis. On a small scale I am centripetal. I am interested in different types of characters and places. I can create physical setting fairly well and have a reasonable if confined ear for speech and gesture. I have very large limitations. I once tried to write a drama, not a novel. Hopeless. I forgot I had people in rooms, interacting, moving around, establishing their differences of character. I just set them all talking, all using my voice; no sense of movement; no dramatic sense for incidents and relationships. One of my touchstones for all that kind of thing, in the novel rather than in drama, is the scene in *Middlemarch* where Mrs Bulstrode confronts her husband with his sins. What power, and complexity and insight into personality; and sense of space and place and time. [Long after this interview occurred a colleague wrote to me: 'I have thought, like many others of your readers, that there is a novelist *manqué* in you; but I would now revise that to describe you as a literary practitioner of the character-study in the seventeenth-century manner.']

I have been reading a lot of Nadine Gordimer recently and wondering why she is so impressive. The first quality, simple enough to name but very hard to achieve, is that her writing has a great depth of texture. Nothing is simple, two-dimensional. When she is talking about blacks and whites, nothing seems programmed or polemical or ideological or even on the surface political. You feel these are real people who are suffering, living, facing problems, moral problems. Doris Lessing creates a similar effect. I suppose all fine novelists do; it's not a new point nor a particularly subtle one but one can come to such insights belatedly and unexpectedly. As I've said, it came suddenly to me only after reading several of Nadine Gordimer's novels in fairly quick succession. It almost made me think that I *should* try to write a novel. Raymond Williams wrote several but I do not think his novels work; they are complicated, even complex, but they do not have the living texture I am clumsily pointing to. In their own way they are interesting but you can see the schematic bone structure underneath. If I did start a novel and suddenly discovered that I had forgotten what it was I had thought I was doing, that it had taken off and away from me, I would be delighted. If I found each morning that I had to crank up the machinery, I would wonder whether it was going to work.

I'm slightly sniffy about the amount of attention paid to the novel today. So very many are published that you wonder how many can clear their costs; and so many are hailed as the best this and the best that. So you look at a few at random and find them quite unremarkable. Of course, there are a few new novelists who are truly interesting, but in the nature of things not many among the forest of names offered to us today. There are, by contrast, some extremely good biographers; better than the autobiographers, who often can't achieve the right distance from the self.

I wonder whether the problems of writing autobiography are any less than those of fiction – problems of structure, tone, selection, distance, angle. Not long before he died, Lionel Trilling said he thought we were going to move into an era where socially descriptive non-fictional writing would again reveal its strengths, which had been disregarded. I hope he was right.

Nicholas Tredell: Isn't one of the problems with that kind of writing that it leads sometimes to unwarranted inferences and generalisations? Doesn't this happen at times in *The Uses of Literacy*? – for example, in your memorable description of the juke-box boys in the milk bar, where you say: 'Compared even with the pub round the corner, this is all a pecu-liarly thin and pallid form of dissipation, a sort of spiritual dry-rot amid the odour of boiled milk. May of the customers – their clothes, their hair-styles, their facial expressions all indicate – are living to a large extent in a myth-world compounded of a few simple elements which they take to be those of American life.'

[I had been wondering whether that old chestnut would come up. Nicolas Tredell as compared with some others does at least call the scene 'memorable'; I think it is, if overdone. This little incident also illustrates a bad habit among some critics. The ticking-off criticism of what came to be called 'the juke-box boys' scene was passed from hand to hand, virtually unaltered.]

Richard Hoggart: I had watched those young men several times, as I was waiting to go to my Goole class; as a novelist would; but if it had appeared in a novel people would not have spoken of 'unwarranted infer-ences and generalisations'; it would have been accepted. Several people criticised it on the grounds that I did not recognise the richness of British youth's pop culture at the time. Their chronology was all wrong. I was writing of and at a time (early fifties) when the Beatles and much else in British pop music were a good many years off and American juke-box culture was still dominant. More important: there is a tendency – it is a side-aspect of political correctness on the far left – to avoid criticising any aspect of working-class culture. Ironic, that, since I have also been called romantic or sentimental in my descriptions of that culture. The passage was also, usually implicitly, felt to be anti-American; another sacred cow of conventional intellectually correct opinion. I stand by what I wrote;

those young men were, to anyone who wished they had a fuller life, deeply deprived, and without many expectations. I feel less sorry about being misread than about the evidence from some responses here of the casual picking-up of fashionable opinions at second or third or fourth hand.

Nicolas Tredell: That prompts my next question, because you're the great founding father of cultural studies in England. *The Uses of Literacy* is one of its great founding texts; and you began the Centre for Contemporary Cultural Studies at Birmingham at a time when there was nothing else like it. Much of the work you've just described and criticised is precisely the work which comes out of modern cultural studies. What do you think of the way that discipline has developed?

Richard Hoggart: Let me go back a little. I gave an inaugural lecture at Birmingham in which I tried to set out what I was up to. I wished to set up a postgraduate centre for Contemporary Cultural Studies which would essentially begin by using the methods of literary criticism and analysis – listening to words, to the different textures of language and tone – and applying them to the study of society. That was one central point. The second, just as important, was about the need to *look* at people and places; with as much sympathy as you could summon. I had learned a lot from Leavis but was here modifying his approach along the way.

I thought, and think, that literature, the language of literature and the insights of literature, are key ways of understanding society. Incidentally, people had said to me apropos *The Uses of Literacy* and the setting-up of the Centre: 'The sociologists will slay you.' They didn't; on the whole they were generous. There was the occasional number-cruncher who said: 'Oh, mere impressionism', but most sociologists did not react in that way. The French reception was marvellous; they were reacting against their own theorising and were much more receptive. If anyone grumbled, it was a few Eng-Lit people. I remember one very superior professor saying: 'You do realise, don't you, that your graduates won't get jobs.' Not from him, they wouldn't. He look off for one of the great traditional American universities – 'Wouldn't you know?', as the Americans say on such fitting occasions.

I asked Stuart Hall to join me. I admire Stuart; he is much more theoretical than I am and, I suppose, much more to the left. We worked together well and never quarrelled. When I had left for UNESCO, at first for three years, and Stuart was holding the fort as acting director of the Centre, a PhD candidate – a bright, middle-class girl – said they now no longer had time for the 'Matthew Arnoldian liberal humanism of Hoggart'. I took that as a compliment. She was right from her perspective. She thought the Centre should now be a 'Red Cell' and ought only to admit people who were already committed on the left. I thought that fundamentally mistaken. I would admit people because they seemed gifted and likely to advance things eventually. Stuart and I did not question candidates' politics. Several of the people we admitted – not, we learned later, all on the left – produced some of our best work in cultural studies.

After I left, the Centre was, then being directed by a considerable and well-known theoretician of the left. So, clever postgraduates already inclined in those directions sought the opportunity to work there. Once I had agreed to stay for two extra years at UNESCO I resigned from Birmingham. The rest is an old story. The new vice-chancellor did not like the Centre and set up an external committee to examine and report on it. Apart from two quite fair criticisms, it reported extremely favourably, so Stuart directed the Centre from then until he left for the Open University. I wasn't very close to it during that period but I understand that two of the main new elements Stuart introduced and which were questioned by the committee, were first, working for higher degrees in groups. This was often in what one might call genre studies; e.g. on race or feminism or authority (the hegemony) or youth. Group study can be helpful, of course, but it cannot take the place of the solitary preparation of the first thesis; that was, I assume, their point.

The committee's second doubt was about the excessive use of the abstract language of theory (an opponent might say, of 'jargon'). I thought, and think, since the habit is still there in much cultural studies across the country, that there was too great a fascination with that abstract language. That is why, when I do sometimes speak to groups about cultural studies today, I tend to hammer on about the need to look first at people and things so that you do not run the risk of seeing people and things through a preformed theoretic prism. 'In the destructive element immerse.' 'Open your eyes before you open your mouth.' I don't think I have much effect. I probably have even less when I insist on the centrality of literature to the work. Rip van Winkle waving his stick. Still, the Centre throughout Stuat's time did a lot of good work and, so far as

I know at second hand, still does. And its alumni do get jobs in spite of the dire predictions of the professor mentioned earlier.

Nicholas Tredell: There is now a strong movement in higher education and indeed in schools to assimilate the study of literature into cultural studies, so that literature will no longer have the autonomy and high prestige it once enjoyed. What do you think about that?

Richard Hoggart: It will be clear from what I have said so far that I would greatly regret any movement to reduce the prestige of literature. As I say boringly often, our literature is our greatest artistic achievement and an unparalleled way of extending our understanding of our relationships, personal and social ('if we wish', one always has to add). That is why it was fair to call me an old 'Matthew Arnoldian' and why I put it at the heart of the Centre's work from the start – which greatly surprised some of the students: 'What, a poem of W. B. Yeats for study in a seminar before *Coronation Street!*' I am sorry it is no longer so central. Endless studies of soap operas without a prior understanding of literature will be two-dimensional, lacking essential critical and linguistic apparatus, without deep imaginative background. In any serious discipline we all need yardsticks; without them we will have ragbags; a few cultural studies courses in Britain and elsewhere are just this, fashionable, jargon-ridden ragbags.

But I think that many traditional ways of studying literature, and many traditional Eng. Lit. programmes in universities and elsewhere, were overtraditional and overconfident that they had got the definitions and boundaries absolutely right. Any proposal for change is 'unacceptably radical' – if not subversive. It's a fast-bound set of conventions, and unacceptable to me and many others. There are Departments of English to which no different kind of thought has yet penetrated. I am not invited to speak at those! I believe cultural studies can help and do help to break those rigidities open, most valuably; but they should not do so at the expense of literary studies in a more imaginative sense.

Nicolas Tredell: You've also attacked that kind of abrogation of value judgements on the public library service. Could you talk about that?

Richard Hoggart: Yes, it's going on now in the public libraries. They say they are suffering because they are short of money and that is true, but not the whole or the most important truth. Many working in the library service do not know why it was invented and so what is their role. They do not know, let alone argue about, the fact that libraries have stood for something beyond bestsellerdom; that they have stood for the conviction that some books are better than others and that as many people as possible should have free access to them. If they do not have that fundamental sense of purpose, they will merely follow existing majority taste and buy twelve copies of the latest Jeffrey Archer and say they haven't enough money to buy, let's say, a single copy of a book by Iris Murdoch. The library service is as full of self-consoling myths, as are most of our cultural institutions today. 'If we tempt them in with Jeffrey Archer they will go on to better things; if we dare use the word "better".' Untested and untrue; merely a comforting assumption.

Worse is to come. If you offer even such simple truths in a librarians' professional journal, you will receive abusive letters from schools of librianship on these lines: 'Does Hoggart not realise that the public libraries were a soporific invented by the bourgeoisie to keep the workers quiet?' The parliamentary debates when the service was being initiated show that some people held that view; some others opposed founding them, on the ground that reading might lead the workers into revolutionary thoughts. Yet others thought they would enrich the lives of readers. It seems that students come out of some schools of librarianship reciting ideological gibberish. It appears that few were introduced to the idea that public libraries were also founded on that third belief above: that reading, reading what their supporters might have called 'nourishing' books, would help the workers the better to control their own fates.

Other librarians today, uncertain about matters of judgements of worth in their work, take refuge in information technology. That is easier than recognising that George Eliot was/is more than a bourgeois writer for a bourgeois audience, much more; and so has to be on the shelves. If you use that kind of language today, you will be dismissed by on the one hand the deconstructionists and on the other by cultural materialists. For some, books are the property of their readers, who constantly remake them in their own images; for others, books are made by and must reflect, the dominant hegemony. I sometimes think that we should all, before we enter that argument, sit down and write forty pages of autobiography; we would then come face to face with our own limits, prejudices, vulnerabilities; we would be facing a deeply personal set of moral questions; which no one can appropriate, and which are both internal to and external to us and to our society.

Nicolas Tredell: You've been much concerned in your work with the quality of a society's conversation with itself. In your more recent writing, particularly in the third volume of your autobiography, *An Imagined Life*, there's a strong sense that you feel that the quality of that conversation and indeed the quality of life in this society has deteriorated a great deal in the 1980s.

Richard Hoggart: Yes. There are many aspects, such as the way new divisions are succeeding those of social class but with hardly any gain, the increasing triviality of the popular media of communication, and so on. In particular I've grumbled about the extent to which so many writers, intellectuals and the like, do not play much part in these debates and do not try to reach a wider audience outside their kind of people. There are of course notable exceptions; I think first of Margaret Drabble and Michael Holroyd. But in general the French have something to show us there. I dislike very much the phrase 'the chattering classes', which must have been invented by a tabloid journalist. I of course avoid so far as possible the word 'intelligentsia'. I like Colderidge's word 'clerisy' but it's not useable; nor is 'clerks' as in 'The Treason of ...'.

My grumble is founded on the belief that there is still a sizeable cohort of intelligent lay readers out there who would value a wider and better-fed argument. Apart from the libraries debate, an outstanding example is that about broadcasting in which the public service idea – like the Open University, one of the best British social inventions of the century – is increasingly going by default. Meanwhile, we trot up to Broadcasting House to deliver our bright ideas, with little thought that broadcasting's public service world is closing in.